At the Edge of Ireland

At the

HARPER ● PERENNIAL

NEW YORK ● LONDON ● TORONTO
SYDNEY ● NEW DELHI ● AUCKLAND

Edge of Ireland

Seasons on the Beara Peninsula

Written and illustrated by

David Yeadon

HARPER  PERENNIAL

FIRST EDITION

Designed by Emily Cavett Taff

Library of Congress Cataloging-in-Publication Data is available
upon request.

ISBN: 978-0-06-115127-9

09 10 11 12 13 NMSG/RRD 10 9 8 7 6 5 4 3 2 1

In loving memory of my wife Anne's late father,
Sydney Coultish
whose Yorkshire humor, courage, and warmth
remain as examples to us of a full and fine life.
He will be a vital part of our lives forever.

Also with wonderful memories of the late
Theo Westenberger
dear friend, photographer supreme,
and creator of beauty, magic, and mystery.
You will never be forgotten.

Also in admiration of the late
Tommy Makem
"Mr. Ireland" himself, renowned singer,
songwriter, author, philosopher, compatriot of the
beloved Clancy Brothers, and friend.

The Beara—a haunting array of scenery—least toured but most spectacular of the southwestern peninsulas, showed herself to be an eerie beauty of the mists, especially suited for the ghosts and fairies who live there. . . . Wind, fog, sea and craggy rock crescendo here and the wildest of Ireland's wild moors give testimony to the mysticism of the land.

—JILL AND LEON URIS,
from: *Ireland: A Terrible Beauty* (1975)

Contents

☩

SPRING
The Season of Imbolc

✠

SUMMER

The Season of Beltaine ("Bright Fire")

✠

AUTUMN

The Season of Lughnasa

✠

WINTER

The Season of Samhain

List of Illustrations

A Note on Research

FIRST, I'M SURE THAT CONNOISSEURS OF Irish history and the country's socioeconomic subtleties will find a few places in this book to let fly with contradictions at my gleaned research. The problem with Irish history is the viewpoint. This of course is what led Henry Ford to the blunt conclusion that "history is bunk," based largely on the fact that historical facts are malleable, selectable, and notoriously unfactual (a quandary obvious in any law court every day). Ford also pointed out that history and the facts to support it were invariably compiled by the victors or survivors of any particular battle or other shifts in the status quo, not to mention the personal spins of the historians' political/social biases and regular revisions in the context of longer term hindsights and perspectives and shifts in power, control, and politics.

So—generally speaking I've taken what one might call the "cautious" path with Irish and even local Beara history. I've tried to avoid putting my own overly neophyte spin on things (despite arduous research that inevitably made it even more difficult for me to arrive at any hard and fast conclusions). I thus left it largely to the locals—some very opinionated locals usually—to give me their erudite and effervescent summations. And in terms of their and everyone else's words in this book, I have relied primarily upon transcripts from my beloved little microtapes, used whenever I chatted with potential contributors. In most instances they were fully aware of the taping, and I respected their wishes for anonymity whenever (rarely) requested, by modifying names a little or merely paraphrasing their inputs.

Also, to all those who shared their views on and love for Ireland and the Beara Peninsula—thank you all for your invaluable assistance. This book would not have been possible without you. And you know who you are . . .

Finally, "a thousand thanks" to Bridget Allen, my loyal partner in manuscript production; to Hugh Van Dusen, my longtime (and long-patient) colleague and editor, whose advice and support are always vital; and to my wife—Anne—traveling companion, gentle critic, spirit nurturer, and best friend without whom all my ventures and wanderings would be hollow shards indeed.

A Note on the Illustrations

I AM CONSTANTLY INSPIRED BY THE amazing artistic work and publications of my friend Neil Watson. In his most recent book, *Drawing: Developing a Lively and Expressive Approach*, I noted a series of suggestions that helped redefine my usual approach to book illustration:

> Our mechanisms of visual perception do not result in an innate ability to copy things visually, but rather to experience them, react to them, respond to them, interpret them. . . . The human mind excels at interpretation and imagination so it makes sense to play to those strengths when we come to embark upon any form of personalized graphic expression, rather than to become bogged down in over-descriptive draughtsmanship.

> Be still and just look. Let the subject speak. Constantly ask yourself what your drawings are about, their purpose and intent.

> And in the end—be enthusiastic. It is contagious!

So—I've tried something a little different with the illustrations in this book.

In my previous self-illustrated publications I've tended to select a specific medium and—for want of a better word—a "style" and use them consistently through each specific book.

In this instance I've taken a different approach. Or, maybe more accurately, a different approach has taken me in new directions. As I began sketching, particularly "on site," I found that the power and impact of each subject tended to suggest its own distinct medium and its own "style." My materials consisted primarily of various blendings of pencil (HB to 6B), charcoal, pen and ink, monochrome brush washes, bamboo pen, and a range of paper textures. I found great freedom and joy in letting the subject speak to me and guide the combination of hand, brain, and eye from fast—even frantic—flurries of lines and shadings to far more measured articulations of form, texture, and dimensionality.

The process has been both fascinating and satisfying. Boundaries have been pushed out in terms of my own learning and technique experimentation. Some may find the intended inconsistencies and permutations of style a touch bizarre—maybe even a little self-indulgent. But I blame Beara itself. The power and intensity of both the land and the people are such that I celebrated the subjects imposing their uniquenesses upon me. Ireland had that effect on my spirit.

And it also had that effect on the spirit of my longtime friend and coartist, Celia Teichman. She joined us with her husband, Robby, on Beara for a spate of sketching and produced such fine portraits of three of our friends—Danny Quinn, Michael Murphy, and Julie Aldridge—that I asked if I could include these in the book. She agreed—so thank you, Celia, and may your art continue to be ever inspired by the unique essence of Beara.

Little Insights on Ireland

Edmund Spenser, poet, 1596:

Ah to be sure it is yet a most bewtifull and sweete country as any is under Heaven.

A Quandary: *Southern Star* 5/13/06:

The enthusiasm surrounding the launch of a new marketing tool for Cork-Kerry Tourism was offset by the confusion surrounding the upcoming disbandonment of Cork-Kerry Tourism.

Benjamin Disraeli:

Ah Ireland . . . That damnable delightful country, where everything that is right is the opposite of what it ought to be.

Brendan Behan:

Sex is still in its infancy in Ireland.

Weather, *Irish Times*, 17 May 2006:

There will be early morning showers becoming heavier and more persistent as the day progresses. This is now the 22nd consecutive day of this forecast.

"Water and Whiskey," from *St. Patrick's People,*
Tony Gray. Macmillan, 1996:

Irishmen don't take much water in their whiskey. They're deeply prejudiced against it, perhaps for the very good reason

that there's far too much of it about. You can't get away from
water in Ireland.

Shane Connaughton:

Jesus must have been an Irishman. After all, He was unmar-
ried at thirty-two years old, still living at home, and His
mother thought he was God.

Patrick Murray:

God created alcohol just to stop the Irish ruling the world.

Introduction:
Where and Why Beara?

A NUMBER OF YEARS AGO I spent a week or so roaming the wild moorland hills and ragged coastline of County Kerry's Dingle Peninsula. Set deep in the southwest corner of Ireland, far above and far less discovered than the overtouristic Killarney and the Ring of Kerry (aka the Iveragh Peninsula), The Dingle is the northernmost of the five mountainous peninsulas that thrust out like ancient gnarled fingers into the Atlantic. It was, as far as I can remember, a most intriguing if rather predictable romp of village dances, stout-drinking nights in lopsided pubs rowdy with Irish folk music, quaint guesthouses serving true Irish "comfort food" (heavy on "salt-meadow" lamb, just-caught fish, and such strange vegetable concoctions as *boxty*, *pandy*, *strand*, and *fadge*), and locals whose ability to befriend with good-humored graciousness softened the dramatic desolation of the moors and mountain ranges all around.

After that week, The Dingle seemed to me the epitome of an authentic Irish experience. One that I promised myself to repeat, and maybe I would even trace my own Anglo-Irish roots to learn something about my father's mother's County Mayo heritage. And I did indeed return—to prepare a chapter for my book *The World's Secret Places (National Geographic)*—only to find that, while still majestic in its scenic appeal, the Dingle had gone tourist in ways that had blurred and distorted its original unfussy, unself-conscious appeal.

I was ready to move on and out until the owner of a small B and B in Tralee suggested that "if it's in search of the 'real Ireland' that

y'are, y'd best be sneakin' a peep at Mór Choaird Bheara, the Beara
Peninsula, before that gets 'Dingled' too!" Actually his advice was a
little more succinct: "I'd bugger off to Beara, fast as y'can now, before
that fella over there sees y've bin chattin' up his bird . . ."

I was going to explain that my "chattin' up" was merely an innocent discussion about the Dingle's recent and remarkable surge in
popularity when I spotted the boyfriend pushing up his sleeves in a
particularly determined manner . . .

My journey was not wasted (as obviously I could have been).
Beara is certainly a long way from being "Dingled." "Stubbornly and
gloriously remote at the edge of the world," was the way one local
described it at MacCarthy's Bar in Castletownbere. William Makepeace Thackeray was a little more flowery, as befits that famous
nineteenth-century author: "Here is a country the magnificence of
which no pen can give an idea." Leon Uris in his book *Ireland: A
Terrible Beauty* writes more recently: " 'The Bere' [local spelling] is
the least toured but the most spectacular of the peninsulas and
shows herself to be an eerie beauty of the mists, especially suited for
the ghosts and fairies who live there . . . Wind, fog, sea and craggy
rock crescendo here with the wildest of Ireland's wild moors, giving
testimony to the mysticism of the land." Mysteries that have also
lured here such other notable writers as William Wordsworth, Anthony Trollope, Sir Walter Scott, Alfred Tennyson, and much more
recently, Daphne du Maurier, George Bernard Shaw, James Joyce,
Samuel Beckett, Brendan Behan, W. B. Yeats, J. M. Synge, Sean
O'Casey, Seamus Heaney, and many others. A fine host of mutual
Beara celebrants!

H. V. Morton, in his classic book *In Search of Ireland*, suggests:
"Here [on Beara], away from the roads and among mountains that go
down sharply to the sea, you understand why in such lonely places
the Irish believe in fairies and things not of this earth . . . High up
on the hillsides, there is a reek of peat and the distant creak of a cart
grinding the dust of the road, then silence deep as the ocean—the

silence of enchanted hills, the silence of the sky." Morton admits to being utterly seduced by this beguiling region: "It encourages fantastic thought . . . There is one sign that a writer is beginning to enjoy Ireland: he stops writing. There is another: he disappears. This generally happens when he enters County Kerry!"

George Bernard Shaw

Other writers, however, were a little less gushy. Dublin-born James Joyce, who spent little time in the country, dismissed the whole of Ireland as "a mere afterthought of Europe." And Louis MacNeice wrote: "The Irish have nothing but an insidious bonhomie, an obsolete bravado and a way with horses." But, there again—he was from Belfast in Northern Ireland, a whole different kind of country.

So Anne, my wife and favorite traveling companion, and I plan on following H. V. Morton's example and . . . disappearing. Although the writing will continue, here on this thirty-mile-long peninsula, with a population of around 14,000 (in a nation of around four million), half in County Kerry and half in County Cork. Beara is blessed with some of the finest Gulf Stream–bathed coastal scenery in Ireland: glacier-gouged mountain passes and trails across the Caha and Slieve Miskish ranges on the 125-mile-long Beara Way; prehistoric remnants and stone circles; bird and seal colony islands; whale-watching perches on the 700-foot-high Mizen Head cliffs; color-bedecked villages (tiny Allihies and Eyeries also have small but flourishing artist communities); ancient castles and manors—and, of course, history. The full gamut of that riotous Irish heritage of revolutions, decimations, evictions, emigrations, famines, and ultimately celebrations of hard-won freedoms that are at the very heart of Irish poetry, literature, and folk songs. Songs that can make you weep, laugh, curse, and cheer all in the flow of a few melodic stanzas while the stout pours out, thick and black, in the traditional grocery store–pubs that are the focal point of every village on this "secret" peninsula.

I remember one splendid folk song about St. Brendan, who set off in a tiny *curagh* (a wattle and cowskin boat) and supposedly discovered America. Apparently it was not unusual for monks who sought to bear witness to their faith to set sail without food, water, or any means of steering. This sometimes proved a remarkably convenient and rapid way of getting to heaven rather than to the New World. Or anywhere else for that matter.

Castletownbere

And while significant tourist trappings in Beara are a long way off yet—due in part to the narrowness of its roads and the rugged nature of its topography—it's good to know that the charmingly unspoilt town of Kenmare (population 6,500 or so) offers some of the finest dining outside Dublin, not to mention some of the best handmade lace in the world. In addition the villages here, while simple and remote, are celebrated for their beauty and authenticity. Quaint Castletownbere has one of the busiest fishing harbors in the southwest, along with its beloved ultratraditional famed MacCarthy's pub offering pure Irish ambience—what the writer Pete McCarthy describes as: "The dream Irish pub of the popular romantic imagination."

So who's this Pete McCarthy? you might well ask.

Well, sadly he's now the late Pete McCarthy, who passed away from cancer in 2003 at far too young an age. But from all accounts he lived a full life as an actor, writer, professional scriptwriter and comedian, BBC radio commentator, traveler and travel filmmaker and TV travel program presenter (and seemed to possess the potential for a dozen more multi-incarnations). And it was his hilarious and very popular travel book, *McCarthy's Bar*, that was another reason Anne and I felt lured to Beara. Pete had set himself the enviable task of meandering around the west of Ireland in search of bars that bore his surname. Despite an Anglo-Irish identity, he had a strong leaning toward the latter and was an enthusiastic proponent of the "eighth rule of serious travel": "Never pass a bar that has your name on it."

So—using a montage of extracts from his book—this is how Pete came to discover the magic of Beara for himself:

> *[An impromptu conversation with a builder in a bar.]* "So, looking for ya roots are ya? Like all them poor feckin' Yanks in Killarney . . . Where you heading next then? Have you been out to the Beara Peninsula?"
>
> I never have; a piece of news which is greeted by sighs of

pity and incredulity all around. I've heard about it all right, a
wild strip of land poking out into the Atlantic off the Western
fringe of Cork.

"It's a beautiful place. You'll find plenty of McCarthy's out
that way to make you feel at home."

It's a nice idea but there just isn't time to go to Beara.

"And there's a MacCarthy's pub out there, real old style,
never been changed."

"I really couldn't change my plans now."

"Why the feck not!"

[Another customer joins in.] "I reckon there's only two
kinds of people, the Irish and the wannabe Irish."

Clearly she's one of the former, but what if I'm one of the
latter?

Pete finally has to make a decision in the gorgeously verdant,
Gulf Stream–lapped town of Glengarriff. Go north to the Ring of
Kerry and the Dingle Peninsula or be serendipitous and take the
narrow road west down into Beara.

A man after my own wanderlusting Anglo-Irish heart, Pete decided to go west into

an altogether wilder place . . . with stark mountains of
biblical ruggedness . . . Radiant shafts of sunlight pierce the
dark bruise of cloud cover and hit the water with a metallic
flash, as if to prove there is a Creator and his taste is for
random and terrifying beauty. By heading for Beara instead
of following my intended route I suppose I'm hoping to leave
the world of plans and arrangements behind, lay claim to my
share of Ireland's spontaneous and disorganized ebullience
and see if I really fit in. I'll simply turn up at MacCarthy's
bar and see what happens. If nothing does, I can go away
again.

So God bless you, Pete, for following the finest of travel instincts
and spontaneously pursuing the hidden and the authentic—and in

doing so, encouraging us to follow you in your serendipitous adventures into Ireland's "hidden corners."

And this is what I'll be describing in this book—how a nation, currently booming with newfound prosperity as part of the European Union, and known proudly now as the Celtic Tiger—still manages to hide away such little gems of authenticity and awe as the Beara Peninsula. But from time to time, Anne and I will also "disappear" and just like Yeats dreamed:

> *I will arise and go now, and go to Innisfree,*
> *And a small cabin build there, of clay and wattles made,*

(at least we'll build it in our imagination . . .).

And we'll be celebrating the unique spirit and humor of Pete McCarthy too. May you rest in peace and also continue to share your laughter wherever you are . . .

SPRING

The Season of Imbolc

⋮

ACTIVE LIFE IN THE IRISH COUNTRYSIDE *explodes (something of an oxymoron in a nation renowned for its laid-back approach to life and living) after St. Patrick's Day, on March 17, and that old Gaelic greeting once again celebrates the arrival of spring—Céad Míle Faílte—"a hundred thousand welcomes."*

When the wild and pagan-tinged Imbolc and Brigid's Feast festivities are over (much to the relief of the local Catholic clergy), and the shamrocks drooping from buttonholes have finally wilted—the year unveils itself again, and the rush of new life truly begins.

The three incarnations of St. Brigid are revitalized—the inspired poet and keeper of ancient traditions; her creative strength of the blacksmith; and her nurturing hands of a healer and midwife. The spirit of Taispeach—the great fertility and fresh-life romp—surges across the land. The fields and the ribboned roadside hedgerows

St. Brigid

see their first flush of color, the daffodil. The winter winds have abated, the land is warming up, giving way to budding foliage and swathes of primroses that carpet the ditches with creamy yellows and the softest of greens. Even the bare boglands and the hump-backed mountains behind them and the cozy white cottages and the dark fortifications of old peat turf-mounds that seem like the flame-blackened ruins of once mighty forts—all these are now sprinkled with glittering Seurat-like pointillisms of sun-flecked color and the bouncing white dots of newborn lambs.

Curlews and cuckoos call, and ravens replenish their nests. The blackthorn blossoms powder the field edges, followed in mid-May by high flurried walls of white thorn and hawthorn and all their explosions of berries, devoured in their billions by the field birds. Gorse blooms fresh-golden on the moors and bluebells carpet the small woodlands. At this time of the year the air is heavy with heady aromas—not the turfy smoke of winter but rather the life-stirring fragrance of fresh growth following sudden short April showers. And the ocean too. That aroma too is different—particularly the first earth-breath of morning rolling in with the vast Atlantic undulating under a huge pearlescent sky. And along the water's edge, tiny dunlin and sanderlings skitter in hyperactive clusters and village children play in the rock pools and, way out there, on the horizon's edge, and along the beautiful Allihies beach, the great colonies of kittiwakes, razorbills, guillemots, and gannets regain and aggressively retain their precarious perches on Little Skellig and other offshore sanctuaries.

And we smile. The bone-chill and blackness of winter are gone. The days are warmer, longer, and full of fresh beauty and hope. And we're moving in . . .

Sláinte!

1
Comín_G ínto Dublín

WAY BACK IN MY NEOPHYTE DAYS as a wannabe adventure-travel
writer, a curmudgeonly editor of a long-defunct travel magazine
once insisted that I should avoid all negativity in my submissions
because "people reading pieces such as yours really don't need to
hear about the 'reality' of places—just give 'em the cheerful, positive, upbeat stuff," he said. "Tell 'em only what they want to hear."

In hindsight I realize that most of my erratic life has been based
on the motto "learn the rules first and then break them fast." So I
begin this particular chapter awash in negativity. For example: it was
not a good idea for us two neophyte "blow-ins" (tourists, visitors,
and other "outsiders") to head straight into the heart of Dublin on
our first hour after arrival from New York in a hired, right-hand-drive
car with manual shift and all the turbo power of an egg-laden sea
turtle. In fact, following the dire warnings from the rental car staff
about Ireland being one of the three most dangerous places in the
world to drive in and about how all credit cards, even the elite platinum cards, refused to provide ancillary insurance coverage in the
country—it was possibly *not* a good idea to hire a car at all.

We even began to have doubts about the country itself as we de-
tected little from airport personnel of the "Warm Irish Welcome"
that we'd been promised in all those positive brochures. And it was
not a good idea for me to say to Anne, "Look, I found the street on

the map where our prebooked hotel is located, so all you have to do is to guide us there." It was *not* a good idea first, because Anne hates reading maps and will sit slightly traumatized staring at all the colored squiggles and barely legible type and forgetting to actually lift her head to check the passing scene for street names and the like (not that it would have made any difference in Dublin, because the street signs are either nonexistent or so small and cramped with bilingual Gaelic translations that you can't read them from a moving car anyway).

Second, because Dublin is the proud possessor of one of the world's most illogical and diabolically confusing one-way-street systems, which makes you wonder how even experienced residents ever find their way to anywhere around the inner city. Even the taxi drivers are flummoxed to the point where we later found it useless to request their services. They were invariably more confused by all the one-way systems than we were.

And third, because despite a very enticing Web ad that had lured us to advance hotel booking, the hotel was actually not a hotel at all, but merely a front office for a random scattering of rentable apartments all around St. Steven's Green park. And the office, of course, had a different name from the one on the Web site. And the nameplate was so small and insignificant that when, after hours of inane looping around downtown Dublin, we were finally parked outside the office, and it was still impossible to confirm from the car that we had in fact arrived. And, in fact, we hadn't. We signed in, parked the car in one of the murkiest, deepest subterranean garages it has ever been our misfortune to negotiate, and then followed a poor immigrant from Nigeria who had been sent to manhandle our luggage along almost half a mile of sidewalks to a tiny, disheveled apartment that was to be our home for a few days. We complained vehemently about the garage, the luggage system, and the apartment and—our first break of the day—we were rewarded with far larger and newly refurbished accommodations.

And it was *not* a good idea to go in search of the Irish tourist office. "Sure, it's just a little stroll down the street and across the bridge," said the girl at the hotel reception desk. But it turned out to be a very long hike, and the office wasn't there anyhow. It apparently had been closed up for weeks and vanished without leaving so much as a relocation address (a rather odd debacle in a country so dependent upon the goodwill of tourists).

And it was *not* a good idea for me then to look at the map and say, "Well, why don't we have a stroll into town . . . It's just a short walk across St. Steven's Green." It was, in fact, a major ambulatory expedition along broad streets lined with officious-looking, Corinthian-columned, neo-Stalinist monoliths until—ah! the relief of it all—we suddenly entered that oasis of green calm. There were bubbling fountains, chirpy choruses of birds, and cool shade beneath enormous oaks and beech trees whose branches curved gracefully to caress velvety grasses and vibrant flower beds. A small sign announced we had discovered—almost by chance—this beautiful twenty-two-acre Manhattan Central Park in miniature created around 1880 courtesy of the Guinness family, prime doyens of Dublin's affluent aristocracy.

Statues abound here—including (of course) James Joyce, a Henry Moore memorial for W. B. Yeats, and a huge monument to Wolfe Tone, one of Ireland's greatest nationalistic leaders. A band was tuning up on the delicately filigreed bandstand. But most appealing were the people—locals sprawled on the lawns eating their sandwich lunches, lovers nestling and nudging beside the winding footpaths, travelers of all ethnic and national origins slowly wandering and wondering at the encyclopedic array of plants and trees—and Anne and me, utterly beguiled by this mellow, magical place.

The mellowness ended abruptly as we emerged on the pedestrianized Grafton Street, whose gay (in all its interpretations) intimacy, retail hoopla, street-busker rowdiness, and crowded youthful brouhaha, complete with tumults of giggling teenettes zigzagging about with hen-party abandon (if you've never seen one of these events—don't!), made us realize that, finally, we had found the heart, or at least one of the three hearts, of Dublin. And although it was *not* a good idea to have left the umbrella back at the apartment because of regular tumultuous downpours of spring rain, we still laughed and hugged in delight at finally sensing the enticing people-powered spirit of the city.

And where better to celebrate our belated arrival in this place of creators, writers, con artists, and cock-a-jays but at John Kehoe's little pub on Anne Street South right next door to the tiny and oh so gorgeously redolent Sheridan's Cheese Shop. (This immediately became our favorite retail focus, with the possible exception of the nearby Marks & Spencer Food Hall.) And what a greeting we received at that pub, one of over a thousand within Dublin's city limits. People turned and smiled; the barmaid welcomed us as if we'd been regulars for years, and in no time at all, our very first beautiful, black, smoky-flavored, cream-topped pints of Guinness were set before us. Although here I exaggerate a little. It wasn't really "in no time." It was actually quite a few expectancy-laden minutes because we'd forgotten the ritual three-stage (sometimes even four) process of stout pouring, whether it be Guinness, Murphy's, or Beamish, the three traditional choices across the country, none of which are actually produced, sadly enough, by an Irish-owned company.

Our initiation into pub protocols began as we watched the ritual of "the pour," which is enticing yet very deceiving. The barmaid's first pull fills a pint glass rapidly and you're licking your lips, waiting to plunge into that semisolid cream-foam head. But then her pull ceases when the glass is two-thirds full and it's set down "to rest" while she's off serving someone else. Eventually, two long minutes later, she's back and slowly easing the remaining third of the stout into the glass . . . almost to the top. But it's that "almost" that'll drive you mad with pent-up desire because you have to wait again—sometimes for up to another full minute—until a final ridiculous little flick of the pull-lever injects that last ounce or so of black liquor to provide a perfect cream topping, which she may or may not skim with a knife, in a final finessing flourish before handing you your reward for almost unbearable patience. And so I celebrate the daily patience of all those other "punters" who wait at each of Ireland's 25,000 Guinness "taps" for their glasses of "black." And each pub seems to have its own little pouring idiosyncrasies and customs. Some in Dublin insist that the best places are Neary's, Long Hall, and Stag's Head; others, particularly the writers and journalists, insist it's Doheny and Nesbitt's, but in terms of an overall favorite, it's invariably the mighty Mulligan's, founded in 1782 and still said to offer "the best pint in the whole city—and maybe the whole of Ireland!"

Is it worth the wait? Indeed it is, although to reduce further waiting time, it's best to order the second pint immediately upon receipt of the first.

We had been dreaming of this moment for months, but first, permit me a pet peeve.

As any regular bar-frequenter knows, there are thousands of erzatz versions of Irish pubs around the world complete with elaborate etched glass; brightly burnished quaint shamrock-adorned signs for O'Shaunahay's, O'Flanagan's, or O'Doherty's; antiqued Guinness signs; pseudo bar pulls; red-haired (dyed) non-Irish colleens; lots of diddle-di, diddle-da music; and inane signs inviting customers to KISS ME I'M IRISH. They're everywhere. Some even have genuine Irish pub doors ripped off some poor bankrupt place in a godforsaken Irish bog-village no one's ever heard of. Others boast fiberglass yellowed oak beams (to suggests eons of tobacco-pub-fug), a dartboard or two, and maybe even a few clay spittoons scattered about, although no one ever seems sure what to do with those.

And it really doesn't matter. Because it's all a load of "feckin eejit junk" that bears no more relationship to a real Irish pub than a tame house cat does to a wild savannah leopard. And having got all that off my chest, let me introduce you to the truly authentic Dublin watering hole of Kehoe's, just a short stroll off Grafton Street.

We couldn't have found a more Irish city pub than this one, described in one revered guidebook to Ireland's taverns as "possibly the best pub in the world." (Similar accolades celebrate the eight-hundred-year-old heritage of the nearby Brazen Head, long regarded as the hotbed nexus of nefarious plots to rid Ireland of the hated British.) And according to a sign outside on the side wall, even the great "*Ulysses* man" himself, James Augustine Joyce, wrote that "in the particular is contained the universal. Kehoe's with all its charms and beauties will surely live for generations." And indeed it has, with its aged yellowed ambience, old wood paneling, etched glass, ancient worn floorboards, and a clientele that knows this is one of the best places in town to enjoy the best of times. Even to the point of offering impromptu hugs, which I received from one charmingly exuberant youngish lady who said she loved my white beard and "lovely tummy" and had always wanted to say a special thank-you to dear old Santa Claus for all his kindnesses. So—as we were leaving—she did just that, which halted our departure for a while longer as we chatted with her coterie of female friends (three more hugs here—I tell you, this Santa beard is a keeper for life! Not too sure about the tummy, though . . .) and managed to squeeze in another pint or two before we finally eased ourselves painlessly out the door as they all wished Anne and me a very good night—*oíche mhaith duit!*

Despite the abrupt deluges, which were interspersed in schizoid Irish fashion by brilliant periods of bright, hot sun and blue skies, the exuberance and vitality of the crowds on Grafton Street washed us northward into the tiny squares and courts of the Dickensian Temple Bar Quarter and eventually to the River Liffey itself.

Writers often make this stream seem as imposing as London's Thames or Manhattan's East River, but in actuality it is an enticingly modest stream crossed by stubby bridges that provide easy intercourse between the twin urbanities on either side.

We strolled on past the great Dublin landmarks—Christ Church Cathedral, the stately composition of Dublin Castle, the National Gallery, and the architectural extravaganza of Trinity College, meeting and melding place of Ireland's greatest artists, writers, and statesmen. Finally we circled around to the great O'Connell Bridge. Here we crossed into O'Connell Street, that gloriously broad avenue that is featured so prominently in Dublin's turbulent history, a history that was now being flaunted from banners and poster and placards declaring the celebration of the ninetieth anniversary of the great Easter Rising of April 24, 1916—one of the most spectacular, if ill-organized, of Ireland's attempts to throw off the scourge of British imperialism.

And guess what day it was? It was April 12, 2006, and the Easter Rising celebrations had already begun and were an incessant generator of discussions, documentaries, and political diatribes for another three weeks!

And if that wasn't enough, it was also the centenary of the birth of Samuel Beckett, that maverick poet, playwright, and novelist,

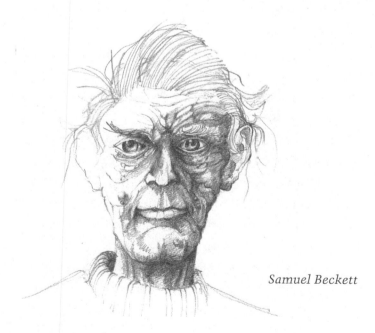

Samuel Beckett

once described by Nancy Cunard as having "the look of an Aztec eagle and a feeling of the spareness of the desert about him." His *Waiting for Godot* and a score of other minimalist productions still confuse the uninitiated, delight his disciples, and create infinitely more pompous pontification and pseudo-intellectual blather than all his own strange pieces combined.

Beckett left the city—"this nothing of a noplace"—without ever adequately explaining any of his work, except to hint that maybe his whole genre and oeuvre was a send-up of the very idea of genre and oeuvre—and pretty much of life and living in general.

And it was ironical that he and fellow Dubliner James Joyce became companions and strong coworkers in Paris during the late 1920s. There was Joyce, renowned with his *Ulysses* and his impenetrable *Finnegans Wake* for putting everything into his works (at almost seven hundred pages, *Ulysses* covers only a single day in Dublin), whereas Beckett took just about everything out. A review of *Waiting for Godot*, which was running at a city theater during our visit, read: "Each fresh viewing sheds new light—on nothing."

And yet despite the differences in their works, they were very similar in other odd respects. As one biographer suggests, they were both: "agnostic, polyglot, metaphysical, apolitical, numerologists, superstitious, and humorous."

So we had arrived in the midst of this zany carnival-like celebration of a key historic and political event, on that fateful day in April 1916, that was in truth an utter confusion in terms of organization, public interest, and comprehension. Then this was coupled with a second event that honored a writer who, according to one critic, epitomized "organized disorganization" and certainly generated enough public incomprehension about "nothing and nothingness" to guarantee his celebrity for a second centennial.

Swimming about for a couple of days in such dichotomous tides of "un-history" and nonsensical rhetorical contradictiveness, we felt we were touching something of the true wacky and audacious spirit of this compact and cohesive city (cohesion that, alas, collapses into utter confusion, of course, when you get behind the wheel of a car).

Joyce, who wrote the ultimate "Dublin novel" in his *Ulysses*, despite the fact that he lived most of his life out of the country, captures the rambunctious stream of glorious consciousness here. In fact, so richly descriptive of Dublin is the book, that Joyce claimed, if the city were ever destroyed, it could be re-created through the pages of his *Ulysses*.

So—here are a few fragments of his homage to Dublin:

> *The gray warm evening descended upon the city . . . The streets swarmed with a gaily-colored crowd. Like illuminated pearls the lamps shone from the summits of the tall poles upon the living texture below, changing shape and hue unceasingly.*

In a second vibrant vignette:

> *The air without is impregnated with rainbow moisture, life essence celestial, glistening on Dublin stone there under star-shiny coelum. God's air, the All Father's air, scintillant circumambient cessile air. Breathe it deep into thee.*

And from another of his beloved books, *Dubliners*:

> *It was noon when we reached the quays and we bought two big currant buns and sat down to eat them on some metal piping by the river. We pleased ourselves with the spectacle of Dublin's commerce—the barges signal from afar away by their curls of wooly smoke. The brown fishing fleet beyond Ringsend, the big white sailing vessel which was being discharged on the opposite quay . . . Looking at the high masts I imagine the geography which had been scantily dosed to me at school gradually taking substance before my eyes . . .*

Then we walked through the flaring streets, jostled by
drunken men and bargaining women, amid the curses of
laborers, the shrill litanies of shop boys who stood on guard
by the barrels of pigs' cheeks, the nasal chanting of street
singers, who sang a come-all-you, about O'Donovan Rossa, or
a ballad about the troubles in our native land. These noises
converged in a single sensation of life for me.

There's something utterly enticing about Joyce's rich ramblings that resonates here in the city. They are perfectly suited to one another—the prose and the zany realities. You want to go about reciting aloud his observations and celebrations, sharing them with the smiley-faced people on Grafton Street, watching their eyes light up when they see how his bouncing words and rhythms pick up and toss like bright baubles all the sensations, sounds, and sights that surround us. You want to shout out "D'ya see it?" "D'ya feel it?" "D'ya understand what he's painting in words?"

But instead of shouting we shuffled off instead to a church where, it being the Easter season, one of many services was in progress. Easter is one time in the year when even the most recalcitrant churchgoers finally bow to guilty consciences and bend a humble knee. And we were no exception on this particular occasion. It is also the one time, on Good Friday, when all the eight thousand or so pubs in Ireland are closed and there's a national panic over booze—or the lack of it.

We entered the church and, despite the excellence of the choir and the rapidity of the Communion that in an Anglican Church with five hundred congregants could have taken a good hour or more to get through, the long service inevitably developed a droney, droopy pace and mood. And I caught myself remembering the flash and flourish of Joyce's religious revivalist rhetoric in the turbulent middle section of *Ulysses*, and wondered how this would go down if read aloud here in the church instead of yet another dirgy psalm:

Hush! Sinned against the light and even now that day is at hand when He shall come to judge the world by fire. Pflaap! Elijah is coming! Washed by the blood of the Lamb. Come on, you wine-fizzling, gin-sizzling, booze-guzzling existences. Come on, you dog-gone, bull-necked, beetle-browed, hog-jowled, peanut-brained, weasely-eyed flower flushes, false alarms and excess baggage! Come on, you triple extracts of infamy. The Deity ain't no nickel dime bum show. I put it to you that He's on the square and a corking fine proposition. He's the grandest thing yet and don't you forget it. Shout salvation and King Jesus. You'll need to rise precious early, you sinner there, if you want to diddle the Almighty God. Pflaaap!

It didn't happen, of course. Instead the congregation began one more murmured recitation of the Our Father, and I felt the yawns easing like sleepy cloudscapes over me. A little Joyce would certainly have juiced up and jollied the process along, but as this period is the most sacred of the Catholic calendar, maybe it was best to stick to the tried-and-true. After all, I convinced myself, we were going to need all the blessings we could engender during this new adventure of ours in a new country—and by the sound of it, most

James Joyce

particularly on the racetrack roads where we'd been told many drivers were unlicensed, uninsured, and far too often, unsober.

And so back to Beckett, who, like Joyce, spent most of his life out of Ireland and was typically obscure when defining the settings for his works. This fragment possibly captures something of the spirit of Dublin that we sensed during our own brief introduction:

Apologies. As another editor emphasized to me eons ago, authors should not play games with their readers. But—this tease of blank space could be interpreted literally. I honestly couldn't find, in all of Beckett's works, a single reference that seemed to have any relevance to our reflections upon Dublin. Or any other recognizable place on our earth, for that matter. On the other hand, this space could be interpreted artistically as a recognition of the minimalist blankness, the emptiness, the near vacuum, the void that permeates almost all of his plays: *Acts-Without-Words, Roughs-for-Theatres, Roughs-for-Radios,* and even his forty-second contribution to Kenneth Tynan's *Oh! Calcutta!,* "written" in 1969 and titled simply *Breath.* This work consists of a curtain raised up with a faint light falling on "miscellaneous rubbish" scattered across the stage followed by "a faint brief cry," an expiration of breath, and then silence, before the curtain drops again. Some claim it's actually been performed in just over twenty seconds as opposed to the forty seconds estimated by Beckett. Undoubtedly a relief to many in the audience.

What a bizarre nonworld the Nobel-Prized Beckett offered to a confused public—minimalistic tableaux of suspended heads with frantically chattering mouths; people in overgrown plant pots; characters immersed in sand; two Chaplinesque tramps waiting by a solitary tree for someone or something that never comes; a man feverishly winding and rewinding a recorded tape searching for . . . the truth, the meaning, or perhaps just the meaning*less*ness of man's existence. I find his work irritating, absurd, pretentious, arrogantly elusive (and illusive), ambiguous to the point of total nonsense—and utterly, gloriously enticing. Even if I can't call up the necessary rigorous attention his plays need, I still sense fundamental truths, humor, and deep eternal perceptions floating by, tantalizingly just out of reach. Or certainly *my* reach, and certainty, or the lack of it, seems to be the elusive essence of many of his works. As one of the *Waiting for Godot* characters exclaims: "To have lived is not enough for them . . . They have to talk about it . . . To be dead is not enough for them."

With all the frenzied forelock-tugging of the metropolitan literatae and Habling-bling bloated reverential piety about Beckett mushing around the city, it was refreshing to read one critic who wrote that "the centenary celebrations are almost enough to put most off literature for life." Nevertheless, a Beckettian spirit was definitely flowing through downtown Dublin that Easter week (you could hardly escape posters and banners of his tumultuously wrinkled and time-worn face), characterized by sequences of bizarre non sequiturs.

First came flurries of little girls frolicking by in neon pink, meticulously embroidered costumes and heavily made up, carrying skirt-shaped bags for all their inordinately expensive outfits. They were here for some important Irish step dancing contest (now thanks to *Riverdance* and clones, an international passion) and accompanied by proud and occasionally stressed-out parents who seemed far more nervous than their tiny, decked-up offspring.

And then came one of Ireland's oddest ball games. I'd seen Irish football before and rather liked its odd, rugby-soccer-basketball maneuvers and speedy flow. So different from the lumbering, tough guys' scrums and touchline tumbles of the traditional rugby games I used to be involved in. But I'd never seen a hurling match before and sat fixated by the TV in our room, which showed one of the fastest, most bizarre, and seemingly most dangerous games I've ever experienced. Harry Potter would love it. Fifteen men a side hurtled by and into one another in seemingly total Hogwartian disarray, flailing long *cáman* paddle-sticks on which they carried—yes, carried—a small white leather ball (*sliotar*)—although in the truly wild days when the game first emerged I heard it was often a human skull. And then, while running pell-mell, they tossed the ball off the tip of the stick and whacked it with all the force of a top-flight tennis player to another team player fifty yards or more down the field or, if they could, over the posts at the far end of the field to score points.

In minutes I was hooked. The constant frantic pace and ability of the players to avoid regular decapitation by swirling sticks and supersonic-speed *sliotars* amazed me and left me utterly exhausted by the end of the first half. As a result of watching the game, I fully understood the remark of an elderly gentleman in another of Dublin's fine Irish pubs, Ryan's, on Park Gate Street, when he chortled: "Ah well, this game and our other ancient village game of 'road bowling' explains it all, d'y'see. You English play cricket, which is a waspocracy gentleman's game of patience and fair play, and we do the hurling, which is an ancient bogman's game of pure unrestrained, skull-crushing passion. No wonder we didn't get along with you lot for centuries!"

"Well—thanks for explaining that . . ."

"*Tá fáilte romhat*—you're very welcome, good sir!"

FINALLY, WE DROVE SOUTH out of Dublin, leaving behind the tortuously tangled one-way traffic systems; the glorious pure-Irish pubs, and the earthy redolence of fresh-poured pints of thick black stout; the pedestrianized people-powered streets full of music and mirth; the sudden passing vehemence of a tanked-up local calling the whole world "ya feckin' eejits"; the cultivated calm of the St. Steven's Green gardens; and all the big burly-pillared and porticoed neoclassical public buildings and the dainty, decorous streets of Georgian refinement.

And we were sad, despite the fact that we'd barely touched the place in our brief stay. As had so many others, our hearts had warmed immediately to the heart of Dublin. We could have done, however, without the endless outer eddies of suburban "semis" financed by the surging economic tsunamis of Ireland's "Celtic Tiger" affluence, with their pristine privet hedges and eye-blurring stamp of bland sameness and keeping-up-with-the-Joneses mundanity. And we also tried hard to ignore the bizarre, carnival-colored bungalow mania that seemed to characterize the outer-outer neighborhoods. The riotous riches of downtown Dublin remained with us as we curled on through the high Wicklow Mountains with the radio playing either endless recountings of the Easter Rising or "let's pretend we understand" discussions and diatribes about Beckett's intentionally ambiguous and obscure works that were apparently not meant to be "understood" but rather "un-understood" by the hoi polloi.

"We'll be back," said Anne when we finally switched off the natter-chatter.

"I'm still there," I said. And I meant it.

AND I INDEED FELT we were "still there" a little later that day when we paused on the quay in the pleasant riverside town of Wexford to while away an hour or so over lunch before continuing our drive to County Cork and the Beara Peninsula (a seven-hour drive we managed to stretch into a leisurely three-day backroading odyssey).

Hardly had we ordered a platter of "toasties" (those ubiquitous toasted ham and cheese sandwiches that are a staple of pubs everywhere here) than we became aware of a real Irish brouhaha at a nearby table. The subject (of course) was the Easter Rising again, and the pro-and-con arguments were so complex in the Beckettian sense that I was convinced we were back in one of those gloriously intimate and intense little pubs just outside Trinity College where feisty debates and furious beer-imbibing are the order of the day. Every day.

It quickly became apparent that the distinct lack of concerted conviction on the part of the public in support of the Rising still lingers on today. I tried to keep notes on the group's arguments, but they spoke far too fast (a frustrating national problem over here) and the dialect was far too thick (another problem). But I did find, the following day, parts of a Sunday *Times* editorial that seemed to strike a reasoned balance in all the blather and blarney:

> *Twenty-first Century Ireland is an independent, proud and prosperous republic, and the world's tenth wealthiest nation. Its economy is thriving, its culture is vibrant. Other societies now look to Ireland as an economic role model and covet its confidence and accomplishments. Irish people no longer need the dubious myths and shibboleths of the past to bolster their identity.* [By the sound and fury of the adjoining debate, one could seriously question such an optimistic statement.] *People who see the world today through a republican lens complain that it has taken far too long for the modern Irish state to acknowledge formally the undeniable courage and idealism of the men who led the insurrection on that fateful April morning in 1916.* [The debate at the nearby table continued: "It had officially been canceled, for God's sake! They couldn't get enough support," claimed one of the men at the table. "It was only the crazies who kept going, and if the stupid Brits hadn't executed them in the stonebreaker's yard at Kilmainhan Jail and made martyrs of them, they'd all be long forgotten today!"] *Those who believe this bloody and divisive rebellion had a malign effect on modern Irish history meanwhile argue that the celebrations glorify political violence and send out dangerous signals to unrepentant advocates of the physical force tradition.* [At the table again: "We got the freedom we wanted, though!" shouted one of the group. "Only after massive slaughter and a bloody civil war that split the country down the middle for years," said another. "As the

great John Lennon said," quipped a third man, " 'Time wounds all heels'—and the British heels certainly got their comeuppance!"] *Immigration is changing the complexion of our country and with so many diverse cultures now, the ancient quarrel between nationalists and unionists seems increasingly irrelevant, if not absurd. However, the 1916 Proclamation of Independence remains an impressive document and the citizens of 2006 are the first in Irish history fortunate enough to be free to appreciate all that was liberating and outward-looking about the Easter Rising, while rejecting all that was destructive and narrow-minded.*

We hoped the editorial writer was correct. We had no desire to spend valuable pub time over the next year or so of our stay in the country listening to incessant replays of domestic Irish history, but only time would tell, and, indeed, the later release of Ken Loach's film *The Wind That Shakes the Barley* was indeed one more dramatic and bloody replay of that terrible divisive era. Only time would tell if this would be a major theme of our journey here or whether we could focus happily on the many other intriguing and true aspects of Irish life as it's lived today here in this utterly captivating little country.

2
"Blow-In" Initiation

:
:

I DON'T THINK I'LL EVER DO it again. At least if I do, I'm not sure I'll be around later to tell the tale. I suppose I escaped this time only because, first, it was relatively early in the evening and the little time-worn pub in the heart of Wexford barely contained a quorum of imbibers, and second, because I managed to turn my inane question into a lousy wimpish joke that generated enough dismissive sneers and sniggers to dispel, or at least divert, the threat of malicious mayhem. Of course it also got me labeled as a loopy "blow-in" tourist— harmless and certainly not worth correcting in the traditional Irish manner. Which can be a rather messy business, what with all that threatening verbosity followed by the bludgeoning, spurts of blood, splintered cartilage, purpling bruises, and facial lumps the consistency of extremely hard-boiled eggs.

And what, you may well ask, was this question that could have brought about such a potentially traumatic and painful termination to an otherwise very pleasant evening?

All I did . . . honestly, this is the whole thing in all its naïve simplicity . . . I asked the barman—"Is it possible that you have a bottle of Sam Smith's Ale . . . or better still, a Newcastle Brown?"

Now, I asked this, not for any troublemaking reason or devious intent, but merely because I was, despite my growing enjoyment of the ubiquitous Guinness, longing for a good old pint of British ale, preferably one brewed in or near my home county of Yorkshire or certainly somewhere in the north of England.

There was a sudden somber silence. You could have heard the legendary pin drop, although a sharpening of ax blades might have been more to the point.

"Wha' . . . wha's that yer askin' fer?" asked the barman, preceded by a sly malicious wink to the cluster of arm-flexing, Guinness-chugging giants by the counter.

"Er . . . just, ah, a bottle of Sam Smith's? Pale Ale will be fine—or a Newcastle Brown . . . Even a Worthington would be okay if . . ."

More silence. Of the sinister, sniggery kind. And then: "So—that's the way then, is it? Guinness is not good enough f'ya, then? Is that it? Or Smithwick's or Harp. Or Murphy's. Or Beamish. In fact, it seems t'me like nothin' made in our beautiful country will suffice? Is that right? Y'll just be lookin' exclusively f'yer English piss-water, it seems. Puttin' our poor lads at the breweries here out o' the business while y' be asking fer yer own imported rubbish instead . . ."

"Look . . . listen . . . if you don't have any, it doesn't—"

"Don't have any?! As if I'd let anythin' with a name like Sam Smith's or Newcastle or Worthington get into my cellar while my lovely barrels o' the black stuff rest there waitin' t'be appreciated by them's as knows their beer an' their stout . . ."

I began to suspect that I was becoming the butt of some stupid insider joke or the recipient of a silly little hazing ritual for blow-ins with a hankering for the great British ales. Or maybe it was my accent. Very obviously British. Sort of middle–working class with overtones of grammar school. But definitely not that upper-crust tone, all clipped, authoritative, and dictatorial—the one that conjurers up days of Empire, Rule Britannia, Churchillian bombast, and Prince Charles's speeches. "You're not being serious . . . ," I suggested with a kind of "that's enough now—just pour me a pint" nonchalance.

A nonchalance that was not reciprocated. "So, what's it t'be then?" The barman had an unpleasant habit of stroking the underside of his chin with his finger, sliding it about like a short but deadly knife.

"Well, I guess if there's no Newcastle in the house . . . I suppose a Murphy's stout will have to do."

"We don't sell Murphy's."

"Beamish then?"

"We don't sell Beamish."

"Smithwick's Bitter?"

"Out."

"Harp Lager?"

"Out."

"Look—why don't I just try the place across the road . . ."

"One more guess. Y'get one more," said the barman with a menacing leer that suggested no contradiction.

"Okay—right. Fine. I'll take a pint of your Guinness, then."

Utter transformation!

"Well! Yessir! O'course, sir!" He smiled his best "at your service" customer smile. "A pint o' Guinness it is, then, and a fine choice, sir, if I and my colleagues here might say so. It'll just take a couple o' minutes. T'get the top right. 'S'not Guinness without its proper head, y'understand."

"Yes, I know. I'm quite familiar with Guinness by now."

"Well—are ya, now? I wouldna known that from what it was y' were askin' for a minute or two ago . . . maybe y'were just havin' a little confusion of the mind . . ."

And that's when I should have left. But he was already pulling the pint and the black stuff was pouring in with its surges of infinitesimally tiny brown bubbles and that creamy head building. And it looked as good as all the ads you see on television, particularly the one shot in sepia colors with a young guy mesmerized by the gradually rising nectar of his stout and a bead of anticipatory sweat easing

Barman in Pub

slowly down his forehead to the tip of his nose as the glass gradually fills . . .

Finally the pouring ritual was over, and as I reached to pick up the glass, I sensed a concerted gathering of onlookers around me at the bar. They seemed to be watching me and my drink very expectantly. Well, I thought—I guess I'll show this crowd I can drink a pint of Guinness just as well as the next man. This is no wimpy blow-in here. So I picked up the glass and slowly downed the whole pint without a break for breath or anything else for that matter. Then, when I'd finished, I placed the empty, froth-laced glass back on the counter, wiped my mustache and lips with my left hand, and smiled. "Not bad . . ." I mumbled while half turning toward the door. It was only ten or so broad steps away, I gauged, and there was no one blocking the exit. Maybe I could make it because I certainly had no intention of hanging around this malevolent place—an obvious bastion of blow-in bashing if ever I'd seen one.

"So," sneered the barman. "Y'seemed to enjoy that right 'nough, then . . ."

Go for broke, my proud little Yorkshireman whispered internally. So I did. "Well, t'be honest . . . a pint o' British ale obviously would've been far better, but . . ."

I think the *but* was actually delivered as I reached the door, flung it open, and rushed out into the dark streets. I expected a clatter of feet behind me, but fortunately, no one seemed to think the chase was worth the trouble. I'd survived this little unexpected brush with mortality.

Which of course I hadn't because . . . I'd left my bag on the barstool and had no choice but to go back and retrieve it . . . but that, as they say, is another story . . .

3
Irish History—Fast

He said his name was Liam—Liam Farrell—but to me he looked more like Liam the Leprechaun. He was little—very little—with sharp ferret eyes, a purple nose, strangely long and thin fingers, and a definite preference for shamrock green in his clothing. Not a very clean green, in fact a distinctly grubby green, but close enough to traditional leprechaun getup, I suppose.

We met kind of incidentally. I was sitting on one of the benches by the Waterford waterfront wondering which restaurant Anne and I should grace with our presences for dinner when she'd completed her "shopping" (always a mysterious process. Beyond a diminished bank account—I rarely got to see the results of her retailing pursuits. Especially in the clothing area when, if I see her wearing something new, she'll inevitably respond with a dismissive—"Oh, darlin', I've had this *ages* . . . don't you remember . . ."). Anyway—next thing I knew, this little man had slid into position beside me and was offering me something that looked like a once-white peppermint now coated in thick pocket-dust.

"Er . . . no thanks. I'm fine . . ."

"Oh, I can see that. You're lookin' very fine indeed, sir. Are you touristin' round here then, is it?"

"No, no. We're driving down to the Beara Peninsula. I'm just about to go and buy a couple of books. On Irish history."

That was my first mistake.

"Ah—the Beara Peninsula, is it now? Fine, fine choice indeed, sir. One of the finest spots in the southwest. Very . . . authentic, one might say . . . very wild. And—well now—that's a true coincidence . . ."

"A coincidence? How's that?"

"Well, y'won' need 'em now, will y'?"

"What?"

"Y'books. On Irish hist'ry. 'Cause I'm a walkin' encyclopedia of Irish hist'ry. Y'couldn'do any better than ask me anythin' about Irish hist'ry."

"Okay," I said politely (hoping to get rid of him—and wondering if maybe he was just a few slices short of a full loaf). "I'd like a nice accurate summary of your history."

I should never have said that.

"Would y' now—well, d'y'wan' it fast o' slow?"

"What?"

"Hist'ry—our hist'ry. The grand hist'ry of our fair land."

"Well, let's start with a fast version, and then I'll flush out the details later when I get the general hang of it."

"Oh, that y'll never do!"

"What?"

"Get th'gen'ral hang of it, like y'jus' said sir. Likely hang y'good self in all the complexities of the whole t'ing."

"Well—the fast version's fine for the moment. I'll leave the big books 'til later."

"Right y'are then, sir. Very good decision y'made there or I'll be talkin' at y' 'til the fairies pop out with the stars . . . Not that I'd mind, mind y', because y'seem like a decent enough fella an' it'd be a pleasure . . ."

"Thanks, that's very nice of you, so . . . any time you're ready . . ."

"Ah, I see y're a man who gets t'th'point, so t'speak. T'th' nub o' things, and I like that. Can't stand people prattlin' on about nothin' an' never getting started . . . so much time a'wastin', don'cha think? So much paddywackery in a lot of the Irish blarney . . ."

"Yes, I do. So let's not waste time. Let's get to the nub and hear your fast version."

"Ah yes—a man after me own heart y'are, sir. So all right, then. This is how it goes . . . thousan' plus years in a nutshell, so to speak. Although, I must admit, I never really understood that nutshell thing. D'y'think maybe . . ."

"Whenever you're ready . . ."

"Ach, y're a real cracker, sir. Okay, here goes. It seems that after all the great times of legends and the mighty magical worlds that wrapped our little Ireland in shrouds of mist and mysteries . . . should I tell y'more about that time . . . before the coming of the Celts . . . I've got some wonderful tales of far off down all the years . . . tales of our ancient rulers, the Tuatha Dé Dannan, who were defeated by Milesian invaders around 250 BC and went to hide underground and became our fairy people. And all the great stories of that time like *Táin Bó Cuailnge—The Cattle Raid of Cooley*—or lots of others and Finn MacCool, our great warrior hero, and the Druids . . ."

"Let's maybe come back to all that fairy stuff later . . ."

"Ah, sir—be careful now. You don't mess about with the fairies—you never know when they're listening and they're devilish clever, and cruel when they get upset. Oh yes indeed . . ."

"Okay, point taken, but let's start with the coming of the Celts. When was that?"

"Well, they sorta crept in like from around 600 BC. Not like later fast invasions—the 'casserole of the cultures,' as they like to call these times. Slowly they got rid of the ancient Stone Age–type tribes, and after St. Patrick arrived in AD 432, they kind of merged their old Celtic and Druid pagan ways with the new Christianity coming over from Rome. 'Course by that time, there wasn't much of Rome left. The barbarians were flooding in—including a few of the old Asian Celtic tribes, and you'd be right in thinkin' where the heck was Jesus when he was needed, especially as Constantine had made the Roman Empire Christian! Bit of a letdown there, I'm thinkin'. Anyway, so the Celts settled down nicely as Christians and built churches and monastaries despite what happened later on, they gave the Irish—us—a deep love of language and poetry and mysticism and music and all that good stuff . . ."

"So what happened later on?"

"I'm comin' t'that. Don't rush the storyteller once he's off and runnin' . . ."

"Sorry."

"Right. Well. Anyway, so what happened was that the damned Scandinavian Vikings at the end of the eighth century came roarin' in. Sailin' by with their huge boats, pillagin' and plunderin' and messin' up the whole Celtic world here. They were a restless bunch to start with—makin' off with our women and all the rich stuff from the monasteries—even burning the books our monks had copied from libraries brought over here from Rome, which was in a real mess. Most famous is that Book of Kells in Trinity College Library. Beautiful, beautiful thing. And then there's that book writ recently—*How the Irish Saved Civilization*—that tells if it wasn't for our monks in the monasteries in lonely places here, we'd have lost most of the world's classical learning. Think of that! Little old Ireland savin' the whole cultural world! Anyway, the Vikings were a real nuisance and a threat to the Church, so around AD 1169 the pope, who just happened to be English at the time, granted the Anglo-Norman King Henry II—you'll remember the Normans had conquered England in 1066—everybody remembers that date. He granted him the whole of Ireland as an 'inheritance' to protect his churches and whatnot."

"The pope just gave it to the Normans—despite all the powerful Celts and Vikings still living here?"

"Tha's right. Jus' gave it. He was the pope—the big boss! So—when Strongbow the Norman invaded to claim the king's 'inheritance,' it turned out he had a pretty easy time taking over the whole place and building mighty castles and dividing the land up between all his Norman barons. And there's an old saying that they liked the place so much that they became 'more Irish than the Irish.' "

"And that was it? The Irish just accepted things . . ."

"Well, there was a bit of a ruckus when Scotland tried to attack us in AD 1315 and boot out the Normans, and also Richard II, who tried twice in the 1390s to remind the Irish who was boss but made a real mess of things and ended up with only Dublin and the Pale—a small area around Dublin—as his little tiny empire . . ."

"So the English Normans were booted out?"

"Well, not quite. It looked bad for them for a while, but then Henry VIII, after his break with the Catholic church—you remember, because the pope wouldn't allow his divorce from two of his wives, well—he and his Protestant church of Englanders came over and grabbed all the land back. And then his daughter Queen Elizabeth I sent in massive armies in the early 1600s, then James I packed Northern Ireland, you know, the 'six counties'—now called Ulster— with English and Scottish Protestant settlers. And then in came Oliver Cromwell in 1649 and his vicious army, which pretty well wiped out all Catholic power. And, oh God, was he cruel—massacring the population of Drogheda, slaughtering hundreds of women in Wexford, expelling all the Catholics from cities like Cork—just booted them out. I remember my mother's warnings when I was young—'Cromwell'll get you if you're bad!' "

"Poor old Ireland. What a lousy history."

"Oh my, sir—I've hardly begun! It goes from bad to worse an' then even worser! Especially when James II was king from AD 1685, and he was Catholic, would y'believe, and tried to be a bit nicer to us, but he got the boot too, and in comes William of Orange with his huge army and smashes us to pieces at the Battle of the Boyne in 1690, and then later at Aughrim and Limerick. Then he, William—once again—hands out lands to his most powerful 'Protestant Ascendancy' supporters,

Liam Farrell—
"Historian"

enforces the terrible penal laws to destroy Catholic power, and right
through to the 1850s the Protestants and 'Orangemen' fight off rebellion after rebellion—Henry Grattan, the Society of United Irishmen,
the 'White Boys' and 'Ribbon Men,' Daniel O'Connell, and on and on.
And then comes the worst thing of all."

"Let me guess. The great potato famine?"

"Spot-on, sir. Ah, so y'do know a bit of our terrible convoluted
turmoil then. Although no one can truly know what a black time
that was from 1845 to 1850. They called it *Gorta Mór*, the great
hunger, when almost our whole potato crop failed every year for six
horrible years, and well over two million people out of a population
of eight million starved to death, or were evicted by Protestant landlords and sent off on emigrant ships to Canada and America. An
unbelievable disaster, and all the while our food—grain, cattle,
sheep—was being shipped off in the thousands of tons to England
to—as they said—'maintain the economy of Ireland.' Maintain my
bloody . . . you know what . . . if you'll forgive the expression, sir.
There was a popular saying at that time—'God gave us the potato
blight but it was the English who gave us the famine.' While they
were glorifying in their world empire, gentrified affluence, and pedi-

greed aristrocracy, we were trying to stay alive by eatin' grass and leaves.

"It's amazing we ever recovered from all this horror, this pernicious scythe of death and human decimation that swept across our poor little nation—but by God we did! Irish emigrants abroad sent money back here to support nationalistic groups like the Fenians, the Manchester Martyrs, and the Land League, all demanding independence and home rule. Except up in Ulster, of course—Northern Ireland—they didn't want to be split off from Britain, and so they had to battle on and on with Sinn Fein and the IRA.

"And then came the glorious Easter Rising of April 24, 1916, in Dublin, which was actually a bloody fiasco, except that the stupid British executed sixteen ringleaders and made them into instant martyrs. So this was followed by the start of the 'Troubles.' First, a two-year war of independence led by Michael Collins—y' remember him? Very famous. Very popular. Then a peace treaty with Lloyd George, the British prime minister in 1920. But that wasn't much use. Ulster was still left as a British colony, y' might say, but a lot of southerners wanted a united Ireland. So what happens? We have another damned war—the Civil War—us fightin' ourselves, can y' believe, until Eamon de Valera—our *taoiseach* (prime minister)—says, the heck with it, accept the bloody treaty, we'll become the Irish Free State and we'll deal with Ulster later on. And well, y'know that story. Decades of Catholic-versus-Protestant slaughter and bombings up there around Belfast and Derry until today, when we're a republic and—God willing—the power-sharing peace treaty in Ulster might actually work now. But you'll notice—I've got m'fingers crossed. And that last bit—from Civil War 'til t'day, especially that time they call 'The Troubles'—has filled a thousand books describin' the unbelievably tangled shenanigans of politicians and freedom groups and just plain terrorists. I couldn't even start to give it to you straight. And anyway, you asked fer a fast version an' that's what I've given you."

"So that was the fast version then?"

"Fast as I could do it."

"Well—thank you, and thank God I didn't ask for the slow one."

"Aye, well—y'd've been here fer another few hours, tha's fer sure . . ."

"You must be very thirsty by now."

"Well—b'jeez at last! I thought I'd never ever hear the offer of liquid sustenance, which I am more than ready to accept, kind sir!"

I FOLLOWED UP ON this brief introduction to Irish history from my diminutive friend in Waterford with far more extensive readings and now wholeheartedly agree with his description of his poor country's fortunes as "our terrible convoluted turmoil." One of my favorite must-reads, of course, is the long—very long (in dealing with Ireland how could it be anything else?)—epic *Trinity*, by Leon Uris. His book generated the full spectrum of reactions from horror to hurrahs when it was first published, but as I came to realize that every resident here has his or her own take on the nation's history, such discordant reactions were obviously to be expected.

A slightly less contentious nonfiction book by Uris is *Ireland: A Terrible Beauty*, completed with photographs by his wife, Jill Uris, in 1975, and I use his words to summarize the traumatic fate of this tiny nation:

> *Over eight hundred years of occupation and four hundred years of intense colonization, Ireland has been cruelly and stupidly administered and her people shamefully persecuted, with every sort of indignity brought to bear. The most wanton penal laws legislated by a civilized western nation (Britain) denied the Irish Catholics every human and material right. In the mid-Nineteenth Century the Great Famine was little more than a subtle, or not so subtle, exercise at "gentlemen's genocide." The land had been*

stripped naked through court intrigues and run red to the sound of clanging armor and bellowing cannon in an epic of boundless bloody greed . . . This stricken land, a ponderous religion, and a tortured foreign occupation have made it impossible for decades of Irish to exist in their own country . . . Yet it has become a depository of the folkways of a dozen cultures, the haven of the last great peasantry of the west. All this, mixed in with their own Celtic bizarreness and the deeply practiced mystical aspects of Catholicism, has given them the universal image of "leprechaun people" . . . They are as warm and lovely as any on earth. Their wit is incomparable. Their use of words and language has enriched life wherever they may have touched it . . . Through it all a magnificent people have survived with their own identity intact!

I couldn't say it better myself.

So I didn't . . . except to add a celebratory postscript on Ireland's recent economic and social good fortune after joining the EU in 1972 (previously the EEC—European Economic Community). Once the penurious basket case of Europe, the "Celtic Tiger" has led the whole community for years in booming economic expansion, international business investment, reverse emigration (Irish workers returning home), and "best place to live" appeal. As the popular saying has it—"There are only two kinds of people on this earth—the Irish and those who wish they were"!

The only problem is that when tiny, dilapidated row houses in Dublin sell for well over a million dollars, both groups are finding it harder and harder to afford even the most modest accommodations in the major cities. Nevertheless the momentum of ambition, accretion, and affluence moves this proud nation forward, and you can almost hear the little green leprechauns giggling with delight as they watch all the gold rolling in and the coffers filling and swap tales of the Irish buying up fancy apartments in Manhattan and second homes all along the Mediterranean coast.

Even back in the peasant-poor Middle Ages, poets like Edmund Spenser celebrated Ireland's enduring charms: "Ah to be sure it is yet a most bewtifull and sweete country as any is under Heaven."

And today—in celebrating the "Celtic Tiger"—it's a hearty *Sláinte!* again, a booming *Céad Míle Faílte* ("A Hundred Thousand Welcomes"), and this popular blessing too:

> *Health and long life to you*
> *Land without rent to you*
> *A child every year to you*
> *And if you can't get to Heaven*
> *May you at least die in Ireland*

4

The Ring of Beara
Our First "Loop" Adventure

:::

THE PERCEPTIONS OF "BLOW-INS"

DESPITE ALL THE "CELTIC TIGER" TALES of progress and prosperity
and Ireland's pulsating aura of newfound confidence (some even
claim it's becoming cloyingly complacent at times—others claim
"the bubble has to burst soon!")—in places like Beara you still sense
a timeless quality in those great elemental aspects of shattered mountain ranges, sea-gouged cliffs, black water lakes, vast moors, and
miasmas of peat bogs. These have always been the true touchstones
of this strong and ancient land—this haven of great poets, artists,
and writers, whose works resonate with primal energies and the
ancient pagan rhythms of long-forgotten languages and legends and
the horrors of their decimated, diaspora-plagued heritage.

No matter how capsulized you make these Irish histories, how
euphemistically you paraphrase the sequences of ethnic "displace-
ments," cultural annihilations, endless centuries of occupations and
Troubles, heart-shattering poverty, the terrible famines, the mass
emigrations, the constant battles against the state and the Catholic
church for freedom and liberation—the emergence of the "peaceful
and prosperous" nation of today is a nonfictional gothic melodrama
far more complex and convoluted than any novel could ever be.

The recent transformations here have been miraculous and yet tinged with ironies. In a land now flush with new affluence and with more Mercedeses per capita than any other country on earth, including Germany, you can still see the Angelus bells being rung on TV twice a day and people pausing to pray in the street to the Blessed Virgin. And out in the wilder parts of Connemara, Donegal— and Beara—visitors still seek out scenes and experiences of the "old ways"—the *ashling*—of simple sustenance lives lived close to the earth and the ocean and within their own remote, close-knit communities.

It's always fascinating to see how our tastes in and reactions to landscape and travel in general have changed over the centuries. To-day's first-time "touchstone-seeking" explorers of Beara are invari-ably enchanted by its bold, burly mountains, its wild heather and gorse-strewn moors, and that magical sense of discovering secret Brigadoon valleys glowing with that iridescent sheen of green that is pure Emerald Isle.

But it was not always so. Even a superficial search of reactions from celebrities and historical figures over the last couple of centu-ries reveals far less rosy-hued accounts and opinions. While today, for example, most of us are bemused by the little, narrow, winding, and vegetation-crammed boreen lanes here, Prince Hermann von Pückler-Muskau portrayed his journeys around Beara in 1828 as "indescribably difficult." And William Wordsworth, whose purpled poems often exceeded the normal bounds of adjectival and emo-tional restraint, limited his comments on Beara roads to a single word: "Vile!" Sir Walter Scott, however, was far more enthusiastic, describing the scenery of Beara and County Kerry as "the grandest sight I have ever seen."

And then, of course, there's the weather. The plans of poor old Theobald Wolfe Tone, who attempted to harness a French armada here to drive the English from Ireland in 1796, were decimated by Beara's notoriously fickle climate. "Dreadfully wild and stormy and easterly winds which have been blowing furiously and without intermission since we made Bantry Bay, have ruined us," he wrote before being captured and executed in 1798.

Similar outrage also pours from countless early "travel memoirs," although one of the less voracious commentaries by the novelist Marie-Anne de Bouvet (1889), attempts a more balanced summation: "The climate of Ireland is vexatious rather than absolutely bad, and it has consolations the more delightful because they come unexpectedly." A splendid example of damning with faint praise.

And then came such social commentary as this 1818 description by Georgiana Chatterton of the local Beara people in her best-selling travel book, *Rambles in the South of Ireland:* "They were the wildest-looking people I ever beheld . . . and the appearance of the dwellings of the peasantry was more truly wretched than I have ever seen . . . Some of the younger children were completely naked."

Rose Trollope, however, wife of the famous novelist Anthony, obviously had a tolerance for Beara, as they both enjoyed several family holidays in Glengarriff. Anthony quickly absorbed the nuances and subtleties of Irish life in his official position with the post office in Banagher, which he portrays vividly in his novel *The Kellys and the O'Kellys.* However, in 1849, Anthony's mother, Fanny (herself a distinguished author), did not share their enthusiasm and found: "the food detestable, the bedrooms pokey, turf fires disagreeable, and so on, and so on."

Virginia Woolf, like so many other celebrities of the time, also enjoyed a vacation in Glengarriff in 1934, and although she and her husband, Leonard, toyed with the idea of buying property here, she also saw the "underbelly" of life in the country, which she described in her typically terse and acerbic manner: "How ram-shackle and half-squalid the Irish life is, how empty & poverty-stricken." (Interesting how she makes "half-squalid" sound far worse than just simply 'squalid.')

As the twentieth century progressed and conditions improved along the peninsula in terms of roads, housing, and employment, especially in fishing and the British naval yards at Castletownbere, the mood and reactions of visitors began to improve. One particular commentary by Sean O'Faolain in his book *An Irish Journey* (1941) combines the direness of the past with a new romantic effervescence celebrating the power and majesty of this remarkable corner of the country: "If there is in Ireland a harder world than the Bere Peninsula, a tougher life, a sterner fight against all that this loveliness of nature means in terms of poverty and struggle and near-destitution I have yet to find it." But then he switches tone and lets his eloquence flow:

> *Few more lovely seascapes exist in Ireland than that which unfolds itself on the walk to Glengarriff and beyond . . . The sweeping grandeur . . . the vast elemental infinities . . . the Glen, as we call it in County Cork, has three things peculiar to itself. It has tiny refuges of inlet nooks and coves where the mind can dream itself into a drowsy peace for days on end, hidden low-tide or high-tide lagoons, lovely at any season, little islands where one can bathe and bask, silent but for the cry of a curlew or gull, or the chattering of herons or the suck-suck of the seaweed caressing the rocks. It has foliage of a tropical variety in abundance. It has a climate so mild that the place flowers with rare flora, and on the more moist summer days, the bay lies heavy as molten metal, and the very rocks seem to melt, and everything swoons in a land-locked sleep.*

Ironically, while the Beara has remained relatively aloof and unexplored, it is seen today by many to capture the very essence of the Irish people and the enormous power and beauty of the land itself. "Beara," I was told by one proud resident, "is just quite simply the best place in the whole of Ireland." And by the time Anne and I left at the end of our seasons here, we were of course in total agreement with such sentiments.

SCURRYING FROM KILLARNEY
AND THE RING OF KERRY

AND WE ARE BOTH in total agreement about Killarney and the Ring of Kerry too that runs around the Iveragh Peninsula. Out of season, if the weather holds, this is indeed an enchanted realm of soaring mountain ranges with such entrancing names as Macgillycuddy's Reeks reflected in broad forest-edge lakes and a tumultuous chiseled coastline pounded by the Atlantic Ocean. A dramatic dreamworld indeed that conjures up all the boisterous charms of the Ireland of popular inspiration.

But come during the peak late spring to early autumn season and you'll need to brace yourself for a traumatic transformation when the charmingly upmarket and architecturally flamboyant Victorian town of Killarney itself, with its plethora of palace-like hotels and resorts, suddenly becomes Ireland's most popular tourist nexus after Dublin. The relatively narrow roads that encircle the Ring of Kerry attract dawn-to-dusk processions of bumper-to-bumper coach traffic, all visiting the same "top spots" (the National Park, Muckross House and Abbey, the Ladies' View panorama, Ross Castle et al.).

For those whose images of Ireland conjure up shamrock-garnished horse and carriage rides, leprechaun-filled souvenir shops, pseudo-*céilí* concerts in "traditional pubs," KISS ME QUICK I'M IRISH souvenirs in every imaginable guise, and an exuberance of blarney that even make Japanese tourists wary of overkill hype—then this will be seen as some kind of paddywackery paradise.

For those, however, who are willing to work a little harder to discover a more authentic Ireland—may we gently continue to entice you to travel a score or so miles from the crush of Killarney and venture south to the next peninsula, which offers a far more authentic experience altogether.

Here on Beara the scenery is as rugged as a rhino's carapace and formed largely of sandstone, with slate and igneous intrusions, all bent, buckled, and fissured by the Armorican tumult of over three hundred million years ago. The land is creased, incised, and gashed by constant conflicts with the oh-so-Irish elements of rain, frost, and that miasma of "mizzle" (mist and drizzle) that cocoons the high ancient places.

But we don't mind at all. We're out of the Killarney chaos and into the wild country now, switchbacking up the steep narrow road to Moll's Gap and a quick pause for a gourmet snack (one of the thickest, creamiest, and richest quiches ever) at the famous Avoca Café perched on the scoured treeless peak here.

And then it's all downhill, looping and laughing together as we see signs for Kenmare and the Ring of Beara. Anne reads a short outspoken commentary from one of our guidebooks:

> The Beara peninsula is as beautiful as the Dingle, far to
> the north, but it is perhaps the least known of the western
> peninsulas. It is more rugged and till now lonelier than the
> others. Its fate is being argued. One faction, led and supported
> by conservationists, tourists, and many German, Dutch and
> English "blow-in" settlers, is for keeping things much as they
> are. The other, including a number of influential locals, want
> the god Development: roads, houses, hotels and industry
> to match Ireland's economic surge of the 1980s and 1990s.
> Having fouled up your own countries, these Irish seem to be
> saying, you want to stop us fouling up ours, and that is for us
> to decide.

"I assume this 'fouling' business doesn't refer to our peninsula," I said.

"Oh—so it's 'our peninsula' now, is it? Getting a little possessive aren't we, especially as you haven't even see the place yet!" Anne said, laughing.

"Well—it says 'least known,' so I guess we've picked the right one . . . and I've heard nothing about any 'fouling.' "

And Kenmare certainly appears foul free. In fact, after all the hype and hullabaloo of Killarney this is a model town of decorum and grace. Hidden back behind the cozy little cluster of downtown stores are two of Europe's most prestigious hotel-resorts. First is "High Victorian" Park Kenmare tucked away at the top end of main street, laden with antiques and tingling with olde world country house charm. Then comes Sheen Falls Lodge, definitely one of those "if you have to ask the price here you can't afford it" places set on a three-hundred-acre estate with tree-shaded walks down to the long, ocean-lapped bay known somewhat misleadingly as the Kenmare River.

From even a superficial glance at this coy little town you sense a distinctly non-Irish heritage here. And so it was. In fact the notorious diarist Macaulay, ever prone to vast exaggerations in his writings, described predevelopment conditions here in the seventeenth century when Sir William Petty arrived to "make profitable sense of the country. For having been awarded a large grant of land for services to the Cromwellian conquest of Ireland, he had to face half-naked savages, who could not speak a word of English and who made themselves burrows in the mud and lived on roots and sour milk . . . scarcely any place . . . was more completely out of the pale of civilizations as Nedeen" [Kenmare's original name].

So—as happened all across Ireland when the "let's get things organized here" Britishers moved in—Sir William set about creating ironworks, lead mines, fisheries, and other industries and, in 1670, founded a very English-like village in a tree-laced hollow. He even tried to entice scores of "doughty maidens" from England to come and "civilize our local natives" and set up a flourishing Protestant society. Things didn't quite work out in so utopian a manner, but the place began to truly flourish under the Marquis of Lansdowne, who created a new town plan in 1775. Almost a century later, in response to the dire unemployment and starvation conditions of the Great Famine, Kenmare became renowned for the superlative quality of its local handmade lace sponsored by the Sisters of the

Poor Clare Convent. It's still being sold today in the town's Dickensian-flavored stores and exhibited in Kenmare's Heritage Center and occasionally in the town's remarkably eclectic array of fine restaurants.

Just outside town and across the bridge over the Kenmare River is an alluring sign pointing westward to the Ring of Beara.

"What d'you think?" asked Anne (already knowing the answer). "Go south to Glengarriff and then into Beara. Looks like a pretty wild drive over Caha Pass and through some rock tunnels. Or turn here?"

It was a larky-spirited no-brainer. To the south were ogreous tumblings of dark clouds over a hulking muscular mountainscape. The sun seemed hostaged in a tomblike fug. To the west, however, a narrow road meandered past tree-lined meadows into a misty haze of pearlescent light. Smoke-serpents curled languorously from the chimneys of small cottages . . .

So—west it was. And we congratulated ourselves on our choice as the light brightened and the wind-rippled surface of the bay shimmered in gold-platinum undulations.

The first few miles were mellowed by woods and copses, but slowly the trees thinned out and the shattered fangs and stumps of a far more ancient and broken terrain rose up through the winter-bleached swirls of moorland grasses. We passed a solitary standing stone locked in place by rugged drystone walls. Sunlight bathed its sturdy flanks in lacquered luminosity.

"That was a fast change of landscape!" said Anne.

"And just look ahead . . . ," I said, pointing toward an abrupt clustering of ominous bare-rock bastions rising precipitously out of the narrow, ocean-lapped plain.

"That's our route . . . over those things!?"

"You've got the map. Do we have an option?"

"Well, there's a road that seems to twist all along the coast, but it's shown as one lane and not recommended for large vehicles . . ."

"We're not that large . . ."

"You feel like playing around backing up on one-lane Irish roads with Irish drivers honking away at us . . . ?"

"Not particularly," I admitted.

"So—I guess it's the mountains then!"

At least it was scenic—according to Anne. I wouldn't know. My eyes were fixed firmly on each of the fifty or so switchbacking twists and bends that Irish drivers seemed to treat with glorious devil-may-care abandon. It didn't make the slightest bit of difference that the road had two distinct (admittedly very narrow) lanes divided clearly

Standing Stone

by a solid yellow line. Most drivers seemed utterly oblivious to our presence as they wheelied around the bends way over on the wrong side, with tires screeching in Steve McQueen madness.

All this came as something of a shock, as I'd read the famous author John B. Keane's eloquent description of Kerry and your typical Kerryman and expected a little more decorum and decency on the highways here:

> The County of Kerry is distinguished by a gossamer-like lunacy which is addictive but not damaging. It contains a thousand vistas of unbelievable beauty . . . The Kerry attitude is spiced with humor and we tend to digress. To a Kerryman life without digression is like a thoroughfare without side streets . . . He loves his pub and he loves his pint and he will tell you that the visitor, no matter where he hails from, is always at home in the Kingdom of Kerry . . . Being in Kerry, in my opinion, is the greatest gift that God can bestow on any man . . . In belonging to Kerry you belong to the spheres spinning in their heavens.

You just can't beat that Irish blarnied eloquence. And after such praise, I can only assume that the mad drivers were all from County Cork.

Lauragh came as a great relief. Not that there's much to see here except the enticing subtropical exuberance of Derreen Garden. Like Kenmare, this was the outcome of another Cromwellian gift to a loyal British henchman, this time the conqueror's trusted physician. And also, as with Kenmare, it came under the Lansdowne family's control in 1866, which proceeded to create this masterpiece of a rhododendron and Australian and New Zealand tree fern estate in a moist, mossy microclimate on the south side of the Kenmare River. A perfect enclave in which to recover from the manic antics of those drivers.

We agreed to keep on driving westward down the peninsula

toward Allihies and Dursey Island but were fully aware of a most tempting alternative. Right by the turnoff at Lauragh to Derreen Garden, a sign pointed toward the great granite wall of shattered Caha peaks and jagged purple shadows rising abruptly from wild swathes of boggy moorland. The sign read HEALY PASS and was cluttered about with warnings for narrow roads, dangerous bends, sudden climatic shifts, avalanche tendencies, and man-eating sheep. Sorry—slight exaggeration here. It was actually a warning that the sheep up on the high fells tend to regard the road as part of their pasturage and, particularly on warm days, enjoy sunbathing on the heated tarmac and are often reluctant to move, despite their possible imminent and messy demise. A more promising sign indicated great photo ops of Glanmore Lake, the barren bastion of Knockowen, the dramatic profile of the Iveragh ranges, and the majestic Macgillycuddy's Reeks way to the north on the Ring of Kerry.

After Lauragh the low road scenery became distinctly less dramatic to the point where we both wondered if we should have chosen the Healy Pass route. Of course—as the seasons rolled on—we drove that wildly exhilarating sequence of serpentine switchbacks many times, deep into the high heart of Beara. We found it one of the most beautiful and dramatic drives in the whole of the southwest—a wild, empty landscape full of ghostly presences. But if

Old Gas Pump near Healy Pass

we'd done that on this first day of our Beara experience, we'd have missed little Eyeries.

And little Eyeries should definitely not be missed, from its handful of traditional pubs and small stores (some great homemade sandwiches here) to the superb contemporary stained glass in the bright lemon-painted Catholic church. Of course, in a village renowned for winning national awards for "prettiest," "tidiest," and "most colorful" community, one expects to find not only a vibrantly hued church but also a whole village gone Fauvist color-crazy. Which of course it had.

"Gorgeous!" gushed Anne.

I must admit, I didn't altogether share her unrestrained enthusiasm.

Quite honestly I'm not too sure about all these fairground regalias of colors found nowadays in most villages across the depth and breadth of Ireland. At first I thought—now here's a quaint tradition reflecting the Irish love of jollity and gaiety. "Perky as a parrot's plumage," I scribbled in my notebook. But my initial impression was quickly corrected by an elderly gentleman near Skibbereen on the fringe of the Mizen Head Peninsula (southernmost of the five southwest peninsulas), who, with a wide smile and all the dancing-eyed charm of a bar-hugging raconteur, stated that "the whole damned place's gone crackers with colors you'd only see on a baboon's ass. Y'see," he continued, "not so long ago it was all nice and simple— whites, beiges, grays, and maybe just once in a while a touch of canary yellow. More like cream, really. Double Devon, y'might say . . ."

"So why the change?"

"Who the feck knows. M'be they thought they'd got to compete with Italy and Spain for the tourist money . . . Or m'be they just got bored and wanted to liven things up a bit. Whatever—it's got nothing to do with Irish customs and traditions. It's just a load of tourist . . ."

"But y'know," said Anne. "I like it. It seems to capture the Irish character. Colorful . . . and a little rambunctious."

The old man paused and then smiled sweetly at Anne. (Many of them do. It's something I've learned to live with.) "*Rambunctious* . . . tha's a fine word . . . I never thought of it that way a'suppose . . ."

"Well—what's the harm in it?" Anne continued.

He laughed a loud belly laugh. "Ach, there's no harm. No harm at all—let 'em have their crazy colors . . . Life's gray enough as it is!"

Well—that's as maybe mate (old Yorkshire expression), but things were certainly not gray now in this little rainbowed village or across the surrounding smooth-crowned hills. The sun had finally graced us with its full presence. No more elusive hints of brilliance and warmth; no more pale light touching the tops of diffuse mists drifting in cupped bays of brittle, broken strata; no more rain-drippy cathedral-gloom naves of pines in the wooded places. Now we had azure blue skies and shrilling sunlight. Everything glowed. Cobwebs strung out among roadside bushes displayed beads of dew along their filaments, which flashed and sparkled like an Aladdin's cave of diamond necklaces.

"Fickle, schizoid climate here," I said.

"Maybe that's why the Irish have this reputation for humor and an ironic outlook on life. If their moods changed as fast as the weather they'd all be bipolar manics," said Anne.

"If you listen to Sam Beckett's plays you'd think they already were . . ."

"I thought Beckett spent most of his time in France."

"Well—sometimes you can see things more clearly from a distance . . ."

"Like those sheep ahead . . . which by the way are getting less and less distant!"

She was right. The pewtery sunlight was in my eyes and I'd failed to notice a fluffy family of Blackfaces settled comfortably in the center of the road and showing no intention whatsoever of making way for anybody.

"Stupid sods," I mumbled, making a hasty loop around their sprawled forms.

Anne sat silently, smiling to herself, but I could hear every word she was thinking. And they were not very complimentary words.

Her silence continued as we entered a rather more trepidatious portion of our "Ring" drive. Our underpowered car struggled to grapple with a tortured terrain of ragged hills fringed with black precipices of broken rock, and a serpentining road barely wide enough for a single vehicle. Scores of threadlike runnels and streamlets chittered down the fractured strata, leaping off ledges in fanlike filigrees. The landscape possessed almost surrealistic Joycean images. I seemed to see slow-moving figures—great shambling forms—in the rock formations towering above the moor. There were crepuscular presences here. Then suddenly over a hump came a farm, compact and clustered up to the very road itself, and a towering white wall immediately ahead of us.

Anne gasped—her silence broken by an alarmed "Whoa!"

Where the hell had the road gone!?

And then I spotted it—disappearing around the corner of the farmhouse at an abrupt right angle. Brakes on. Skid and wriggle. Wait to hit wall. Wall vanished. Car made the turn all by itself. And then stalled. Facing a long uphill.

"Jeez!" I think I said.

"Ditto times ten!' said Anne breathlessly.

"What a stupid bl—" I began.

"Well, look at it this way." Anne is always the optimist. "A bend like this means there'll never be any tourist coaches doing round-the-loop, Ring of Kerry–type excursions here on Beara!"

"Good point," I agreed. "But a bit of a warning would have been nice."

Anne smiled: "There was one. I assumed you'd see it."

"How big?"

"Apparently the normal size for Ireland—'bout the size of your average dinner napkin!"

THE DRIVE NOW WAS truly serious. As the weeks went by this became one of our favorite parts of the peninsula—an adrenaline-stimulating rush of a romp through its wildest heart—a land of diminution of self. But our first introduction was just a touch too much on the precarious side. And parts of the problem were the glorious vistas that kept zapping our senses around every white-knuckle bend. Great glowing panoramas of purpled ocean, soaring cliffs, high moorland, the dark broken teeth of ridges draped with cloud-shadows, mountainsides seemingly torn by the claws of enormous primeval beasts, and that emerald shimmer of greens so richly varied and vibrant. You can't help humming a chorus or two of "Danny Boy" and "Four Green Fields," that amazingly moving anthem of cruel Irish history from the heart and pen of the late Tommy Makem—a man we were proud to know for a number of years before his recent death.

Anne spotted Allihies first. "Here comes another color-cluster village." She laughed. And she was right. Eyeries possibly wins out in terms of the overall brilliance of its hues, but Allihies had selected a more modulated range of tones that blended well with the surrounding landscape. With one notable and renowned exception— the bright Venetian vermillion red of O'Neill's Bar and Restaurant right in the center of this small, compact community. Little did we know how this beloved nexus of local *craic*, *céilí*, and occasional dance *hooley* with its roadside trestle tables, cozy bar rooms, and rather more elite upstairs restaurant, Pluais Umha, would quickly become a home away from home for us (along with the adjoining smaller Lighthouse and Oak pubs). Of course neither did we know at that point in our adventure that Allihies itself would also become the base for most of our time here.

O'Neill's seemed a good place to pause for a ritual pint o' the black stuff and, following the recommendation of a hiker sitting at an adjoining roadside table, two gargantuan platters of delicious fish 'n' chips pub grub. All around the northern fringe of the village rose huge black cliffs pockmarked with shadowy tunnel holes. We later learned that this was the Puxley Family Kingdom, where an affluent Anglo-Irish family, the Puxleys, had put to good use their know-how from their Cornwall copper mines in the eighteenth century and made a fortune from reserves of copper and silver discovered here.

Of course most of the money went directly into Puxley pockets, and the local workforce of up to 1,300 men, women, and children were as powerless as penned hens and had to endure starvation wages, appallingly dangerous working conditions, and cruel crushings of even the most modest of their pleas for improvements. The Puxleys' importation of skilled Cornish miners also caused considerable outrage locally, particularly as they were lured here by higher wages and even new comfortable housing in a villagelike setting up on the hillside by the shafts.

Old Copper Mines—Allihies

The ruins are still evident today, as are remnants of the old engine houses and the shaft holes. The main one, fenced off for safety, is an eerie invitation to a vast underworld of labyrinthine tunnels. All around the shadowy maw are turquoise-hued strata indicating the rich presence of copper. Such temptations have lured speculators into occasional and more recent reopenings of some of the mines, but so far the rumored "great vein" of undiscovered ore is yet to be found.

In later weeks Anne and I returned to wander the wild, broken terrain here. We also listened to the stories of John Terry in the local grocery store and tales whispered in the Allihies pubs of strange nighttime sightings of "things best not talked about . . . ," disappearances of "blow-ins" among the unmarked shafts, and spectacular "secret" finds of silver that one day might bring an instant Klondike of untold riches to this modest little village.

There were all kinds of other tales too floating around about the mines. One of our sheep farmer neighbors later told us about sacrifices of food and whiskey that used to be made in the mine to ensure against mechanical failures and accidents. Others told us about secret tunnels linking some of the shallower shafts with the ocean cliffs and used by smugglers.

On this first visit to Allihies we happened to meet Tom and Willie Hodge, owners of a farm near the village's enticingly white sand beach of Ballydonegan. "Our pasture's only thirty-six acres—with a lot of rock in it—and sixteen cows. Not much of an outfit really," said Tom. "Ah reckon we must just like cows!"

Conversation with the two of them was made difficult by their unique accents—a sort of combination of Irish and what sounded like Cornish brogue. Apparently many of the people here had relatives who had come from the tin mines of Cornwall in the nineteenth century and had worked in the surrounding shafts.

"There's still plenty of copper left," said Willie. "If it gets to a good commodity price someone might try and open it up again.

There's always rumors—even about finds of gold and uranium—but there's been no real interest in the place since 1967. They're supposed to be opening a museum about the mines just up the road here, but the funds seem to keep running out. And they've spent quite a bit on the main engine shed up on the slopes there, but it's so crazy-dangerous around the big mine hole—the one with all the copper streaks in the rock, great blue bands of it—that they say they may never open it to the public."

Ballydonegan Beach and Allihies

Daphne du Maurier's world-famous classic *Hungry Hill* is a pretty accurate tale of the Puxley family history here but with considerable added melodrama and geographic dislocation. (The actual Hungry Hill, at 2,260 feet the highest point on the peninsula and famous for its towering waterfalls, is almost twenty miles to the east near Glengarriff.)

Du Maurier's description of the results of a "workers' rebellion" here is typically evocative of her style: "The mines on Hungry Hill had ceased to work. The fires went out at last, and the smokeless stacks lifted black faces to the sky. The whine and whirl of the machinery was still. A queer silence seemed to call on the place. The mine had a deserted air. The door of the engine-house swung backwards and forwards on a broken hinge."

The enormous Puxley mansion, described by one outspoken writer as "a grandiose pile and lump of gross ostentation," was built a few miles east of the mines. It adjoined the tumbled remnants of the medieval O'Sullivan Bere Castle of Dunboy perched on a Norman-styled motte-and-bailey mound surrounded by ancient yews and huge splays of rhododendrons overlooking nearby Castletownbere and Bere Island. This must have been a sturdy and most imposing monolith if the ornately decorated gatehouse here is anything to go by. But in 1601 the O'Sullivans unfortunately sided with the Spanish against Queen Elizabeth I and were largely massacred. A heroic remnant of a thousand or so supporters led by Chieftain Donal O'Sullivan sought sanctuary hundreds of miles to the north in Leitrim but were largely wiped out on their terrible "long march."

A couple of miles beyond Allihies, past that beautiful beach, and almost at the tip of the peninsula, a narrow lane leaves the main loop road and heads down through bosky, sheep-dotted hills. A sign reads DURSEY ISLAND and offers a rough handpainted timetable for the infamously tiny cable car contraption (the only one in Ireland) linking the peninsula with this tiny four-mile-long island. We made a mental note to visit sometime, little knowing what a ghastly

Pandora's box of cruel history we'd discover here. But that, as they say, is another story.

THE ROAD NOW SWUNG abruptly eastward as we began the second segment of our "Ring" drive, traveling along the southern shore of the peninsula by the broad, sparkling Bantry Bay. Moors and meadows suddenly opened out into truly majestic vistas. The land dropped away abruptly into small farms and grazings. To the south we could clearly see the last two of the five peninsulas of southwest Ireland— Sheep's Head (very rural) and Mizen Head (celebrated by more discerning travelers seeking respite from the self-conscious charms of Cork, Cobh, and the Kinsale region).

Closer in we finally spotted the capital of Beara, the lively fishing community of Castletownbere nestled beneath the Slieve Miskish mountains and sheltered from erratic bay weather by the languorous green dome of Bere Island. This was once a major Royal Navy base when Britain and Ireland were united, until its closure in 1938. The British were most reluctant to leave what was generally recognized as being the largest natural harbor in Europe, and it took more than a decade to organize their final departure. Winston Churchill was particularly anxious to keep it as a base during World War II and even hinted at a return of Northern Ireland to the Republic—a deal that never materialized. Fortunately, around two hundred devoted residents have discovered what an enchanting hidden place this is (in the midst of the larger hidden place of Beara itself). It's served by two regular ferries from Castletownbere, dotted with late-eighteenth-century Martello watchtowers; a Bronze Age "wedge tomb" thought to date from around 2000 BC; a prominent ten-foot-high standing stone; and remnants of British gun emplacements and forts, all still in surprisingly good condition.

Castletownbere itself (also once known as Castletown Bearhaven) is a pure delight, particularly in terms of sketch-worthy subjects when the huge, often Spanish and Portuguese fishing trawlers cram the harbor wharves here. But equally appealing are the more hedonistic aspects of life here—the town's pubs, restaurants, and stores—and, for the truly overindulgent and overaffluent—the reincarnated Puxley mansion at nearby Dunboy Castle.

When we first arrived on Beara there were only rumors and whispers of bizarre schemes to reuse the shell of the mansion, destroyed by the IRA in 1921, long after the Puxleys had left and closed the disappointingly nonproductive copper mines in 1884. Many of the unemployed miners immigrated en masse at that time to Butte, Montana, and Beara families still maintain close ties today—including one moving and live video reunion we attended organized in Castletownbere.

Eventually plans were published for a $100 million "six-star" resort hotel featuring Ritz-Carlton management, and imaging itself as a "secret hideaway" for celebrities seeking solace from the ubiquitous paparazzi, a Michelin-starred restaurant, pools, luxury spa facilities, a vast wine cellar vault, and, naturally, a helicopter landing pad—even a special house for the colonies of Lesser Horseshoe bats that once occupied the ruined mansion. All were part of this very non-Beara type of project.

Some locals thought the whole venture was merely a clever "never-happen" gimmick to spur speculation in the proposed mini "leisure-village" developments on the peninsula—but apparently not. The project is now completed, and while rather alien to the "undiscovered" ambience here, its exclusivity, according to the developers, will ensure "minimal disturbance" to the everyday life of Castletownbere ("except m'be make us a little richer for a change with all those new jobs and whatnot" according to one of the locals here).

There's none of this "starred" nonsense, however, in the restaurants and watering holes in town, most of which are clustered around or close to the main square. In addition to the now world-famous red-and-black facade of MacCarthy's Bar and Grocery, it was reassuring to find a cornucopia of culinary delights in the form of O'Donoghue's, O'Sullivan's, Breen's, O'Shea's, The Copper Kettle (great soups and fruit pies), Murphy's, The Hole in the Wall, The Olde Bakery, Cronin's Hideaway, Comara, Twomey's, and Jack Patrick's, run by the local butcher and his wife and renowned for its traditional Irish cuisine. And then of course came the two hotels—Beara Bay and Cametringame, complete with their own bars and nightlife enclaves.

One of the most popular local dishes in the pubs and restaurants here is the ubiquitous Irish mixed grill. And according to the celebrated writer John B. Keane, this is the ideal list of key ingredients: "A medium-sized lamb chop, two large fat sausages, four slices of pudding—two black and two white—one back bacon rasher and one streaky, a sheep's kidney, a slice of pig's liver, a large portion of potato chips [French fries], a decent mound of steeped green peas, a large pot of tea and all the bread and butter one could wish for . . . authorities are divided as to whether fried eggs should be included or not." So—there it is. A gourmand's checklist to ensure no culinary short-changes!

And what a gourmand's checklist of Brit-Irish goodies awaited us when we had a quick walk around the town's compact and cluttered supermarket: crumpets, Birds Eye custard, Callard & Bowser's butterscotch, sandwich spread, Marmite, HP sauce, treacle sponge and spotted dick in cans, piccalilli, jelly babies, Oxo cubes, Fry's cream bars, Gentlemen's Relish, Rolos, pickled onions, Lucozade, Robinsons Lemon Barley Squash, and on and on. Gorgeous!

For a community of fewer than two thousand permanent residents (itinerant Spanish, French, and Portuguese fishermen and "blow-ins" of all nationalities rapidly increase the population), Castletownbere was a true *ceadsearch* (sweetheart) of a town that gave us many memorable evenings of *céilís* and *craic*. On one occasion a barman showed us a descriptive clipping of the town dating back to 1920 with the comment that "ah can't see as things have changed much in nigh on a century!"

> Thirteen trawlers from Bilbao, Spain, arrived today and the streets were crowded with brown men, holy medals around their necks, deeply religious oaths on their lips, merriment and good nature in their eyes, bundles of silk stockings and bottles of lethal Iberian brandy under their jerkins. The stockings and the brandy they would barter for anything available. The dances in the hall beside the harbor were a sight to see. You wouldn't know under God what country you were in.

Whatever country it is, it's certainly going "green" rapidly and responsibly. In the grocery stores you pay a fee for every plastic bag you need; NO SMOKING signs are everywhere (despite the threatened bar-boycotts by petulant puffers), and just on the edge of town is one of the most sophisticated recycling centers we've ever seen anywhere. This is no simple triparate glass, metal, and plastic depository. Instead there are over twenty separate collection sections for four different oils; three different glass types; five different paper bins, plus special containers for "small computers," "large TV sets," aerosol cans, car batteries, domestic batteries, fluorescent lights, and even plastic bottle tops!

EASING EASTWARD OUT PAST the town's modern hospital, a scattering of sedate B and Bs, a couple of enticing arts and crafts galleries, and a very appealing golf course overlooking Bantry Bay, we became increasingly aware of numerous small roadside signs for archeological sites.

"It says here in the local guide map," Anne told me, "that 'over six hundred sites have been identified so far on Beara, ranging from wedge graves, stone circles, and ring forts to ancient church sites

and, at seventeen feet high, the world's tallest ogham stone just outside Eyeries.'"

"And what pray tell is an ogham stone?"

"Just a minute—I've seen something . . . ah—here . . . it says,
'There are over three hundred still existing in Ireland and they usually mark important graves . . . The vertical script carved into the
stone consists of a series of twenty different incisions based on Latin.
The notches represent vowels and the slanting or straight strokes
are consonants. The words themselves are usually found to be old
Irish and are considered proof of a literate society dating back at least
to 400 AD.'"

"Fascinating."

"Yes, it is. And y'know, there's something really magical about
this whole peninsula. You feel as if you're being lured into a very
ancient place—a place that was possibly much more populated in
prehistoric times than it is today. Presences . . . I can sense them.
Can't you?"

I'm not normally very tuned in to such psychic nuances, but I
had to agree with my ultrasensitive partner. There was definitely a

Derreenataggart Stone Circle

sense of well-organized layers of historic occupation here—or maybe, as a friend of ours used to say, "a captivating casserole of primitive cultures."

And if we'd read the guidebook a little more carefully we'd have realized that we were only a few miles from one of the most significant sites in southwest Ireland—the great Derreenataggart Stone Circle—a place we later came to know well.

We passed the great gray bastion of Hungry Hill with its famous seven-hundred-foot waterfall (Europe's highest) fed by two small lakes, and laced with waterfalls following a sudden rainstorm over the Caha range. Tumbling streams cascaded down the deeply gullied, elephant-hide-like strata, then split and splintered into sheened silver cascades. At the base of the mountain they surged in peaty froth and fury and raged down narrow serpentining streambeds across the long slow slopes of brown-green moor. Whirling like out-of-control dervishes, the streams roiled around boulders bigger than Beara's famous standing stones, ultimately surging under and occasionally over the coast road and out into the vast stillness of Bantry Bay. It was a most impressive sight, and we wondered at the fury of the storm as it ripped across the bare rock summit. That was not a place, we agreed, that we'd like to be.

The terrain then began to stretch itself languorously into a wider coastal plain dotted with farms and sleepy communities like little Derreen, Adrigole, and Tratrask. Once again we were tempted to turn inland and cross over the peninsula on the dramatic Healy Pass road but resisted, promising ourselves a more leisurely trip later on in the month. We continued along the coast road, past the impressive bulk of Sugar Loaf Mountain and—finally—down a long winding descent into Glengarriff, end point of our first "Ring" drive.

Like Kenmare, this is definitely a town of Victorian distinction and self-conscious promotion. It boasts fine hotels and restaurants for "main highway" trade on the dramatically tunneled Caha Pass road to Killarney and beyond. The pubs are plastered with signs for "authentic Irish folk music *céilí* evenings." Souvenir stores do a roaring trade in everything from hefty Aran island sweaters, hand-carved shepherd's crooks, and Waterford crystal to budget bins full of fluffy little toys with Irish Tom O'Shanter hats, dainty shamrock-decorated spoons, and the inevitable black T-shirts with prominent GUINNESS IS GOOD FOR YOU logos. This is no longer wild Beara country, but despite all the commercialism (and notorious plagues of summer midges), it does offer three distinct attractions. Perhaps best known is Garinish Island, locally called Illnacullin, where a quirky Gulf Stream microclimate of high humidity and almost subtropical temperatures enabled the creation of an internationally renowned Italianate "Garden Paradise" on a tiny island a short distance from the shore of Bantry Bay. This unique little masterwork of exotic flora and fauna was created around 1910 and later became a favorite hideaway for George Bernard Shaw, who ac-

cording to local lore wrote much of his play *Saint Joan* here among the exuberant gardens and delicate architectural "follies," while amused by the antics of seal colonies on the rocky shoals around the island.

An even more exotic creation is the nearby Bamboo Park heralded by a large Japanese gateway and offering meandering

The Bamboo Park—Glengarriff   paths and bay vistas

framed by explosions of bamboo groves and tropical jungle enclaves.

But perhaps the most enticing—and authentic—attraction here is
the Glengarriff (or Gougane, which translates as "rugged glen")
Forest Park, a large swathe of rare native oak woodland that once
covered much of Ireland. This was a favorite haunt of such celebrated
authors as William Makepeace Thackeray and Sir Walter Scott, and
today hikers and avid nature lovers can vanish for days in this vast
scenic—almost subalpine—wonder world of wild streams, shadowy
gorges, waterfalls, and a silence that is so refreshing after the in-
season tourist crush of the town itself.

Signs at Glengarriff pointed enticingly southward to Bantry, a
delightful market town (famous for the produce stands of local
cheese makers and other artisans) arced around the eastern tip
of Bantry Bay and watched over by the graceful Queen Anne–styled
Bantry House, built around 1700 and home to an eclectic collection
of art and ornate furnishings, and magnificent gardens. The two remaining southwest peninsulas of Sheep's Head and Mizen Head are
to the south, and then eastward are Skibbereen and ultimately Kinsale, Cobh, and Cork. All very tempting destinations. But Anne, as
usual, was the one to return us to a semblance of normalcy:

"Excuse me, but I wish you'd stop dreaming of driving south.
We're here on Beara and there's now the rather significant question
of precisely where are we going to live!"

"Live?"

"A house, a cottage, a bungalow. Y'know, preferably near the
ocean, near a village with decent pubs and a well-stocked grocery
store, and . . ."

"Ah, yes . . ."

"Y'remember now? We're got nowhere to live at the moment . . .
like tonight, for example!"

"Well, the lady we spoke to on the phone said she had a couple of
options . . ."

"Yes, that's true. So how about if we turn around, head back to Castletownbere, and go and take a look at what she's offering. They all seemed very charming on her Web site, but we need to go and check them out. Let's go . . . it'll be fun!" (Anne is always very convincing when she plays the role of trip coordinator.)

"Yes. You're right. Check them out. Definitely. Great idea."

No reply. But it didn't matter, because I knew she was raring to set up a new home in a new place, with new places to food shop, new dishes to cook, and with who-knew-what experiences ahead.

And what the charming lady with the bungalows to rent had said to us about her properties turned out to be absolutely true.

Within a couple of hours we'd selected an almost brand-new fully furnished bungalow for a "just-affordable" rent close to that beautiful white Ballydonegan Beach just below Allihies. By sunset we were sitting at our outdoor picnic table sipping a fine fruity pinot noir together as the brilliant flare of evening light turned everything golden. Shadows eased slowly across amber grasses and we could hear the soft susurrus of surf on the sand and we were very, very happy, bathed together in tranquil splendor.

We had arrived safely on Beara, made our first "loop" journey, and were falling in love with the place already. And we still had months more to explore and learn all the nooks and nuances of this unspoilt "best secret place in Ireland."

So—once again—*Sláinte!*

5

The Magic at MacCarthy's

EARLIER I PAID SINCERE HOMAGE TO the late Pete McCarthy and his splendid romp of an Irish travelogue book—*McCarthy's Bar*. I also thanked him from the bottom of my soul for luring Anne and me here. "Here" being Beara, Castletownbere, and most specifically, MacCarthy's Bar on the main square in this hectic little harborside town.

MacCarthy's is the kind of Irish pub you enter and fall in love with in nanoseconds Pete was no exception, and I quote once again with great affection and respect from his book:

> I can sense that this place might be a contender in the Best Pub in the World competition. MacCarthy's is an effortless compromise. The front half is a grocer's shop with seats for drinkers; the back half, a bar with groceries. On the right as you enter is a tiny snug, once a matchmaker's booth where big-handed farmers arranged marriages between cousins who hadn't met. Aluminum kettles and saucepans hang from the ceiling, not for show, but for sale. Drinkers sit under shelves of long-life orange juice and sliced bread. There is a fridge full of dairy products. The well-stocked shelves behind the bar display eggs, tinned peaches and peas, Paxo stuffing, custard creams, baking powder, bananas, Uncle Ben's rice, nutmeg, onions, olive oil, Brillo pads, and soap: good news for hungry drinkers who need a wash.

MacCarthy's Bar

The dense, luxuriantly-sculpted pint of stout is five minutes in the pouring, the precise amount of time needed to confess your entire life history to the skilled Irish bar person. I was jolted out of my introspection by a seventy-two-year-old woman who stood on a chair and sang "The Fields of Athenry." She was a bit wobbly on her pins, on account of having suffered a stroke the previous week, but it went down well anyway. Everyone followed with songs of their own . . . I was in the dream Irish pub of the popular romantic imagination.

And although Pete, from what I remember, didn't use the word *magic* in reference to this little gem of a watering hole, you could sense that aura in his words, and I will certainly use it. You see, that's the thing with MacCarthy's. You just never know when you open the creaking doors, swinging like those saloon bar doors in a spaghetti western and set in the pub's bold red-and-black facade, what little dramas and complexities of the human condition you'll find within. Sometimes, particularly in an off-season afternoon, it'll be like it used to be, with a couple quietly sharing a pot of tea at a small chipped table in the front snug room where marriages were once arranged like barter-transactions in an Arabian bazaar and where a selection of those vital groceries and other household necessities are on permanent display behind the counter and also over their heads, precariously balanced on little shelves. In the back room, divided from the front by a halfhearted attempt at a screen a yard or so wide and just enough to block the shenanigans of ardent beer-huggers, there's invariably a couple of local crusties, maybe a shepherd, a farmer, or a fisherman—one of those who sailed in the "small boaties" before the mammoth EU-approved megatrawlers appeared. And the conversation would be slow, measured, and full of serene pauses for joint mental cud-chewing to ingest the riches of shared information or age-honed insights.

And once in a while, a halfhearted attempt at a joke will rise like a semi-inflated balloon. "So—what's the definition of an Irish queer, then?"

An expectant silence.

"A man who prefers girls to drink."

Grins and groans and more orders for stout.

And while nothing much was going on, the ladies who run this place, Adrienne MacCarthy and her sister Nicola, would make regular appearances to see if anyone had any sudden impetuous requirements in terms of groceries or Guinness or their glorious crab sandwiches with brown bread and lashings of Irish butter or the need for a little across-the-counter banter. They were always around. I never saw a man behind the counter and never asked why. It seemed just fine the way it was.

Of course there are occasions when a man's bicep-backed authority would be needed to separate a couple of tanked and cantankerous post-teenager town terrors. And it inevitably came from one of the regulars who, with a polite "by your leave" nod to one of the ladies, would launch into the fray initially with a "Now, c'mon, lads, c'mon . . ." If that failed to calm the pit bull tensions, there would be a stronger indication that the door would be the evening's denouement. Usually things ended in a kind of amicable blur of back slappings and proclamations of undivided brotherhood. In fact I don't think I've actually seen a real Irish fistfight here because, first, it's too small to get a good swing at anything other than your own glass, and second, because the mood is usually so pleasantly benign even when the place is packed. It invariably has the aura of a family gathering or even an Irish wake which, unlike wakes in other countries, are often renowned for their jolly games, pranks, and spirit of upbeat bonhomie. And a third reason too, which is maybe a little more subtle, is what I can only describe as the confessional spirit that seems to float around the tiny space, which is barely big enough for a dozen people comfortably but often hosts three times that number.

Whatever the size and spirit of the *craic* and no matter how intensely earsplitting the din, you'll invariably see and overhear the most personal and intimate of verbal intercourses. Perfect strangers, I should add, not entirely succumbed to the juice of the barley ("He has the drink taken, but not to unseemly excess," in local police lingo), have told me about aspects of their lives that they possibly wouldn't even think of sharing with their spouses. Maybe for them it's a toss-up between a mumbled recitation of sins in the confessionals of the towering gray cathedrallike edifice up the street, or in the more relaxed raconteurship here with someone you've never met before and may never meet or remember again.

However, in the case of Adrienne, I guarantee you'll certainly remember your first meeting. There's an aura about her that lures you to the bar. She looks straight at you—gentle eyes from a pretty but proud face framed by long blond tresses. She exudes kindness, sensitivity, a quiet wisdom, and a sense of fun—frisky and bubbly—beneath her placid demeanor. You feel you could trust her with all your worldly woes and worries and that she'd find time to listen while pulling half a dozen pints, making change, taking orders for sandwiches, and smiling at someone's corny joke down the bar.

Following the publication of *McCarthy's Bar*, with a photograph of Adrienne's colorful little pub on the cover along with a behatted Peter and a nun in her black robe supping a pint of Guinness on a bench outside the front door, the place has become a bit of a shrine with travel book lovers.

"Every day I find I'm talking about him to strangers," Adrienne told me. "I tell them the way he'd pop in after the publication of the book and peep his head around the door and sigh with relief when he saw that nothing had really changed. I think he dreaded that the popularity of his book would spoil things around here. But, except for a few extra visitors and blow-in residents, it's still a place for the locals really. Occasionally we'll get letters from people who loved his book—really sweet messages. Even poems and things. I think it's a great honor for Pete—and for us—all this affection and interest.

"But it happened so . . . accidentally, I suppose you'd say. Pete was at a bit of a loose end. He was working a lot with the BBC but was getting restless. So his agent suggested—with a name like McCarthy and despite a very English upbringing—he should do a book on Ireland. She said—'Just go and you'll know what to write.' And after he'd spent a few days here in Castletownbere, he suddenly knew what he wanted to do, and the book just sort of wrote itself. And he was so grateful—to us—to the whole place. And then—surprise,

surprise!—he called us a year or so later and said 'I've written a bit of a book about Irish bars . . .' and I thought 'Oh yeah . . .'

" 'What do you think about the title *McCarthy's Bar*?"

"And I said 'Sounds great . . .'"

" 'Do you mind if I put your pub on the cover . . .'

"And I said 'No, that's fine. Think it'll sell a dozen or two . . . ?' and then it turned out to be a best seller. It was on the charts for over a year. But you kind of just take that on board. There's no panic about it. It's just nice that people can come and chat . . . I mean, we were here long before Pete made us famous and that's what he liked. He even signed one of his books for me—'To Adrienne, definitely the best bar in the world!'

"It's so nice to have that. We both really clicked the way you do with some people . . . It all began when he first came here. It was my birthday, and he looked a bit low, so I said 'Why don't you come along?' and we had a great time and he just kind of became part of the family. He was quite well known on the BBC doing travelogues, but we didn't know any of that . . . and he was a stand-up comedian too . . . and you could see his wit and timing came through. But then he left after a couple of days and we didn't hear anything until he came back months later with his family. He did that a few times. And then, on his last visit, he said 'You've made me so much a part of your family, and if anything ever happens to you or your mum, please contact me and I'll be right here for you.' But a couple of months later . . . it was me going to his funeral."

Adrienne paused. Her eyes were moist but tears refused to leave the sanctuary of her eyes and she smiled: "Y'see—it still hurts. Even after all this time . . ."

"Sometimes the death of a close friend makes people go off and fulfill a few of their dreams, their life fantasies, before it gets too late. But you stayed on here," I said.

"Well—you're right. And I sort of mixed them up a bit. Y'see, this place is not a family obligation—I love it here. I just enjoy people so much, and despite all the routines, you never know what each day will bring. And I have my adventures too—hill walking in the high Atlas Mountains, in the Himalayas. I finally went to our Skellig islands too—the hard way—climbing all those seven hundred steps to the top of Skellig Michael, where the monks lived in those tiny beehive huts. Most fantastic place I've ever been to. I just wanted to lie down on the ground and cry . . . It's wonderful to realize what we've got right here in front of our noses. I love it all so much. Even if I go to Cork for the day, when we get back to Glengarriff and the whole of Bantry Bay just opens up . . . my heart just goes aaaaaghh! What a place! I need so little. I enjoy life. I'm not interested in a lot of money. I just want to be surrounded by good, interesting people and maybe help bring them together a little. Beara attracts who it needs. There's just so much . . . right here!"

"That's what I'm beginning to find out about Beara—layer upon layer—right here . . .'

Adrienne laughed softly and said, "Yeah, right . . layers . . ."

Then she looked directly at me. (A disconcerting habit of hers. It was almost like having someone step inside your head and root around for a truly responsive self.) "Have you got a few minutes? I'll show you some layers right now, if y'like!"

I had no idea what she was referring to, but one does not reject such an invitation from a lady of charm and charisma.

Adrienne led the way up creaking stairs to the family house above the pub. Then she opened the door on the second floor, held it open for me, and I entered a totally time-warped room. I was back in the 1920s—maybe the end of World War I. Even possibly somewhere around the end of the late Victorian era, if the crush of furniture and trinkets was any indication. Certainly the profusion of gracefully aged armchairs and settees, beautifully carved wooden side tables crammed with photos and family memorabilia, and dark somber oil paintings on the walls above a cheerful peat fire set in an elegant fireplace made it all feel like a refined drawing room in an affluent Dublin town house.

"My grandfather started a store here around 1860 and then later, despite objections from other family members, he got one of the first official licenses to sell Guinness in this part of Ireland. Before that, you mainly got your porter and your *uisce beatha*—your 'water of life' whiskey—from illegal stills and in *shibeen* shacks. So we did pretty all right and then my grandfather made a nice living out of supplying the British navy, who had a base across the channel there on Bere Island until 1939. He had his own bakery here behind the pub, and up in the garden he had the official powder house for the troops. So we had a nice life, which is fortunate, because he had ten children and he furnished the house all fancylike and well . . . it kind of stayed that way!"

For an hour or so we chatted in this Aladdin's cave of a room. Then Adrienne's mother came in, her hair done up in a kind of 1940s style (time-warp time again), with an ornate tray brimming with dainty sandwiches, scones, homemade sloe and apple jam, and tea in hand-painted porcelain cups. She was a delightful person, full of tales of family antics and obviously very proud of her homemade jams. "I'll give you a pot to take with you. It's the gin that really makes it special!"

"Gin in what—the jam?!"

"Of course. Gives it a little kick, don'cha think?"

"Yes, I certainly do and"—I paused—"by the way, there's something over there in the corner kicking too . . ."

Adrienne laughed. "Oh, that's just one of the pugs having a bit of a scratch . . . There's two more around somewhere."

The dog seemed to realize it was now the focus of attention and ceased its flailing and turned its head toward me. I gasped, I think. Certainly I was shocked by the dog's resemblance to an utterly time-worn, exhausted, and ferociously angry Winston Churchill. And then I remembered: "Isn't that the dog on the cover of Pete's book?! The one next to the boozing nun?"

Adrienne laughed. "That's the one. Isn't he a darling!"

Not my choice of adjective, but I chewed on a sandwich and made some kind of acknowledging grunt and we moved on to other matters.

As we chatted, I noticed one corner of the room seemed a little like a shrine to a good-looking man and adorned with swords and medals and newspaper clippings.

"Oh, that's my dad—Aidan," said Adrienne with a grin of pride and affection. "He was a doctor and decided to join the Brits in World War II. Many round here didn't, but he thought he should, and later—thirty-five years later—he finally wrote a short memoir about all the amazing and terrible things he'd seen. I showed it to Pete. He was utterly gob-smacked—so was I when I first read it. He'd never talked much about his experiences. He was a very gentle, modest man. So Pete helped get it republished and it's been on the best-seller list now for quite a while. Look—just read one of the reviews. There were plenty, but I think this fellow—Philip Nolan—got it just about right."

Adrienne handed me a yellowing review clip and I read: "The shelves of the world's libraries are not exactly littered with memoirs of World War II written by Irishmen. After all, the vast majority sat it out on the sidelines watching with a lazy eye as the markers were shuffled across the map like chips on a roulette baize. And what a tale it is. This is a stranglehold of a book . . ."

The reviewer, aware of the gravity and horror of many of Aidan's stories, seems relieved by its lighter moments. For example:

> *Aidan's wanderings around Europe in search of his elusive "senior medical officers' group" in 1939 and the heady days of the "phony war" in France where he was called upon to examine the local prostitutes for infections. He described how ordinary servicemen had to be out of the brothels by 10:30 p.m. to leave the field clear for the officers, thus reinforcing the fact that, even when satisfying nature's most basic urges, the ranks were not allowed to mingle! Then his*

efficiency as a health inspector was so respected that on one
occasion he had over 200 completely naked females lined up
for him at an RAF base in England. Following his initial
surprise and embarrassment, he instructed that bras and
panties be donned immediately. For the next few days, the
incident took a good deal of living down and was the subject
of endless ribaldry in the officers' mess.

But at the heart of the memoir is a traumatic record of his five years of military service, starting with the utter chaos and slaughter of Dunkirk; his attempts to rescue men from a burning plane, for which he received the George Medal; a sudden transfer to Singapore, which fell to the Japanese just prior to his arrival so he was directed to Java, which was also being rapidly conquered by the Japanese. Four long and cruel years of internment followed by a plethora of River Kwai–type horrors, and in a sudden evacuation of prisoners by crazed camp commanders, the ship was torpedoed and survivors were picked up and then carried to Nagasaki just in time for the disastrous atomic bombing of the city on August 9, 1945 (two days after he and all the other prisoners had dug their own graves in preparation for their mass execution!).

His description of the immediate aftermath of this war-ending event is as follows:

We were wildly dashing for the air raid shelters. There was a
blue flash, accompanied by a very bright magnesium-type
flare. Then came a frighteningly loud but rather flat explosion
which was followed by a blast of incredibly hot air. Some of
this could be felt even by us in the shelter . . . Then an
Australian POW stuck his head out of the shelter opening,
looked around, and ducked back in again, his face expressing
incredulity. This brought the rest of us scrambling to our feet
in a panicked rush to the exits. The sight that greeted us halted
us in our tracks . . . The whole camp had disappeared . . .
We could see right up the length of the valley where

previously the factories and buildings had formed a dense
screen . . . But most frightening of all was the lack of
sunlight . . . We all genuinely thought that this was indeed
the end of the world.

Eventually, having somehow escaped the horror of radiation sickness, Aidan sailed back home to Dublin following Japan's surrender—on the *Queen Mary*! But even then—safe at last—a final dagger twist of fate awaited him when he was told by his family on his arrival that his younger brother had just been killed by the last V-2 rocket of the war to fall on London.

And yet Aidan's spirit—a living example of sensitivity and generosity overcoming gross brutality—is captured in the last paragraph of his memoir. Adrienne insisted on reading it aloud as we sat by the fire in that intriguing museumlike living room: "The greatest gift I have had is the appreciation of life around me. To be able to love my wife and children, to breathe the air, to see a tree in the golden stillness of a Cork evening, to take a glass of Irish whiskey, to see my children grow up, to fish in my favorite river—and to see the dawn come up upon each new day."

We sat together quietly for quite a long time by the glowing peat fire.

A WEEK OR TWO later, after many return visits to what had now become our favorite watering hole in Castletownbere (a judgment of course requiring regular resampling of delights at the town's other fine hostelries). I realized I was becoming a connoisseur of conversational tidbits here. Conversations are constantly buzzing around the bar, and amid pauses in my own yammer and blather, I found myself capturing a few pungent aphorisms and gems of societal perception—so many in fact that I wondered about compiling a modest booklet with a title something like: *Overheard at MacCarthy's,*

A Provocative Potpourri of Prepossessing Platitudes and Attitudes.
For example, how about some of these actual tape-recorded fragments to get the thing started off . . .

- "Y'see, the problem is my whole feckin' life seems to go on
  by itself just a little too far out of reach for me to feel a part
  of it . . ."
  "Ah—tha's not a problem, lad. Jus' get y'self longer arms."
- "She keeps on what she calls 'openin' up m'mind,' but
  problem is, there's nothing in there . . . absolutely nothin'!"
- "Y'see, movie stars are the external images of society's
  idealized dreams, fantasies and hopes . . ."
  "Oh Lord, Mr. Redford—say it ain't so."
- "I suppose you've just got to trust things will all work
  out—when I paint, for example, I've got to be convinced that
  something worthwhile will eventually evolve out of my
  mush of a brain . . . so all I can do is go to the edge and jump!"
  "Have a good stiff drink first—in case you hit something
  hard."
- "It's a really great film—it reveals the mask of mediocrity
  that hides an enormous all-encompassing emptiness—the terrible randomness that has spawned us, the ultimate ecstasy
  of exhausted surrender when the fear of death is finally
  conquered by death itself."
  "Oh yeah, right—sounds like a real laugh-a-minute Oscar
  winner!"
- "Our problem is—no one seems to want to vote
  anymore—and those that do are just glassy-eyed media sheep
  asleep in a national trance . . ."
  "Baaa . . . humbug!"
- "You've heard that old sayin' 'Your mistress knows you're
  a feckin' lyin' creep but your wife can only wonder . . .
  endlessly!' "

- "Life's far too damned short and far too much fun to waste time accumulating trinkets and toys . . . especially toys for boys who should know better!"

- "Y'see, I never really noticed him until he was gone and then I forgot all about him until he came back—and punched me out!"

- "I was jus' gettin' worried that there was something a bit wrong wi' me by feelin' this happy and then I got some bad news like I always do, and then I felt lousy, and then I knew everything was okay again . . . so I felt a bit better . . ."

- "Don't know what the hell's happening to the real Irish music—now it's all these overproduced musical blunder-busses with boilerplate plots if any at all, and full of little tweener pop-tarts and snarky little snits all wrapped up in sparkly garishness and lip-synching gnarly nouveau-bog country tunes . . ."

   "Oh . . . I rather liked the show . . ."

- "Poor lad—all he wanted was to be labeled an 'Artist' with a capital *A* so then he'd have all the excuses he needed to behave very badly, drink himself daft every night in Dublin, whore it up whenever he wanted, and die young, penniless and prematurely senile."

   "You call him a 'poor lad'—I'd call him pretty damned smart!"

- "Oh boy—the way that man lived! 'Beaten paths are for beaten men!' he said. I tell you—it was like an ode to the randoming life—a joy-obsessed odyssey of discovery and zany inspiration that made those who met him wonder if they were living as fully as they should—and why they spent so much time and effort stifling all their wonderful reckless impulses!"

   "So why the heck did he jump off those cliffs?"

   "Ah well, yes—you have a point there . . ."

- "Original sin!? A bloody myth! There's never been anything original in Catholic sin. It's all boringly predictable, repetitious, and as old and hackneyed as a senile cart horse!"
- "Y'see, it's all very simple. We humans are essentially the visible tail ends of karmic sequences that stretch back eons of time—even before time existed."

  "Ah well, so that explains this bleedin' eternal backache of mine then . . ."
- "There's no choice s'far as I'm concerned. You've got to live all out for today because you and/or the whole feckin' world could end tomorrow."

  "So what the hell am I doin' wastin' my time talkin' to you!?"
- "I thought I was seein' one of those beautiful 'love at first sight' romances openin' up t'me . . ."

  "Yeah—so . . ."

  "Turns out I was wearin' the wrong specs!"
- "Be honest now—do you ever mean what you say, or say what you mean?"

  "Which would you prefer?"

  "Both."

  "In that case I truly mean and believe that 'Guinness is good for you' and I've been meaning to say that my glass is empty and I'd love a refill. Is that honest enough for you?"
- "You know, it must be the Irish in me, but I'd much rather fail gloriously in what I do than succeed in a mediocre manner."

  "Ah well—in that case—congratulations to you on both counts!"

And so it goes—grins and gleanings of insights and little wisdoms at "the best pub in the world"!

6

An Introduction to
Dzogchen Beara

:::

WINKS, NODS, AND WHISPERS TINGED WITH wonder and awe. These often seem to characterize Beara and the people here who celebrate its diverse layers of realities, perceptions, and meanings. Nothing is what it appears to be in this wild and beautiful place, particularly from the point of view of neophyte blow-ins. Either you accept this and learn or you don't—and thus invariably learn very little and ultimately leave.

This was particularly the case with a very hidden place way off the main road to Allihies. We heard about it initially from one of our very first historian-informants, Jim O'Sullivan. He appeared at the door of our newly rented cottage a couple of days after our arrival and very kindly and unexpectedly offered to help us "get adjusted" to Beara and its oddities. We invited him in for tea, and he sat by the window, neatly dressed, hair combed to perfection, and politely professorial in demeanor. For the next hour or so he presented us with a remarkable array of information and insights on "this unique little finger of land." Also over the next few days he introduced us to a number of individuals such as Gerard ("Gerdie") Harrington and Connie Murphy, who became invaluable informants on Beara history and traditions.

Somewhere in the middle of this preliminary initiation Jim

mentioned the existence of a place—a center of meditation and learning—visited by a wide array of seekers, thinkers, and Buddhist practitioners including some very notable Tibetan *rinpoche* monks (who are believed to be reincarnations of important Buddhist figures) who offered occasional retreats and courses.

"But is there enough interest in Buddhism here on Beara? Where do the people come from?!" asked Anne.

Jim laughed. "Oh, you'd be amazed. People travel in from all over Ireland, all over the world for that matter. Especially when Sogyal Rinpoche comes here. He was born in eastern Tibet and he's said to be the incarnation of a teacher to the thirteenth Dalai Lama. He wrote that very famous book—*The Tibetan Book of Living and Dying.* It's said to be a condensation of over twenty-five hundred years of Buddhist teachings. You've heard of it?"

A bit of an embarrassed silence here, followed by a grunty "Er . . . no . . ."

Apparently Sogyal Rinpoche is one of the most renowned Buddhist teachers of our time and is the spiritual director of this Beara center—known as Dzogchen Beara—in addition to an international network of over a hundred meditation centers around the globe.

"His network is called Rigpa—the Tibetan word for 'informed awareness'—or so I'm told," said Jim.

"You're kidding!" gasped Anne.

"No—that's what he calls it, I think . . ."

"Sorry, Jim. What I meant was . . . I'm sensing some fascinating synchronicities here on Beara. AWARE is the name of the nonprofit organization I founded just over ten years ago. Its main purpose is to increase the independence and quality of life of people with vision loss. Check it out on our Web site—www.visionaware.org—and let me know what you think . . ."

Jim nodded and smiled. It was one of those smiles that reinforce the old adage "there are no coincidences."

■ ■ ■

APPARENTLY THE DZOGCHEN BEARA Center was actually the dream, and eventually a reality, of Peter and Harriet Cornish, who bought a run-down farm of 150 acres here in 1973 on one of the most spectacular cliff-ramparted headlands on the peninsula. Their intent was to create a spiritual home with hostel-like accommodations and even a series of small cottages for people of all spiritual traditions and denominations. Having succeeded, they gifted the center to a charitable trust under the guidance of Sogyal Rinpoche.

"Do they still live there—the Cornishes?" I asked Jim. "I'd like to meet them."

Jim paused. Wrinkles appeared across his forehead. He coughed quietly and then said, "Well, that's a little difficult. Peter still lives there and doesn't see many people now since Harriet's death in 1993. But apparently, the way he arranged her last few days in a hospice in Cork in a room decorated with Tibetan tankas and with her favorite *ngondro* chants playing—it inspired an idea to build a unique 'spiritual care' center on the cliff top here near the dormitories and the main meditation center . . . Just a minute, I think I may have . . ."

Jim delved into a small briefcase he was carrying. He'd already given us a few brochures, but now he pulled out a small booklet. "It's the only one I have at the moment—I'll get you a copy. But I like this bit. 'When we find we have chronic illness, or we are told we have only a few months to live, our lives can change dramatically. There is usually a need to find meaning, resolution, peace, and hope. This search for meaning can be a transformative experience for both the person who is sick or dying or for those they will leave behind. This process may or may not be rooted in a spiritual tradition . . . but the process can unfold itself to ultimately rewarding stages.' "

The room was very quiet for a few moments and then Anne spoke softly: "Beautiful. And that's what they're creating up at the center?"

"Yes," said Jim, "slowly. Like everything they do there. They seem to allow things to develop at their own rhythm and pace. Someone once described it to me as 'spiritual farming'—planting idea-seeds, fertilizing them a little, and then letting them grow according to their own timetables. He also said something I'll never forget: 'Always be generous. Give yourself away because what else are you here for anyway?' . . . But listen. I'm not really the person you should be talking to. I find the place magical—a magnificent place to go, if only to sit quietly on the cliff tops or in the meditation room when it's empty with all those huge vistas of the sky and ocean. But I'm hardly a Buddhist—although there's no proselytizing and that kind of thing there. You can attend workshops and whatnot if you want to—or you can just go there to be quiet. Matt Padwick— he's the one you should talk to. He's kind of in charge of most things there."

"Where is this Dzogchen? And how do we get there?" I said.

"With great difficulty," Jim said, chuckling, "particularly if you've never been there before. There's a sign about the size of a small menu and it's on a bend, so if you blink or get distracted by the view, which at that point is fabulous, then you'll miss it . . . And even when you've found it, you'll wish you hadn't. The track up into the hills is a real shock-smasher."

JIM WAS RIGHT ON both counts. First try—we missed the sign. By a good mile. We were almost down at the rocky beaches near Cahermore before we realized we'd overshot. So—back up the hill between burly boulders and twisted strata to the sign, which was actually smaller than a menu. More like a *Reader's Digest* magazine. And the track—well, at least it was a rental car we were driving, and quite frankly, considering those rip-off rates and obligatory "extra insurance fees"—we didn't feel too guilty about the shock-smashing. After a mile or two of grinding metal and creaking rivets as we switch backed higher and higher across the moors and between scrub-covered rock humps, we arrived in a small parking area surrounded by a thick profusion of trees and bushes. Suddenly and serenely there was silence. Utter silence.

"So where is everything—and everybody?" asked Anne.

"There's a small sign over there," I said, wondering if we'd arrived at the correct destination. Apparently we had. The sign confirmed that this was the Dzogchen Beara. But where was it?

We followed a winding pebbly path and then coyly, little by little, the complex revealed itself. First a tiny store selling an enticing mix of Buddhist trinkets, music CDs, and books on meditation, mantras, and "spiritual medicine." Then came a small administration building, followed by the bright white stucco walls of the meditation space and the shrine room. Beyond that were dormitories and other meeting spaces, and lower down, where the land ended in jagged two-hundred-foot-high cliffs, was a series of small rental cottages. And that was about it. We'd been told there were sacred sites hidden away on the hilltops and in the dense scrub, but we saw none of these. What we did see, though, was almost enough to make us instant converts—at least in terms of the aesthetics of the site. A great green curl of pyramidal hills spun southward, chiseled by deeply eroded black cliffs. Even on this relatively calm day, surf crashed against their bases, spuming fifty or more feet into the air. Farther south, in a blue haze, were the long graceful fingers of the Sheep's Head and Mizen Head peninsulas. And then, as we slowly turned ourselves westward, there was the Atlantic Ocean, striated with purple and turquoise, edging out toward North America in a sheen of burnished silver under a delicate scrim of puffball clouds.

"Next stop, Newfoundland and Labrador! Three thousand miles of uninterrupted brine . . ." I said.

"Beautiful—just beautiful!" said Anne.

Here indeed was a place serenely wrapped in peace and solitude.

Against such terrestrial purity one experiences a sense of cerebral self-erasure, a vanishing into an atmosphere of mirage and mist as you're being gently demoted to the status of a fading shadow . . .

"It is beautiful, isn't it—really!" said somebody else. Behind us.

We turned. A young man with a lean, open face and unusually bright eyes stood smiling at us. "Sorry. Didn't mean to interrupt . . . Matt Padwick. Very pleased you could both make it."

We all shook hands in a welter of grins and "so are we"s.

"You okay out here for a while? My office is a real mess—and it's a great day to be outside anyway."

We strolled slowly down to a low stone wall set unnervingly close to the cliff edge and sat together on the warm grass. Layer upon layer of cliffs shimmered in the soft amber tones of a late-afternoon sun, gradually fading into a purple haze to the south. Matt was immediately honest with us. In fact he seemed to be one of those indi-

Dzogchen Beara

viduals for whom dishonesty would be impossible. "Thanks for calling, but listen, if you've come to hear a long lecture on Buddhism, I'm not the right chap I organize things—keep things flowing—reasonably efficiently! I'm not officially qualif—"

"That's fine with us," I said. "We prefer to do without the indoctrination anyway."

Matt explained that since his arrival here in 1998, his aim had been to encourage open access to anyone and everyone. "To me, some of the most important elements of any belief system are to avoid harming anyone, to increase our connectedness, and to find contentment and meaning within our own selves and not through the pursuit of elusive external things. I've known people—many—who've gone decades without experiencing a truly silent meditative moment. They seem to be driven by some self-created internal 'race.' So I suppose you could say we exist to help slow down—maybe even eliminate—that kind of rather pointless and often damaging race. And that's really what it's all about here. I must admit, though, to being very impressed by Sogyal Rinpoche. I've met him quite a few times now. He really does possess some kind of aura—very peaceful, very focused, and very perceptive. He's not one of those hide-in-a-cave guys—he's right out there, all the time. I love to watch him in action. At some of our workshops, we'll always get people coming in with loaded questions—some that would stump your average theology philosopher. But he responds in such a natural, commonsense kind of way that the questions—the crafty semantics—just seem to flutter away. They don't seem relevant. He disarms people. Totally. Not through clever rhetoric or esoteric learning, but by being completely straightforward and honest. He's a great guy! I get great thoughts when I listen to him, but sometimes, when I try to explain them, my words can vanish into a neurological Bermuda Triangle!"

The three of us sat chatting together for half an hour or more, wafted by cool breezes. The sun was warm, the sea haze had intensified. The land became more mystical, merging seamlessly with the sky and the ocean. It was a most enticing interlude. We felt bathed in peace and the pleasure of quiet conversation. Then, without any hint of proselytizing, Matt explained more about the center and how it had added value and depth to his own life.

"I traveled for ages in my twenties. Around the world and whatnot. I suppose I was a kind of seeker, but I also had a great time just goofing off and adventuring. Going with the flow. I suppose living that kind of money-and-thing-free life, which is what I did for quite a while, you begin to see some of the key problems with modern-day antics—ultramaterialism, accumulation of ultimately meaningless toys, the affluenza contradiction—you know, the more you spend, the less you enjoy it! It's fun at first, I suppose, but then you realize you're in a spiritual cul-de-sac. Going nowhere.

"Who was that French philosopher? Was it Descartes? He said our biggest problem is that we often find it very hard to sit silently in a room by ourselves with no distractions. We're always going after the next thing—the next immediate gratification. Stupid, really. Like rats in cages always looking for the next bit of cheese. Anyway, so eventually I wised up and got a bit more serious. Signed up here for a short retreat. I didn't want to go through this life with a brain full of 'if onlys' and 'I *could* haves.' I told myself I'd give it a week or two, and if nothing happened then—shoot—I'd admit defeat and join the rat race! But then—well, I guess something *did* work, and I also met my wife, Andrea, here. Then my parents came to visit, fell in love with Beara, and stayed. My mum's a reflexologist. She's also become one of the Beara 'healers,' although she'd never really call herself that. The place just seems to lure in people with special gifts—and people who need them! That's why Dzogchen Beara is so powerful, I suppose. It's very hidden away, as you found out, and quiet, but it's known literally around the world. I was very lucky to find a job here. I don't get too involved with the actual teaching and meditation side of things . . . I'm kind of like a lubricant, just keeping the machinery of management moving along quietly and hopefully without too many glitches. And it's a great life. I've met so many beautiful people here . . ."

Then suddenly Matt looked up at the sky. A cloud was passing overhead, quickly darkening. The rest of the sky was virtually cloudless, but above us was this ogreish form, visibly bulging and contorting, as if possessed by some demonic force.

"Oh, boy!" whispered Matt. "You've gotta watch this."

"What? What's happening?" I asked.

Anne stared upward. "Wow, this looks interesting . . ."

"We'll go inside in a minute," said Matt, "but just see what happens. We've got some weird microclimate quirks here. Something to do with the cliffs and the Gulf Stream currents, they say . . ."

"Or maybe the natural forces don't like all these humans here tapping into esoteric spiritual realms," I suggested.

"Y'know I never thought of—" Matt started to respond with a chuckle but was abruptly drowned out in a flailing, crackling tumble of large (and painful) hailstones. "To the shrine!" he shouted, and we leapt up and scampered up the steep slope from the cliff edge past the altar for butter lamps and into the large unoccupied white room with its scores of red cushions scattered around the floor.

This was our first introduction to the Dzogchen's magnificent meditation space with its floor-to-ceiling glass windows overlooking the cliffs, the bays, and the timeless infinities of the ocean. In the midst of the frantic hammering of hail on the roof and the blizzard-like miasma outside, which eliminated views of anything at all, Matt asked with a huge grin, "So whadya think of this?!"

"Amazing—it just came out of nowhere!" I gushed.

Anne was silent.

"You okay?" I asked.

No reply.

"Hello?"

"What's that phrase?" she finally responded. "If you don't like the Irish weather . . ."

"Just wait five minutes," Matt said, rounding off the old chest-nut. I remembered a similar and well-justified sentiment in the Heb-rides of Scotland and also in Maine. And then, being English by birth, I couldn't resist throwing in another favorite chestnut—one of good old Dr. Johnson's: "When two Englishmen meet, their first talk is always of the weather."

"So how did you know I was English?" asked Matt.

"Well, you certainly don't sound Irish! Oh—and I've just remem-bered an old Yorkshire saying:

> 'It ain't no use to grumble and complain
> It's just as cheap and easy to rejoice;
> When God sorts out the weather and sends in rain,
> Why then—rain's my choice.'

Ironically there was latent meaning in the words—a sense of be-nign, smiling receptivity—that seemed most appropriate for our Buddhist shrine room setting.

ON OUR WAY OUT into the now-bright day with a cloudless sky again, I spotted this handwritten message on an index card pinned to a notice board by the door. It seemed coincidentally (but of course, as we all know by now, there are no coincidences) to capture the es-sence of the string of little experiences since our arrival here a couple of hours earlier:

> We may idealize freedom, but when it comes to our habits,
> we are often enslaved. And yet when you look deeply, you
> realize there is nothing that is permanent or constant, not
> even the tiniest hair on your body. Nothing is as it appears to
> be. Opportunities for transformation are continuously
> flowering. The sky is our absolute nature. It has no barriers
> and is boundless. And these great cliffs of Beara are a
> springboard for the spirit. So—Fly! Fly! Fly!

7
Monologue on Mortality

:
:

"Yeah—there is a definite sense of 'flying' here—on many levels. The Karma quotient must be off the scales. A real Richter-buster! For me at the moment, I guess it feels like a kind of floating between two worlds—the Buddhist world of recycling and reincarnation and the Christian world of heavenly hosts and all that kind of thing . . . I don't really see any contradictions between them. I believe they're both intensely personal, enveloping courage, love, and compassion as key ingredients to life and whatever comes after."

He was a middle-aged man, tall and thin—even slightly emaciated—and he walked slowly, with a distinct stoop. We never really introduced ourselves. I just found him sitting on the cliff edge at Dzogchen one late afternoon on my second spontaneous visit. He looked deep in thought—maybe even meditation—but then he turned, smiled a sort of wan smile, and invited me to join him. He was obviously troubled by something weighty. His brow was compressed in furrows and his eyes lacked any kind of life-sparkle. I soon found out why . . .

"The cancers hit me suddenly. It was like what Joan Didion wrote in that recent book of hers, *The Year of Magical Thinking*: 'Life changes fast. Life changes in the instant. You sit down to dinner and life as you know it ends.'

"They tell me I now have four different ones, so I guess my

immediate destiny is pretty much defined. Maybe not quite so fast as the doctors predict, but their job, I reckon, is to err on the side of cautious pessimism once the cards are spread out for all to read.

"At first it was a real death sentence and it sent me into a mad panic. I hadn't prepared for this at all. I felt like a wounded animal. And more than likely heading for a pretty painful end. I'd lived a bit of a riotous, self-centered life. People came and went—women, writers and artist-friends, drifters and grafters, con men and complacent peers, all certain, as I was, of long hedonistic lives lived for the day—and entirely for ourselves.

"And then when the news came, I was suddenly alone—with a sense of slow drowning in this great empty ocean. Dark and cold and endless. The terrible void of utter meaninglessness. Did I grab at religion just to fight this nihilistic horror? I guess maybe I did. At first. You know—anything to believe in, to have faith in, was better than this slow drowning. But then things changed. The adventure—of life and beyond—returned. The realization that even though I'll disappear as a physical entity, there remains the possibility of endless spiritual explorations throughout the hereafter.

"I became intrigued by the prospect. A never-ending expedition into the spiritual universe. A rejection of the naïve 'beginning-and-end' theories and ways of thinking of today's physicists and philosophers. You know—the first big bang explosion leading finally to the final whimpering implosion. The ultimate black hole that ultimately absorbs itself. It all seems too stupid—as if even our greatest minds, being incapable of conceiving 'infinity,' have to collapse the inconceivable to a petty little picture with a neat beginning, a lively middle, and a pathetic conclusion. Why can't we just accept the fact that there are things our minds will never be able to wrap themselves around? Ideas so vast that all you can do is celebrate their immensity and accept the wonderful open-endedness of everything. Including the self and our vast, barely explored psychic reservoirs of past lives and experiences and karmic ripples! That was a time when, to quote someone famous whose names escapes me: 'Mortality rested very lightly on my shoulders!' "

He paused at that point. It was a long monologue, and even he seemed surprised by the scope and sear of it. He blinked, coughed, chuckled, and then leaned forward, half whispering: "I guess it must have been the LSD that did it. Once I discovered the glorious hidden mind behind the mundane day-to-day functioning mind, I knew our adventures—for each one of us—were meant to be vast and all-encompassing. The lowly old joints of marijuana opened quite a few mental doors and shutters too at the start. But LSD just blasts you off into the infinities. Problem is, if you're not careful, you may not always come back. The wonderful thing is, though, when you do come back, you bring a hell of a lot with you. Almost too much sometimes. Your mind can feel as if it's about to fragment into a gazillion pieces with all the new perceptions you discover. It's scary as all hell first time, but you start to get used to it as you learn the stepping-stones out into the universe. It's all so incredible. No wonder they try to ban this stuff. We'd all become so wise and 'Tree of Knowledge' all-knowing that the world as we see it wouldn't exist anymore . . . and most of the things we're programmed to value and revere wouldn't matter a toss anymore. We'd see them for what they truly are—barriers and clamps on our amazing potentials—false gods and fake rewards of materialistic madness!

"Of course, the old, unenlightened self still keeps lumbering out occasionally, even though I like to think I'm far beyond that now. But he's still there—sudden panics at my predicament, great weeps at all my stupid actions and ignorance and lost loves and that kind of thing, whirling fantasies of chasing young nymphets like a rut-minded professor at some flea-bitten college . . . and of course that utter dread that I might be totally wrong. That all this rekindled 'belief in the eternal-spiritual' might be nothing more than just a frantic selfish scramble for a life belt in the face of an inevitable expiration—an end with no purpose, no continuity, no resonance, no nothing."

He paused, as if struck by the horror of his own dilemma—false faith or fatalistic futility. I expected him to weep. Or maybe even scream. But instead he just started to chuckle . . .

Finally I said something. (It's unusual for me to be quiet for so long.) "Maybe in the end that's the best solution—facing life with a wink and a chuckle . . . I've always been fascinated by our inherent impermanence. Sogyal Rinpoche deals with that head-on in his *Tibetan Book of Living and Dying*. I'm reading it at the moment. He uses a wave as one of his examples. In one way of looking at a wave, it has a very distinct identity, a beginning and an end, a birth and a death. But look at it another way and it doesn't really exist at all, but is merely the result of the behavior of water—'full' of water but 'empty' of independent existence. It comes and goes. It's constantly morphing into other forms and other waves—dependent on sets of always changing circumstances and related in its 'emptiness' to every other wave.

"What I think he's saying"—I seemed to be on a bit of a rhetorical roll now—"is that nothing has any inherent existence of its own. Doesn't matter what it is—a tree, a house, a car—or you, even you! The closer you get to the essence of a 'thing' you realize that it's made up of an awful lot of 'no-thing,' identical to all other things. Everything merges into incredibly complex and subtle webs of interconnectedness that link everything with everything across the universe. There's no independent existence for anything. It's all one unified, multidependent, interconnected existence. The butterfly's wing syndrome—the infinities of ripples, the magic dance of genomes, the world of quantum physics. Things have no more reality than dreams. Everything—all particles exist potentially as different combinations of other particles or waves. At the quantum level waves and particles are interchangeable, so they say. 'Death' doesn't really exist in a universal sense. It's merely one more amazing transition—something you can finally accept with a 'wink and a chuckle' because, in many ways, it's already a part of us all."

I think he heard me. He certainly kept on chuckling and staring out across the soaring cliffs beyond the shrine, the broken rocks at their base pounded by explosions of white surf and the vast horizon of the Atlantic under soaring galleon sails of cumulus clouds. But he nodded, as if something I'd said made sense for him. Then he slowly raised his arms as if addressing some great imaginary audience and very quietly, very precisely, he said: "I think I'm really ready for the start of the next journey now . . . Almost . . ."

We sat silently together, letting the breezes stroke our faces and whisper through the clusters of white daisies growing wild along the cliff tops. Slowly I felt myself being absorbed into the silence of the land—an enduring expansive sense of stillness and benign solitude. An odd sense of emerging opened up around me—emerging from the edges of finite knowledge into a more rarefied state of beginner's enlightenment? A freshening of the spirit—a dreamtime of my imagination—a melting or melding into far larger visions—things endless—things with no beginning. Things infinite and full of peace and beauty. Things I hoped my newfound friend was discovering too in preparation for his "next journey" . . .

8

Moments of Meditation

:::

OF COURSE ANNE AND I HAVE dabbled in meditation. Who hasn't? We're certainly old enough, curious enough, and occasionally daft enough to have done enough dabbling for half a dozen lifetimes. And meditation certainly takes a lot less effort than seeking out golden toads in the Costa Rican cloud forests, or hunting for unique species of plants atop the soaring Tepui Plateaus in Venezuela's Gran Sabana, or any of a couple of dozen other zany "pursuits of the almost impossible" we seem to have undertaken in our endless and erratic quests for "secret places" and "lost worlds" described in my previous books.

But unlike those other ventures, in the case of Buddhist-inspired meditation, we never seem to reach any specific destination. Assuming, of course, that there is any destination to be reached. Prior guides we've experienced along the mystical breathe-in-breathe-out route have emphasized that wonderful old saying: "There is no path to happiness; happiness *is* the path," and freely admit that there are many times when they feel the constant dichotomy between ceaseless mind yammer and silent meditative now-ness is one that is ever challenging. "It's a simple art, surrounded by complexities," a colleague once told me after "an amazingly long" weekend meditation course. "I mean, you'd think your mind would actually enjoy switching itself off for a rest. Unfortunately, mine apparently doesn't . . ."

Our guide for the Tuesday morning "meditation for beginners" session at the Dzogchen Center was a blond-haired woman with a captivating smile and eyes that bored into you and never seemed to blink. She definitely looked like a meditation-maven. But she was also disarmingly honest at the outset by admitting, that despite her years of practice, she still had days when she felt herself to be at a novice stage, grappling with a mind so teeming with thoughts and emotions and imagined crises and gotta-do lists that she wondered why she'd ever considered meditation as a practice. "You never get 'there,'" she said with a broad smile. "But sometimes you just know you've moved sideways into a different and far more peaceful space—and that suffices and encourages you to carry on."

Even Sogyal Rinpoche writes in his *Tibetan Book of Living and Dying*:

"There are so many ways to present meditation, and I must have taught it a thousand times, but each time it is different, and each time it is direct and fresh." He goes on to suggest in colorful, honest language that "generally we waste our lives, distracted from our true selves, in endless activity . . . in intense and anxious struggles, in a swirl of speed and aggression, in competing, grasping, possessing and achieving, forever burdening ourselves with extraneous activities. We are fragmented . . . We don't know who we really are . . . So many contradictory voices, dictates and feelings fight for control over our inner lives that we find ourselves scattered everywhere leaving nobody at home." How many times have I thought that! Then I resolve to resolve the "waste" but invariably continue—after a guilt-laden period of nonreform—to continue just as before.

"Meditation," Sogyal suggests "is the exact opposite. It is a state in which we slowly begin to release all those emotions and concepts that have imprisoned us into the space of natural simplicity . . . We return to that deep inner nature that we have so long ago lost sight of. Meditation is bringing the mind back home, releasing and relaxing . . . and ultimately embodying a state of gentle transcen-dence which is why we are all here."

The luminosity of the shrine room here seems to engender tran-scendence. Sometimes silvery sheens of mist or glowering banks of dark cloud can create an otherworldly mystical sense of floating with only occasional glimpses of open ocean or ragged precipices tumbling down to churning surf-spumes. On other occasions the sun can be so dazzling on the sea and the myriad greens of the land that your eyes water with the intensity of it all. You're not exactly crying, although on many occasions, you could indeed be tempted to weep at the overwhelming beauty of it all. On other occasions you might vanish into a dreamtime miasma of your own imagin-ings, living inside your own silences.

On this particular day Anne and I are sitting on small cushions facing the ocean vistas (actually Anne is sitting on a chair because

Skelligs in a Storm

she thinks she'll get cramps!). And it is the light that is the main feature of the room today. The light in the air and on the sea and the distant Skellig islands—that incredible pure molten platinum light that combines the intensity of silver with the sheen of gold but is more powerful than either in terms of its calming quality.

The session begins gently with our guide reminding the dozen or so early morning participants to "follow the breath," the slow, regular, in-out rhythms of breathing that can allow us to circumvent the constant clamoring yammer of the mind and reach a quiet state of timeless now-ness. We've both tried this before, so her instructions are familiar.

"We'll begin now" she says and gently taps the brass bowl with a small leather-wrapped stick. The sound echoes and re-echoes around the sun-bathed space and seems to go on for minutes until finally fading away into a delicious silence. And then of course begins the battle. A battle you're trying to pretend is not a battle at all and doesn't really exist except that pretending something doesn't exist is, of course, already an admission that it does. The mind doesn't like to be sidetracked. The mind is used to being the boss—center of all focus and attention. The mind demands to be heard even when it's offering nothing but jumbled gobbledegook.

"Concentrate on your breathing—the slow in and the slow out—forget everything else," our guide says. So we do, and for a while it seems that the pathetic prattle of consciousness—that messy porridge of lists and forgotten must-dos and should-haves and could-haves and guilts and fears of futures that may never come and fears of repercussions of past action, or fears, as FDR suggested, just of fear itself—the whole ridiculous frantic flurry and scurry—it seems that it might actually be quieting down for once.

For a while at least.

But inevitably I do catch a sneak thought or two creeping in, even as I am studiously not thinking about thinking. I tell myself firmly that I shouldn't think about the thought but instead try to think about nothing until the thought slinks away, unexamined, and leaves me nothing else to think about except wondering when the next sneak attack of thinking thoughts might be on its way. It's that whole elephant-in-the-kitchen thing. Trying not to think about something everyone is thinking about but that you've all agreed not to think about because thinking about it would be a mutual recognition of the elephant's existence, which of course you're all trying to ignore.

I think possibly, maybe, there were a couple of interludes in my half hour of meditation on my little cushion that you might say were blessed by pure unthinking silence. Moments of modest illumination expanding in a place where loose, dangling threads of thought and experience can coalesce into more enduring tied knots of perception and insight. But most of the remainder was occupied by a mental jousting match in which those errant (and ridiculously random and meaningless) thoughts would be challenged by the "wannabe a better me" advance guard of mind-protectors, valiantly warding off invaders but trying not to think about it too much!

Finally—our guide tapped her brass bowl with the small stick, slowly lifted her head, and allowed herself a modest, rather shy smile, and it was all over. Anne thought the experience was great and was eager to return. I thought, maybe—next week, or— whenever . . . but first I need to have a serious chat with this lump of gray stuff that contains my rambunctious, restless mind. Whatever a "mind" actually is . . .

9

A Delicious Work in Progress
Progress
Gastronomic Romps Around Beara

⋮

THE HEADLINES OF A LOCAL NEWSPAPER were blunt: "US foodie magazine says 'Ireland is no gastronomic wonderland' but we beg to differ!"

The editor, with obviously little patience for arrogant American journalists with overblown gastronomic claims to fame, made it very clear in unambiguous terms that, for all the international array of fancy restaurants in Dublin and Cork, there is also a marked emphasis today in Ireland on true "local" cuisine, which in turn has helped maintain local farmers and create new cheese makers and a wide array of other artisanal producers.

After blasting the American penchant for pasteurized, homogenized, sterilized, emulsified, genetically modified, and hormone-pumped food products, the editor suggested that one of the first purist proponents of 'genuine Irish menus" was Hedley MacNeice, wife of the renowned poet Louis MacNeice, at her Spinaker restaurant in Cork. Then in 1964 came the celebrated Myrtle Allen and her extended family at their Ballymaloe complex of restaurant, hotel, and cookery school. They, along with the irrepressible Ryans at Arbutus Lodge, have celebrated the abundance and excellence of Irish native fare and stimulated a well-overdue resurgence of culinary crafts.

In the early days, when Irish cuisine consisted primarily of gargantuan breakfasts with black blood pudding as the featured attraction, watery "Irish stews," and overbicarbonated soda bread, Myrtle Allen was dismissed as a quirkish "middle-aged farmer's wife in the wilds of east Cork."

With the same determination of purpose and emphasis on authenticity as Julia Child, Elizabeth David, M. F. K. Fisher, Alice Waters, and others, Myrtle celebrated the seasonal bounties and varieties of fruits, fish, vegetables, and game. She offered menus of simply prepared dishes redolent with real, not manufactured, mélanges of flavors. She introduced—or actually reintroduced—recipes from the past utilizing often unfamiliar local ingredients such as wild garlic, cardoons, rocket, zucchini blossoms, nettles, flower-flavored honeys, and all those aromatic seaweeds—carrageen, laver, dulse, sloke, sea spinach, samphire and dilisk. Add to all these wild "fingerling" eels, unusual game birds such as snipe, woodcock, barnacle goose, plover, thrush, and even puffin, home-smoked fish and hams and salami-type sausages, wild salmon, crayfish and lobsters, salted herring and mackerel, limpets, whelks, cockles, sprats, periwinkles, rogham (blue octopus), and sea urchins, and you begin to see what a celebration of choice exists. In addition one finds heirloom breeds of farm-raised ducks and chickens, a vast array of wild mushrooms, golden raspberries, boysenberries, worcesterberries, enormous "dive scallops," and some of the ugliest fish I've ever seen starting with the gelatinous mouth-for-a-head monkfish and progressing rapidly into "beyond nightmare" territory.

Then top all this panoply of peculiar—but oh, so delicious—culinary ingredients with such utter delights as marshmallow-tender Connemara lamb, a vast array of potato types, superb freshwater fish, boar, and venison galore—and, of course, fine porters, whiskey, and even (if early promise reaches fruition) regional wines. And what we have here is a nation on the cusp, maybe well above the cusp by now, of an enticing gastronomic revolution.

■ ■ ■

A 2006 SPECIAL ISSUE of *Saveur* magazine on Ireland—the one the local editor had strongly objected to—gave modest, if guarded, encouragement to this process:

> Let's be honest here. When it comes to food, Ireland is not
> France or Italy China or Japan. It has no elaborate court
> cuisine, no lengthy restaurant tradition, no world-famous
> chefs. What it does have is a damp, relatively mild climate
> where things love to grow. It has, in other words, the raw
> materials. Almost everywhere we went we saw things
> happening: rural entrepreneurs building little food produc-
> tion businesses; restaurants revising their menus to take
> better advantage of native bounty; writers delving seriously
> into the history and culture of Irish food. If we didn't exactly
> find a gastronomic wonderland, we certainly found a deli-
> cious work in progress.

Anne and I arrived on Beara quite a while after this long and photo-rich feature was published and were curious to see to what extent the gastronomic wonderland potentials had reached our home in Allihies.

"This is not gourmetland by any means," one local told us, almost offended by the idea. "Although, when they're finished building that ultraposh hotel at the old Dunboy Castle down the road, things could certainly change. At the moment, if you want fancy, you go over Moll's Gap to Killarney or to Kenmare and the Park Hotel. Or closer in you can go to Josie's overlooking the lake at Lauragh or Mossie's at Adrigole—but I've heard that's closing—or that new place over O'Neill's in Allihies. Most local places are more basic—chips-and-peas-with-everything at the pubs and a bit more uppish at The Olde Bakery in Castletownbere. Then there's places like Jack Patrick's—the butcher across from MacCarthy's. His wife runs a small restaurant next door, and she puts out some real solid

Irish dishes—Guinness stews, lovely lamb and pork, *colcannon*, *boxty*, that kind of thing. Nothing too fancy—just good stick-t'-y'-ribs kind of food. Oh, and beautiful fresh seafood too when the boats come in."

"We'd heard there was someone here on Beara who made his own cheeses. You know anyone like that?"

"Ah! Of course—I forgot!" Our informant slapped the side of his head rather vigorously. "Norman! And Veronica. I forgot to tell you about them and their son Quinlan. Out this side of Eyeries. Very nice family and beautiful cheeses. Go and see them—I'll show you where they are."

He drew us a map on the back of an envelope dragged from his pocket. "Now be careful—if you miss this lane here you'll end up miles down the road in Eyeries."

So, inevitably—we ended up miles down the road in Eyeries.

"There's a sign telling you when you've got there," insisted the elderly lady cashier at O'Sullivan's store in the village when we asked her for directions. And after a couple of erroneous attempts, we discovered that she was indeed correct. Norman and Veronica Steele's farm is certainly elusive, although it's only a mile or so west of the village of Eyeries and perched on a steep slope overlooking the local graveyard. The "sign," which read MILLEEN'S CHEESERY, was barely the size of a paperback book and camouflaged by globs of sprayed mud from passing tractors.

"Yeah—I've been meaning to put up something a bit bigger—we love people coming here . . . if they can find the place!" said Norman, a gentle, stocky giant of a man in crumpled jeans and an enormous gray sweater that drooped off his torso like melting lava. He'd emerged from his stone-built house to quiet a ferocious lion-size dog apparently determined to keep us locked up tight in our car.

"Oh, don't worry about that stupid creature." Norman's generously bearded red face crinkled into a chortling laugh. "He's all noise." And we watched bemused as the dog's aggressive, bite-your-arms-off attitude of a moment ago morphed into a cringing, crawl-ing, Uriah Heep–type of creature which, if human, would have been fawning all over us while pulling its forelocks out by the roots.

"Good trick, that," I said, pulling myself out of the car.

"Yes, well, it works both ways. If you're somebody I'd rather not talk to . . ."

"Like an EU regulations cheesery supervisor, for example, I sup-pose?"

Norman's grin diminished somewhat. "Y're *not* . . ."

"Gotcha!" I said. He was laughing again, this time with real Santa Claus ho-hos, and I'm standing there thinking he's a far more convincing Santa than I'll ever be with that expansive beard of his. Not quite ZZ Top–length yet, but certainly a promising start.

"Well, you're definitely a better-looking man in person than that photo in *Saveur* magazine," said Anne with a flirty smile. (She does that on occasion. And the results can be fascinating . . .)

"Oh m'God, have you seen that horror? They just sent me a copy

Norman Steele: Cheese Maker

from the States. It wasn't fair, y'know. They didn't tell me they were photographing, and I'm standing by our cooking stove, which is all clogged up with pans, cheesecloths by the dozen dangling from the rafters, m'shirt hangin' out and trousers with the zipper halfway down, lookin' like they're about to drop off any second and expose all m' crown jewels to all and sundry!"

"That just about sums it up," Anne said, laughing, looking at the photo in the article. "In fact it almost looks as if you're intentionally pulling them down yourself!"

Norman peered at the photograph, one of a montage in an excellent feature on Ireland and its cuisines and farm-based produce that takes up most of the magazine. "M'God! You're right . . . or maybe I was pullin' 'em up."

"Could go either way," said Anne.

"Story of my life." Norman laughed. "So many ways I could have—actually did—go."

"From what we've read in this piece, you certainly seem to have had an interesting existence," I said, remembering Norman's transformations from counterculture teenager to star pupil to professor of philosophy at Dublin's Trinity College to older counterculture New Ager to farmer in the 1970s who found that he didn't know what to do with all the milk from his one-horned cow, so he started to make cheese.

"Yep—I've led quite a dance. But somehow Veronica's stuck with me—in fact, she's really the power behind everything we've done."

"And your son . . . Quinlan?"

"Oh, yes—great lad. He's in the cheesery now, packing the curds into the frames. Doesn't like to be interrupted at this stage. Random mold spores and all that kind of thing. He's not so sociable right now—needs to focus on our two main cheeses: the big yellow Beara made with cooked curds and our Milleen's, which is smaller, flatter, and much more pungent. I guess I'm the front man for this operation—sometimes I'm so loquacious I think I deserve an Equity acting award! Veronica's the one who really got the whole thing rolling for us, though, and for a lot of others with her teaching. I was messing with pigs and all kind of fun things, but she's the focused one in the family. A real determined Dublin lass."

"I love how *Saveur* quotes her," said Anne. "She describes your Milleen's cheese, named after the farm, as a 'brine-washed-rind cheese with a complex floral flavor and a creamy texture—the kind of cheese that wanted to be here.' That's a great description."

"Well, it's pretty accurate. We played around with so many different types—heating the curds to different temperatures, trying a blue or an Emmenthaler style, but eventually we let the milk guide us, and suddenly one day we got this really well-balanced cheese using a salt wash and aging for at least a month. We realized that if we tried to do more than two types, we'd likely make a real hash of it. Too many different spores floating about . . . Come on into the cold room and you'll see how it looks today."

We followed him across the unevenly paved farmyard into what looked like a big white metal box—a giant refrigerator. And there were the cheeses—scores of them—the larger kilo-size rounds being packed into pizza-style cardboard boxes and others—the half-pound rounds—neatly wrapped in transparent cellophane and colorfully labeled.

We, of course, sampled the product, and it was indeed superb—creamily tangy with a flavor that lasted and ended on an enticingly sweet note, almost like a sip of fresh-crushed apple juice.

As we sampled and smiled, I remembered something I'd noted in the *Saveur* article that might explain why it's taken so long for the art of cheese making and fine dining as a whole to be revived, recognized, and rewarded here in Ireland: "The whole idea of eating for pleasure was not accepted until very recently . . . It seemed almost sinful to approach the table with sensual gratification in mind." (And it took a long time for memories of a constant diet of potatoes and then almost nothing at all during the terrible famines of the mid-1800s to fade.)

I reminded Norman of that phrase in the article—"a delicious work in progress."

"That's so right. There are great changes, but they're all very recent. We were just about the first of the new farm-based cheese makers in Ireland," he told us as we stood salivating over the samples. "There are now over fifty, and although you'll think I'm showing off, many resulted from courses that Veronica taught—y'know—the best names—Gubbeen from Schull, Cashel Blue, and plenty of others. Before that, all you could find in most local shops were those ghastly little foil-wrapped triangles of half-synthetic processed glop. Which is surprising, because way back in the seventh century, when Ireland boasted some of the most renowned centers of culture and learning in Europe, it was the monks at our monasteries here who taught the art of cheese making to the Europeans! And particularly the French, d'ya believe!"

"The French?" I almost choked on my cheese sample. "How have you managed to live so long if you preach such heresy? I'm amazed they haven't come over and guillotined you and stuck your bearded head on your own gatepost!"

Norman laughed. "Yeah. It's been a bit of a touchy point with a few of our French friends, but I'm a fairly good professor and I've done my homework and it's a well-substantiated fact. Unfortunately, after the seventh century, though, the Vikings raided our monasteries—destroyed an amazingly sophisticated culture here—and the poor old Frenchies were on their own after that. And," he added with a giggle, "I suppose they've done pretty well all in all, considering . . ."

We left bearing a fine supply of cheeses for guests from the USA and England who had threatened to inundate us during the coming weeks. Norman followed us to the car and invited us back.

"Deal!" said Anne. "Even though I know you only want us back to buy more of your cheeses . . ."

"Of course," said Norman, "y'think I enjoy just raconteurin' here all day long with complete strangers?"

"Yes!" I said, and his beard shook with laughter. "I think you do. And I think you're pretty proud to be a part of all this gastronomic renaissance around here too."

THE *SAVEUR* ARTICLE IN particular had made me realize how, in this little corner of Ireland from here to Cork along the coast, you've got a significant kind of culture-saving trend going on today. There seem to be a remarkable number of people down this way making cheeses, building smokehouses, aging meats, creating sausages and salamis, curing salmon, milling flours, raising heirloom animals and vegetables, and generally restoring artisanal excellence in the southwest.

Norman smiled when I said this. "It's no wonder they call this region the 'California of Ireland'! If you go to places like the English Market in Cork City—fabulous experience—you'll see all their wonderful wares spread out on stalls under a roof of leaded glass and shaped like an inverted ship's keel. Beautiful! Same thing at the weekly Bantry Market just down the road from Glengarriff. Lovely place—fabulous artisanal things from the local farms and cheeseries. The Cashel Blue cheeses, Jetta Gill and her Durrus cheeses, Giana and Tom Ferguson with their Gubbeen cheeses made on their farm on the Mizen Head peninsula and their son Fingal and his beautiful spicy sausages and cured meats—best bacon you have ever tasted! Then there's Sally Barnes and her Woodcock Smokery and Frank Hederman's smokery. Then you've got Maja Binder and Olivier Beaujouan, who collect and sell different seaweeds, make cheeses, and sometimes combine the two! A crazy but gorgeous idea!"

"And from what I understand," I said, "it was all started up by pioneers like Myrtle Allen and her family, and of course you and

Veronica—who seem to have helped a lot of people get started in cheese making."

"Well, we all sort of help one another, and we still have quite a way to go. As the writers of that *Saveur* piece said, we're still 'a delicious work in progress.' "

But every culinary initiative helps nudge Ireland toward its gastronomic wonderworld potentials. Myrtle Allen's daughter-in-law, Darina Allen, in addition to being a renowned chef, author, and TV personality, is also famous for her "foraging walks" from her Ballymaloe cookery school in Midleton, County Cork (not far from Ireland's famous Jameson whiskey distillery). She's encouraging many to revert to "the old ways" of food collection. These walks inevitably involve battles with stinging and scratching plants, peat bogs, midges, wasps, and the occasional irate bull objecting to overt trespassing on his harem-territory. But intrepid participants can return with bagfuls of wild mushrooms, elderberries and blackberries, wild crab apples, damsons, nettles, watercress, sorrel, rocket, samphire, and carrageen moss (a seaweed ideal for aromatic puddings). All these are brought home by the foragers, rejoicing and backslapping, to be transformed into jams, jellies, soups, salads, and—in the case of nettles occasionally—a fine pungent beer that makes most pub brews seem pale and pallid in comparison.

And the meals these ingredients inspired were magnificently man-size. Cooks had little time for the overly decorative miniportions of the nouvelle cuisiners (as Saul Bellow once grumpily remarked—"I see the nouvelle, but where's the cuisine?").

"OH—WE'VE BEEN DOING all that gathering for generations," said eighty-six-year-old Nellie O'Connolly in a dismissive tone.

I met her by chance in the Hawthorn Bar in Glengarriff on a rainy day when I'd planned to visit the Garinish Island—Beara's sumptuous Italian gardens—but didn't.

"In the bad times—and they were mostly bad times—you had to dig deep in the hedgerows and field edgings t'get the stuff y'needed. Meat was very rare—maybe a bit once a week if you were lucky. Mor'n likely, once a month. And it was always just the end bits—pigs' ears, snouts, tails . . . oh! And those lovely *crúibíní*. Always the *crúibíní*—the trotters. Hind ones were best—they had more fat and meat. Nice and salted too, to bring out the flavor. Then y'simmered them up in a big pot with some herbs and spices—allspice was very popular—and when they started to fall apart you could begin nibbling and sucking on 'em—Oh, so so good they were! Or you could do 'em the 'Frenchie' way by splittin' 'em after cookin', fryin' 'em up covered in bread crumbs, and served 'em with a mustard, brown sugar, and vinegar sauce. Oh—and a whiskey or two. Always a nice warm whiskey to wash all the lovely stuff down. Oh, Lord! All Hail Mother of Jesus! I can taste 'em like it was yest'd'y. Y'can keep all y' fancy joints and chops. Give me a plate of hot *crúibíní* an' that's all I need for the day . . . or forever!"

"You're making me very hungry," I said.

Nellie laughed. Her gypsylike, sun-scorched, very wrinkled face broke into a wide smile. Her eyes were witchy with icicle glitters—but not unfriendly. I had no idea who she was or where she lived. I suppose I should have dug a little deeper, but I felt it didn't really matter. When you're talking food—food is really all that counts. And she did that with a captivating enthusiasm, rubbing her wrinkled hands together furiously as she spoke.

"The thing that fascinates me is how much a whole country survived mainly on *praties*—potatoes. From what I've read, you had to send most of your meat—your beautiful grass-fed beef and lamb—off to England to make enough to live on here. It sounded like potatoes were really all you had left."

"Well," said Nellie with a sad smile, "that's true. But we're a canny lot, y'know. Leastways we can be when we have to be, and we certainly got pretty nifty with the old potato. Many times that's about all we had to eat. You're right. 'Specially during the Troubles with the British from around 1914 to 1921. Real difficult times, those were. When y'think that eatin' up to five pounds o' potatoes a day each, if you were lucky—even y'r typical poor *cottie* and all those other landless laborers—y'had to do something a bit extra with 'em. Most of it was pretty basic. Boil 'em up and serve 'em with *anlann*—a buttermilk dip—or onions and a bit of mustard. Some added a meat bone or a few strips of salted herring to the pot to give a bit of flavor. It was strange, though. A lot thought fish— 'specially herring—was rubbish food. They called it 'paupers' porridge,' which is a bit daft when y'think how poor they were themselves! If they'd have liked fish a bit more, they might have got through the great famines of the mid-1800s. Much better than dying by the hundreds of thousands from starvation. Anyhow, where was I? Oh yeah, so—when all the potatoes were cooked, you'd pick one out of the *sciob*, a basket made of sally saplings—some people even grew an extra-long thumbnail to use as a kind of fork. And then you'd peel it as fast as you could so you could grab another one and then you'd dip it in the mix. And you'd go like the devil. Otherwise you'd lose your share. We'd not s' much in the way of manners in those days, I'm thinkin'!"

"But weren't there all kinds of other ways of serving the potatoes? I'd tried something called colcannon in Dublin. It was potatoes and cabbage mixed. A bit like England's bubble and squeak but not fried. Just lovely and creamy . . ."

"If it was in Dublin, they usually add some onions and even boiled parsnips or turnips—but you know what the secret is to really enjoy it? When you cream and fluff your potatoes, you use boiling milk before you mash them. Then you add the cabbage cooked down to a soft mush. Then you make a hollow in a big spoonful of colcannon on y'plate and pour in some melted butter and then spoon up the potatoes and butter together . . . just gorgeous." Her wrinkled fingers were flailing away now.

"My hunger is really getting worse."

"Y'wanna hear a song? Something my mother used to sing when she served colcannon?" Nellie didn't wait for a response. She just sang this little ditty softly and slightly off-key. I was utterly charmed:

> "Now did you ever spoon colcannon
> Made with yellow cream
> With kale and praties blended
> Like a picture in a dream?
> And did you scoop that hole on top
> To hold that melting lake
> Of our clover-flavored butter
> Which dear mother used to make."

"Beautiful!" I gushed.

But Nellie ignored the compliment. She was deep into potato lore. " 'Course, colcannon's pretty easy. But it was always fun serving it around Halloween. You hid a ring and a thimble inside. The one who got the ring was ripe for marriage, but the poor girl with the thimble would be a spinster forever. Although, to be honest—from what I've seen of Irish marriages, she most likely was the luckier one of the two!" Nellie chuckled at her own joke, then coughed and continued. "Bruisy is a bit stronger as a potato dish because you're adding nettles.

Nellie O'Connolly

They have to be young shoots and well cooked to kill the sting. And lots of white pepper. They said it was a very healthy dish because of all the iron. I've tasted some done with spinach, but it's not as good. And then there's *champ*—a bit like colcannon and another popular dish at Halloween. You're supposed to leave bowls of it out for the fairies—usually under hawthorns or whitethorn trees, the favorite trees of fairies. You could add various things to be fluffed up into the potatoes—I use chives, peas, and browned chopped-up onions— and again, you put that hole in the middle with the melted butter. The secret was not so much in the recipe but in the tasting. You could add in whatever you wanted, so long as it tasted good. Like that old saying 'To cook without tasting is like painting a picture with closed eyes!' "

"And what about Irish potato cakes . . . ?"

"Oh—y'mean the *boxty*—the pan *boxty*. Well, they're pretty obvious but—if you add some nice fresh herbs to the potato mash and let it cook in butter real slow for up to half an hour, it's beautiful. My dad used to like *boxty* big—covering the whole pan and about an inch thick and with a real beautiful crisp golden crust. And then he'd have it brought to the table to 'cut *farls* with a *fack*.' A *farl* is a slice and a *fack* is a special spade they used to use to cultivate the raised potato beds—the 'lazy beds'—on the rocky land. They'd be raised up to make very fertile strips of soil with manure from the pigs and cows, and seaweed if you lived near the coast. He obviously didn't use his *fack* for the *boxty*—it was five feet long! He used a sharp knife and—oh, it tasted so good! And so were all the other potato dishes too—all wonderful stuff—*poundies, cally, pandy, lutoga, strand, stovies, fadge, stampee*. And then you had all the soda breads—not just your basic one with plain flour, salt, bicarb, and buttermilk. That was easy. But you had to watch your bicarb. Too much could make it what we used to call 'mouth-pucker bread.' Ugh! Not nice. But other types were your *goaties* made with goat milk, small *gátarí* griddle cakes, yellow buck, *bocaire*, oat bread with lots of rough-cut oats, Kerry treacle bread—my mother was one of the best for this one—potato bread, seedy bread, and my favorite of all—spotted dog. That's a soda bread with raisins and, if you could get it, some molasses or black treacle. Oh Lord, Heaven love us, now I'm getting hungry m'self, too!"

"Nellie, you're a gem. A treasure trove. You should be running your own restaurant . . . !"

She laughed—a deep, rumbling belly laugh that set all her wrinkles wobbling and her eyes gleaming. "Oh—I would have loved but . . . well, in our family . . . the whole idea of eating for pleasure was considered almost sinful. 'You should never come to the table with gratifying your stomach or your taste buds in mind,' m' dad used to say. Almost a mortal sin, it was!"

"But so much of the folklore—your Irish folklore—seems to involve food and feasting. In the long poems like *The Cattle Raid at Cooley* and that great Irish warrior—Finn MacCool. Didn't he celebrate the salmon, claiming he gained all his poetic intuition, his *imbas*, from eating the great salmon of life—*bradán beatha*—something like that anyway . . ."

Nellie looked at me and gave me a coyish grin—which can't be easy for a woman of eighty-six with a very weathered, wrinkled face. "Aha—a reader too! Not just another hungry blow-in!"

I laughed. "Well—I'm definitely a blow-in and I'm certainly hungry . . . so listen, why not join me for a snack or something and you can give me a few more recipe ideas while we try to get rid of this emptiness in our midriffs!"

Nellie's grin became even more coy (and her finger rubbing even more enthusiastic), and off we went together—two new foodie friends—down the street to a restaurant she said had "the best Irish stew this side of Bantry—and a pretty good batter pudding too . . ."

"What's batter pudding?"

Nellie laughed. "It's like the first thing they try to feed you when you're born and the last thing they try to stuff down y'when you're dyin'! It's the same thing as what you'd maybe call Yorkshire pudding—only flatter and floppier!"

Something with the thwack of a virtual mallet whacked the side of my head. A mental breathrough was occurring. A quandary—decades old—suddenly seemed to be resolving itself.

"So . . ." I said to Nellie, "the Irish equivalent of Yorkshire pudding is . . . batter pudding?"

"Yeah," she said. "One's a bit flatter than the other, but they're made with the same things."

I stopped suddenly in the middle of the sidewalk. Maybe I was mumbling something. Nellie certainly seemed a little perplexed. But in fact I was offering a sincere apology to my grandmother. On my father's side. The one with the Irish roots, whose tentacling complexities we are tracing with increasing expertise and flair for genealogical exactitude and technique. In fact, it's an apology about that. About expertise and flair for technique. And about Yorkshire puddings too.

Now, for those unfortunate enough not to be born and raised in Yorkshire, England, the pudding produced there, when done according to the very rigid and meticulous rules, is a soufflé-like masterwork of crisp cumulus-ballooned golden batter with just the suggestion of a softer, more meltingly textured interior. The ingredients could not be more simple and classic—equal portions of flour and whole milk, two or three eggs, and seasoning (some show off by adding a little sage or thyme for pungency), and the mix left to rest and chill in the fridge for a couple of hours. Then oil (preferably beef dripping) is heated in a baking pan to smoking point in the oven, and as the blue smoke roils out of the pan, the fridge-chilled batter is thrown in with gay abandon. A sudden signature snap of oil and batter is indicative of a perfect meld—and then the pan is returned for baking at 450 degrees for half an hour or so until gorgeously golden bronze-brown globes arise and beckon the avaricious palate.

Now that is my mother's (and my own) Yorkshire pudding—to be enjoyed either as an appetizer with thick beef stock gravy or as an accompaniment to the traditional Sunday standing rib roast. (My mother's mother occasionally served it as dessert with trifle or treacle—a very odd habit.)

Unfortunately we often had to endure what I decided was a far inferior concoction at my father's mother's house when we would make our monthly trek for Sunday lunch. It was the same lunch every time—a small beef brisket tied tightly with twine and cooked to stringy gray dryness with vegetables boiled to a tasteless mush (I think she believed anything from the earth was bound to contain impurities and thus needed ritual decimation in cauldrons of boiling water or ovens set at about-to-melt levels)—and of course her so-called Yorkshire pudding.

Only this was no *Yorkshire* pudding. It was more like a thick, gooey pancake, a half-inch slab of barely baked dough with just the slightest pucker of a puffed edge along the rim of the baking tin. The only way to digest it was to slice your square into the smallest strips and try to swallow each with a minimum of chewing lest your mouth become a mess of gooey flour paste.

So why the apology, you might ask?

Well—I had subsequently learned, thanks to Nellie's offhand remark and years after my poor grandmother's demise, that I may have misjudged her doubtless well-intentioned efforts because, according to a most authoritative cookbook authored by one of the doyennes of Irish cuisine, there is indeed a dish here known as "batter pudding" using a similar ratio and range of ingredients as the true Yorkshire pudding. And my grandmother's creation was apparently a pretty accurate interpretation of it, insofar as it did not require smoking oil (lukewarm is fine) and the batter was meant to be flat and un-souffléed and "moist" and barely brown. And while I still find it hard to comprehend such a terrible misuse of a perfectly fine batter when the creation of a true Yorkshire pudding requires so little extra effort—I do ask forgiveness, dear Gran, for my former ignorance and arrogance. You were merely following a time-honored Irish recipe and—while ghastly—it was doubtless a fine interpretation of your odd ethnic rules! (Oh, and I love you too . . .)

So there I was slap bang in the middle of the sidewalk, grinning and chuckling away to myself, and poor old Nellie looking at me in a most peculiar way . . .

"You okay?" she asked.

"Ah—Nellie. Sorry. It was just . . . well, you helped resolve something that's been confusing me for decades . . ."

"Well, that's nice. Now d'y'think we could move on for that snack. Don't know about you but I could eat a nice fat chunk of batter pudding with some thick beef gravy . . ."

"Absolutely!" I said. "And I don't care how flat it is . . ."

Nellie smiled quizzically and shook her head, obviously unsure as to the mental stability of her newfound foodie friend.

10

Padraig O'Reagan
Ireland Then and Now

■
■
■

"Is it that crazy toucan that's wobblin' or is it me?! For more'n fifty years now I've seen that stupid Guinness toucan ad and its bit o' gimcrack rhymin' nonsense—blah, blah, blah, blah . . . *'like a toucan can.'* Never understood it. Fifty years! How the hell does it go? . . . *If he can say as you can, Guinness is good for you. How grand to be a Toucan—just think what Toucan do!* Jeez, it's enough to drive a man to drink which, in my case, is a bit redundant, as I'm up to m'eyeballs in the black stuff as it is and drownin' the days away in thick, sweet darkness. It's jes' like m'mother said when I was younger. God rest her safe with Holy Mary, Mother of Jesus, Saint of all Saints—she said: 'When the drink is taken and the drop is in, all the sense goes out.' But I said back, 'Ah yes—but youth sheds many a skin, so don't worry th'self, Mother, I'll grow up one day.' "

Long pause while Padraig rapidly drains the last of his glass down his elegant, Adam's apple–bobbing throat. Elegant may be an odd word to associate with throats, but his whole appearance and demeanor was a kind of rough-hewed elegance complete with wobbly wattles and just a hint of bulldog jowls. Even his eyes—a hazy green like crushed emeralds—reminded me of a sort of Oscar Wilde character with more masculine Orson Welles overtones until he opened his mouth and, in a voice deeper than a Pennsylvania coal mine, he

Padraig O'Reagan

descended into street lingo with all the flair of Brendan Behan on a binge or Dylan Thomas on a downer—and with a souffléd ego to boot.

We had met by chance in this small, literary-flavored pub in Kenmare complete with yellow-smoke-stained ceiling and booths separated by etched glass screens. Very Irish in a way that so many "Irish" pub chains in the USA try to be. And invariably fail dismally.

"You'll be havin' another one?" I asked, knowing well what the answer would be.

"Now tha's an eejit of a question if ever I heard one. Y'think I'm here just to display my erudite wisdom and counsel and fine eloquent volubilities t'the likes of you when I could be . . ."

A pause. "Could be what?" I asked.

A brilliant smile and a hoarse, smoky guffaw: "Anyway, what was I on about. What the bejeez was I . . . ?" His right hand fluttered over the table like a one-winged butterfly.

"Fifty years—you were thinking back fifty years."

"Ah, that I was. An' what an epic time . . . Ah mean, can y'believe, fifty years. I been through the lot of it—the highs, the lows, and all the boggy bits of our folly-filled land in between. What our fine poet Louis MacNeice calls 'the sob-stuff and swagger.' Jeez! We're such an arrogant, self-centered bunch. The Jews have got nothin' on us, ah tell 'e. We're the chosen people or so's you'd damn well think. Always assuming the world around cares a tinker's ass for all our horrors and terrors and murderin's and bombin's and lost battles that we sing about so proudly. Y'd think we'd won the stuffin' lot of 'em instead of being beaten into the bogs and pulped into purgatory, as we usually were most time if we ever so much as lifted up our voices in protest!"

Padraig had a distinctly pronounced nose with wide hairy nostrils and a tendency to drip. Nothing overexcessive—just the occasional transluscent globule that he removed delicately with a neatly pressed handkerchief hidden in his left hand.

"True—but another one of your famous writers, William Trevor, claims that since Ireland joined the EU in 1973, the country's changed more than any other country he knows in the world."

"Ah, my—so you're one of those Celtic Tiger converts. I can see that. Y'thinkin' it's all mountains o' money, megamartinis, mugs of Moët, and the gleam and shimmer of all those big fat Mercedeses? Y'thinkin' the bogmen and the *culchies* and the Gaeltacht Irish speakers are all a thing of our evil, poverty-laced past. Y'thinkin' that Sam Beckett's endless proclamations 'bout the pointlessness of existence have all been erased by piles of gleamin' euros or that Synge's *Playboy of the Western World* couldn't have his way anymore today with the fair farm colleens of County Mayo because they're all readin' borderline kitsch *Vogue* and *Cosmo* now and pickin' up college degrees like beer mats on a Dublin pub floor!"

I was fascinated by his nose drips, which seemed to intensify with the loosey-goosey vigor of his oratory or the volatility of the subject under discussion.

"Well, it certainly seems to have changed things. You're one of the most expensive countries in Europe nowadays, and house prices in Dublin are higher than just about any other city on earth!"

"Yeah, yeah, yeah—and the Catholic church is going belly-up with its pernicious priests and their pedophile scandals sending young kids into a sexual twilight from which many have never really emerged. No more Christianized coddlin' and canonical clap-trap of the sinful—makin' 'em dependent but feelin' safe and pro-tected. Now there's all these blue, diamond-shaped pills for instant sexual gratification, legalized birth control and homosexuality, maybe even divorce and abortion allowed by the church one day soon! All very naff! And no more of that censorship of books, films, theater— you name it. All gone. Ah tell ya—we're gettin' as heathen and hedo-nistic as the rest of Europe smothered in our contemporary plague of self-preoccupation. Goin' t'hell in a cushy, euro-plush handbasket, some claim. Not me, though. Good on you, I say! Go on—listen to the fast-track entrepreneurs and your Charlie Haughey politicians and the 'new world' Fianna Fáil. Go build y' fancy bungalows by the billion, enjoy your weird music-to-eat-muesli-by, fly high on y'crack and y'*craic*, buy y'second BMWs. Go and liberate y'lovely ladies and let 'em sashay on swishin' and swayin' like sparkle-eyed models in those erotic lingerie catalogs. Let them work themselves into a nar-cissistic lather like all the rest o' them high-tech, nouveau riche lads, barely outa the cradle titans of testosterone, planning to retire as gazillionaires at forty. Then see if the whole shebang makes y'feel any better than the good old days with the carnal density of inter-mingled lives and lusts and a couple o' fields and some sheep and the wife and a carload o' kids and a good sup every night at the local—and then mebbe a real Saturday night dopey stoner session followed by a crash 'n' burn punch-up and a bleary Sunday in church nursing a chewed-up earlobe and a jackhammer headache from too many slugs of poteen . . . and your conscience tellin' you to 'fess up, clean the slate, and start the rampage all over again!"

Another pause. (He seemed to need one badly after that almost pauseless bit of pugilistic punditry.) I wasn't sure how seriously to take Patrick, although I was impressed by his ever-increasing gushings of glorious verbiage. He combined a volcanic intensity that sparked and rusted with raw heat and an almost feminine silky smoothness topped by a Prince Charming smile.

"Ah, man, don't look s'damn serious. It's only a bit o'chat we're havin' . . ." He paused, as if wondering how to continue. "Y'see . . . How shall I say it? Well—y'gotta understand us Irish are all a bunch o' fakes. Even poor old God has his own hell—his love for us Irish! There's two kinds mostly—there's your blue-eyed, red-haired bogman Irish descended from Celts and Vikings and your dark-hair, dark-eye 'Black Irish.' They're said to be descended from Spanish troops marooned here after the British wrecked the Spanish Armanda in 1588 and sent the ships that weren't blown apart sailing all the way round the top of Scotland trying to get back to Spain. Most didn't. A few ended up here. But outsiders don't really notice the difference. People see us as just full of the old blarney and the jokes and the wide-eyed charm and the oh-so-friendly arm around y'shoulder matey-ness, but y'know what we are beneath all the blither and blather? We're sandwiched between boggy blogosphere baloney and big fat slabs of self-inflated, self-indulgent mediocrity. Okay, and superstition too, rearing its creaky medieval head and binding us all in its fearsome tentacles. We're melancholy, moody, self-doubting introverts pretending to be eloquent extroverts—oh, and loquacious liars, too—we invent our own history to suit our needs or our audiences. We're Beckettians as opposed to Brendan Behans. We're cowed Catholic cowards pretending to be playboys and 'princes of the *craic*' We're all O'Casey's paycocks, if y'know what I mean. We're spoilt little mama's boys like those Italian machos—jewels in their mamas' eyes—trying to morph ourselves into a kind of half-ass maturity but still scared to leave home and not marrying until we're way past our prime. Compared to most

Europeans we were true novices in the sexual arena. Even our love poems had to be exchanged in code! Listen to this lusty one—if I can remember it right:

> "When stormy winds are passed and gone
> Shall quiet calm return?
> I often saw in ashes' dust
> Lie hidden coals of fire.
> With good attention mark your mind
> You will a secret question find.
> Sweet is the secret; mark it well
> Heart for heart, so now farewell."

"Nice but hardly lusty, is it?" I said.

"See, you missed it! It all sounds floppily innocent but the key line is 'You will a secret question find.'"

"So what's the question?"

"Well—how about lining up vertically the first word of each line . . ."

"I can't remember . . ."

"Hopeless. S'good job this message wasn't for you—you'd have missed a nice ripe invitation right off! The real 'secret question' reads vertically: 'When Shall I Lie with You, Sweetheart.' Get it?!"

"Aaah! Okay—got it . . . clever trick . . ."

"Yeah—and one that you'd have missed by a mile! Tough luck! Anyway, back to criticisms of my own beloved countrymen . . . We're complex creatures, y'know . . . we'll ask y' questions y' wouldn't even ask y'self and we'll listen with a nod and a wise smile to the answers, or at least pretend to . . . But don't y' try the same thing on us or you'll likely lose a tooth or two. We're kinda pretend-intimate but private as all hell under it all. Hypocrites—the lot of us! Don' y' trust us, I keep telling people, and 'specially the blow-ins, but th' eejits never listen. They've bought all the Irish bullshit hook, line, and baloney; they've read all the tourist bumpf;

and the women, well, they come on over expecting to have their knickers charmed off by folktale-telling, folk-song-singing, sparkle-eyed, curly-haired Adonises all too happy to oblige you daft so long as you don't expect 'em to hang around too long after enjoying the lust o'y'loins, so to speak, because they got to get home to their dotin' mamas. Or maybe they come to hear our horror stories and songs of famines and emigrations on 'death ships' and all the battles we lost and Oliver Cromwell's rape and pillage of our fair land, and the English landowners who saw us as penniless peasants to be worked to early deaths. Keeping them in fine gentry homes and fancy clothes and riding stables big as the Dublin Customs House and all that. And then you've got our rebellions—the Troubles—the glories of the 1916 Easter Rising, the bloody—and bloody stupid!—Civil War—the great day of independence from Britain in 1921 and all of it told and sung a lot like it happened yesterday. All the lead characters—de Valera, our Taoiseach [prime minister] for sixteen years can y'believe, Michael Collins, Sean Lemass, John Costello—talked about like they'll be poppin' into the pub for a glass or two any moment now. And it all still works, 'specially for the blow-ins, who want to see Ireland as an underdog nation fighting for its fragile independence and hard-won survival. But—thank God—for most of us nowadays, and especially for the young kids, it's much more future-looking . . . Some say it's a sneaky form of neo-colonialism, with the Americans on the throne seats suckin' all the air out of our little nation with all their TV programs, megainvestments, and subsidiary companies, and that eternal reminder that over forty-five million Americans—over twenty percent of the population across the Atlantic there—claim Irish heritage, as opposed to our little country of barely four million! Hell—we escaped the British Empire, we're trying to escape the Vatican empire, but now we're as good a part of the American world empire!"

His pell-mell narrative delivery contained the tumultuous spirit of a Brueghel painting. I thought it was time for me to interject, especially as Padraig's nose drips had reached an almost nonstop flow after another long oration. "But surely Ireland's not doing too badly exporting its own culture—traditional *and* modern. Look at the great Irish films recently, great plays and world-famous rock bands—Bob Geldof, Bono, and U2—folklore extravaganzas like Riverdance . . . and Celtic Woman . . ."

"Surely, surely," he said, waving his whiter-than-white handkerchief dismissively. "All impressive stuff, although most of it's real ersatz Irish—more Irish than we Irish ever were. But still, it keeps us on the map, and people seem to like us as passionate eccentrics brimming over with frolic and fun—even if it's fake! Dammit—even the *craic* is gettin' fake! But times are lush and flush now and the lucre flows rich and thick . . . and deep down we still believe that old motto: 'We don't beat the grim reaper by living longer. We beat him by living well—bloody well!'"

We laughed together. For the first time it seemed to be genuine and mutual laughter. I still didn't quite trust my opinionated colleague, though, and felt he was possibly letting off his tirades of blarney-blather at my expense. (So far I'd bought all the drinks, and was even considering the need to bowdlerize some of his remarks to subdue his rousting rhetoric.) But what the heck. I was gaining some insights and certainly viewing the Irish psyche and "condition" from a very different viewpoint than previously.

Then this prince of windbaggery and the pregnant pause was off again. "Y'see, it's the have-nots. That's where the real cancer starts. When the begrudgin' begins. Like that old saying 'The fat and full will never understand the thin and hungry.' Ah mean, y' can understand a guy out in the boggy boonies who can't get his feet on the ladder to the great pot o' gold in the sky. He'll be pissed and rightly so. But the dangerous ones are the ones who're already rakin' it in in a Thatcherite kinda way, but still don't have that real entrepreneurial spirit—y'know—the real hunger for status, power, . . . and big-big cash! The Americans have it in spades and the Germans and they run a lot of the fast-moving companies here . . . But our guys still dither about—that old Irish insecurity—and bitch and begrudge and debunk. And that can be dangerous. We might well castrate our beloved Celtic Tiger If we don't pull our collective fingers out, we'll be sucked back into the slipstream of our own miserable history. The problem is, we won't take chances. Don't or won't make decisions. We forget—if we ever knew—what Nietzsche said: 'The noble soul has reverence for itself.' We fudge about in a stupor of our self-forgiving Catholic ignorance and we're scared shite-less of 'getting above ourselves' . . .''

"Ah," I said, "the tall poppy syndrome."

"What?"

"Tall poppies—it's an Australian saying . . . If you're a boaster, lifting yourself up over others—you get your head lopped off."

"Ah well—that's a fine metaphor. I'll be remembering it . . . But what was I . . . ? Oh, and my God! Even the Poles can show us a thing or two about initiative. They come over in droves and start off at minimum wages. There's over 200,000 of 'em over here at the moment—but you watch 'em wise up and learn the tricks. Our guys are gonna have to stop gawpin' an' moanin' and start movin'. One good example of a 'made it' native is our Irish filmmaker Neil Jordan, and he sees the problem. He says 'We've lost our coherent idealism.' Well, maybe that's the problem when you've destroyed most of your demons. Then you've got to face the challenges of success! Whole new hurlin' match, that, unless you're an Irish horse trader or breeder. Most of us are still getting used to that idea. Roddy Doyle plays around with it in his books and films like *The Commitments* and *The Snapper*. We're doing that old Irish thing again of prattling on with the gab—words never touchin' the ground—to try to find out what we're really thinkin': we're swimming desperately in the muddy waters of social and spiritual confusion . . .''

"Who said that?"

"What?"

"The 'muddy waters' thing."

"I just did. Why, is there someone else doin' the talkin' 'round here?"

"Apologies."

"Accepted . . . So, eh . . . Ah! The muddy waters. Right. And no one's there to help. The government's always five steps behind, so they're no bleedin' use. And the church—the great omnipotent Catholic church, once the bully-dictator of just about everything in our lives—where is she nowadays, I ask? She's in a feckin' mess, is where she is, despite the fact that over seventy percent of the people here still attend Mass, which compares with barely ten percent in Catholic France and not much more in Italy. Oh, and don't get me going about Italy. Land of romance they call it, right? So how come they've got the highest divorce rate and lowest birth rate in the world? Because they're bloody fakes too! Just like us, and so maybe we're fakin' it all again. It's like our thing with fairies and the little people. We claim it's all a load of hogwash and stupid superstition, but we wouldn't dare intrude on a fairy circle after dark—'just in case,' we'd say. And somewhere, deep down, we'd mean it! Same with the church—'just in case' insurance. No matter how decadent our priests get, the people'll still go to Mass because they've been programmed in deep guilt, imprisoned in persnickety protocols of gawping obedience, made paranoid about sex by frustrated celibate priests who know not a jot about the joys and the horrors of marriage and sex and the like. Deep, deep down, we all still truly fear the eternal fires of hell! Wonderful comment from a politician recently on all our moral confusion—'There was no sex in Ireland until the BBC came!' "

"And Gay Byrne with his *Late Late Show* . . ."

"Ah, yes, gorgeous Gay indeed! Bishops used to call his broadcast 'this dirty-evil show' and preached sermons against his discussing just about every 'ethically challenged' taboo subject in Ireland, which at that time in the 1960s and through the 1980s covered a hell of a multitude of mortal sins. Of course that was when contraceptives were illegal, there was no sex education in the schools, priests were supposedly celibate, and the Clintonian version of marital fidelity had not yet crept in! Talk about the blind leadin' the bloody blind. Right off the bleedin' cliff top! [Another deluge of nose drips at this point.]

"One of our best writers—William Trevor—wrote *Reading Turgenev* and shows the horror of a young girl's life without sexual education. John McGahern, Sean O'Faolain, John B. Keane, Edna O'Brien, with her *The Country Girls*, and—of course—O'Casey and Synge. Oh, and Brian Friel's *Dancing at Lughnasa*—all describing the terrible dark worlds of sexual ignorance, incest, and impotence and all that stuff. And it's all so strange. Education has been highly valued in Ireland ever since the secret 'hedge schools' in the eighteenth century when the local priests and other villagers would illegally teach literacy to peasant children. But then the church took over like they took over everything else! You remember that saying: 'If there's a goose to be found anywhere, it'll be on the priest's table'! Anyway, education became more of a Catholic brainwashing process. No use at all for a healthy sex life, but well—maybe it shaped the lives of some of today's finest writers. They saw what booze did to creativity and longevity and they became the 'Ballygowan Boys' . . ."

"What's Ballygowan?"

"Ireland's beloved mineral water! God forbid y'have t'drink th' stuff!"

"Well, that's great," I mused, "weaning them away from the booze. But church censorship can't have done much for free creativity."

"Tha's so true—they were pretty tight. Anything with overt sex, even covert, or implied homosexuality, blasphemy, abortion, and on and on—all banned! Orwell, Huxley, Bertrand Russell, Behan, and all the other great writers at that time—they all got chopped. Even plays at Yeats's Abbey Theatre got axed. Weird, though—James Joyce snuck through. Maybe no one could understand his crazy stuff anyway—'specially *Finnegans Wake*! Or when he got himself labeled 'Ireland's literary genius,' even the church felt it better back off a touch! But again it's that fake Irish thing—he hardly ever lived here! Left Dublin in 1902 at the age of twenty and spent most of his life in France. A lot of it with old Sam Beckett."

"But what about Yeats?"

"Ah—our immortal bard! God! Someone once described him as a technician's techni-cian whose massive output of poetry is a blizzard of stanza shapes and metrical varia-tions. No one dared touch him.

William Butler Yeats

He played a canny game—mixing up very quotable lines with his role as arbiter of the theatrical arts. Y'know he founded the Abbey Theatre with good old Lady Gregory. He was one of the greatest na-tionalistic public figures of his generation. An unbeatable blend. The church couldn't reach him . . . not even when he went a little wacky with his belief in fairies and all that Irish bog lore!"

"So who's the modern-day Yeats now?"

Padraig paused briefly while signaling the barman for two more pints and, miracle of miracles, backing up his request with a bunched ball of euro notes pulled slowly from his trouser pocket along with a set of keys and a half-finished roll of Polo Mints.

"So," he began again, "y're askin' about the modern poets an' I was thinkin' about the whole creative cat's cradle of them—Louis MacNeice, Patrick Kavanagh, Paul Durcan, Austin Clarke, Thomas

Kinsella . . . But I reckon m' favorite fella has to be Seamus Heaney . . . even though he's from the wrong side of the border . . . a Londonderry man . . . when he's not off professoring at Oxford or wherever. Even one of your top American poets, what's his . . . ah—Robert Lowell—he claims Heaney's the greatest Irish poet since God himself, otherwise known as—William Butler Yeats."

"Yes, Heaney writes powerful stuff. I was rereading *Opened Ground* just last week . . ."

"Yeah, fine collection that . . . Very fine!"

"Some of his poem titles . . . they tell you exactly where his heart is—'Requiem for the Croppies,' 'A Loch Neagh Sequence,' 'Bogland,' 'The Seed Cutters,' 'The Toome Road,' 'Bog Oak' . . ."

"Ah, yes—the self-absorption of the Irish again. Inward looking, agonizing over all the dreck of a failed society . . ."

"Who said that?"

"Tha's the second time you . . . Who the hell do y'think said it! There's only me here thinkin' an' talkin' . . ."

"Apologies for the third time."

Seamus Heaney

"Accepted for the third time—but it's the last one y' get!"

"Good brew, this one," I said. The Guinness was finally beginning to take hold.

"A very effective diversionary tactic—but true, although a glass of full-blast poteen wouldn't go amiss—it's all that's needed to hot-wire the tongue and kick-start the human engine into life again! But to continue, maybe it's that self-absorption that sells Ireland, 'specially in the movies. I mean, think of the best ones, starting with John Ford's *The Quiet Man* if y' can put up with John Wayne's ridiculous brogue. Then there's David Lean's *Ryan's Daughter*. John Huston made a beautiful little art film of Joyce's *The Dead*, and then, much more recent, we had two from Roddy Doyle's books—*The Commitments* and *The Snapper*. Then there's Jim Sheridan's *My Left Foot* from Christy Brown's brilliant novel, Neil Jordan's *The Miracle* and *The Crying Game*, Thaddeus O'Sullivan's *December Bride*. Then y' got that romp of a thing, *Ned Devine*, and our latest success—Ken Loach's *The Wind That Shakes the Barley* that won the Palme d'Or at Cannes in 2006, and Frank McCourt's *Angela's Ashes*. And of course my all-time favorite—John Keane's *The Field* with Richard Harris."

"And mine too! I watched it again just last week. Harris does a great job as the mighty 'Bull' with his determination to hold on to a small piece of pasture he's created over a lifetime from the wild moors. And then, of course, in true Irish heart-wrenching melodrama, it leads to the destruction of everything around him and ultimately himself. Reflecting that eternal cry of the freedom-lusting Irish: 'I might as well die if I can't fly!' "

"Jeez, y're soundin' like a real film critic!"

"Feels like that after a fourth viewing . . . And to be honest, I'm a bit protective of it . . . It got panned by some critics for being far too over-the-top. I think with anyone less than Harris, it might have been . . . But he carries that part so powerfully, and despite the fact that he's a detestable character in many ways, he holds you right 'til the end . . . right up to *his* end, flailing away at the waves with his stick, shouting 'Back, back!' in that terrible King Canute kind of madness . . ."

"Well put . . . and I agree. Without Harris it wouldna've worked."

"So Ireland's certainly made its mark on the arts . . ."

"Ah, that it has. Some fine modern playwrights too—Brian Friel, Sean O'Casey, Tom Murphy, Martin McDonagh and his *Lieutenant of Inishmore*. And music, naturally—the Chieftains, the Wolfe Tones, the Dubliners. People sniggered at Tommy Makem and the Clancy Brothers at first, all dolled up in their fancy white Aran island sweaters and puttin' on the brogue and whatnot, but—boy!— they could hammer home our great Irish ballads like nobody else. 'Fields of Athenry,' of course—our national anthem almost—but also 'The Bridge of Athlone,' 'Danny Boy,' 'Four Green Fields'—that last is one of Tommy's own compositions—all wonderful stuff! Bob Dylan loved the Clancys. Said they got him started and kept him going. And then this crazy Christy Moore. In his early days he'd go through a couple of bottles of Irish a night and still get up onstage for three marvelous hours. And then y'moderns—Bob Geldof, Bono and U2, Sinéad O'Connor, the Saw Doctors, Clannad, the Pogues, Van Morrison, the Cranberries, the Corrs—even Muzak's maestro-maven—Enya! Oh! And not forgettin' Cathal Coughlin—his *Clock Comes Down the Stairs* is one of the best Irish rock albums ever. 'S'all terrific stuff. Ireland's a major force in the music field. But y' also get Tad Meyer, the real traditionalist, too . . . the unaccompanied *sean-nós* singers, the *uilleann* pipes, the players of harps, tin whistles, fiddles, the *bodhrán* goatskin drum, the preservers of the *céilí* and the *seisuin* and the *fleadhanna* music festivals. Thanks to organizations like Comhaltas Ceoltoiri Eireann (CCE, the Irish music movement), the ancient music has been preserved. So now we've got both—the old and best and the new and best . . ."

"You'd never get high marks for modesty!"

"Credit where credit's due, lad. You ever watch a Riverdance audience and the smiles that appear like magic on people's faces when the Clancys used to start one of their toe tappers? There's no music in the world like our music!"

"No," I agree. "And when it's sung in the original Gaelic, just watch the tears roll."

"Tha's true! Though barely one percent of the country can understand the Gaelic and the Gaeltacht regions like Donegal, Galway, and parts of County Kerry and Cork are fast shrinking . . . except— and this is really odd—except in the cities. Some state-backed schools teach all in Irish now. Our former president Mary Robinson always was keen to keep it going. The English tried to kill it, of course, in the bad old days, but de Valera, after independence, wanted us to be a fully Irish-speaking nation. Problem was finding teachers! And parents too—they spoke mostly English. Sean O'Faolain called Irish 'a buried part of ourselves.' The British had certainly done a number on us. With their nihilistic selfishness and papier-mâché bravado, they almost completely decimated our culture. But we had a good go at kickin' 'em out—the IRA in Northern Ireland and down here the burning of all those fancy Ascendancy mansions—the homes of the British aristocrats—in the 1920s—places like Dunboy and the Puxley place in Castletownbere. They say there's only thirty or so o'those huge mega-palaces around today out of over two thousand. But somehow we never really got the power back. And so nowadays, for all the bullshit rhetoric and platitudes, it seems a waste of time teaching kids Irish when they could be learning some useful language, like French, German—or even Chinese Mandarin, f' God's sake. Course, these could never have the pride and power of our great Irish language poets and writers. They'd never capture the spirit of mystery and magic that flows through the Irish language—you're always on multilevels of consciousness when you listen to it . . ."

"Yeah . . . y'know, even though I can barely speak a word of it, you can hear something magic in the sound and rhythms of the stories and songs. It's quite strange, there really is a sense of multilevels."

"Ah well, tha's jus' us, isn't it? Strange . . . and magic . . . and multilayered. Schizoid romantics gliding insecurely through the days on pillows of positive affirmations! Pragmatic sentimentalists! And stupid proud of it . . ."

"All over the world!"

"Ah yeah, our mighty world diaspora of emigrant-loyalists! Without them, we'd be a little forgotten island. Those forty-five million or so in the USA alone, like I said. Can y'believe, a third of Australians too—even a sixth of Norwegians—all Irish descendents. I guess that's the Viking link . . . from their raids in the mid-800s, and it all started with the famines and the 'coffin ships' in the 1800s. Over a quarter of the population either dead at home or emigrating to build a new world despite our terrible reputation for the drink and the punch-up and the 'no Irish need apply' prejudices and our huge Catholic families spreading across uncharted lands like algae on still lakes . . ."

"And then comes your reverse immigration . . ."

"Wha'?! Ah! Right. See what y'mean. The Celtic Tiger an' all that. And a brain drain in the opposite direction with our well-trained young'uns comin' on back from Europe and the USA. Isn't that jus' peachy . . . and along with 'em come all the bloody tourists and blow-ins—busloads of Irish and wannabe Irish, all looking for roots on Grandpa O'Connor's little farm out there on the boglands and puttin' on the brogue and actin' up more Irish in the pubs than the Irish themselves . . ."

"And proud of it!"

"Ah, well, yeah yeah. I think so. Although we got a bit of a reputation in Europe for money-grubbin'—and grabbin'—y'know the expression 'Rip-off Republic,' right? We got more handouts from the EU than any of the other needy countries . . . until a new batch of really poor places like the Baltic States and Poland came in . . ."

"Didn't the Irish government try to veto them being allowed to join the EU?"

A hesitant pause and then: "Er . . . right . . . well, that was indeed not exactly our finest hour. We were scared the tap might be turned off for us a bit too sudden-like, y'see."

"And was it?"

"Well . . . yes and no . . . We did okay, really. And by that time the ball was really rolling over here . . . and it still is. Sometimes—with the crazy property prices in Dublin and just about everywhere you look—you wonder if there's a great bubble about to burst. But until it does, I guess we'll go on spendin' and drinkin' and singin' and laughin'. Just so long as we don't overdose ourselves with too many newfangled dot-com geeks, metrosexuals, femocrats, Eurotrash, brain-iacs, starchitects, and dummy-dweebs. After all, this is still Ireland and we still love livin' the good old Irish life while we can."

"Celebratin' the *craic* forever!"

"Indeed!" he shouted (in one last shower of nose drips).

And so I eventually left this courtly and ponderous character whose lightness of soul and deep frivolity kept him bobbing serenely on great waves of culture, charm . . . and charismatic check!

"Farewell Patrick, and thanks for all the insights."

"Ach—I'm hardly started, but I suppose you blow-ins have to be indoctrinated slowly."

"And indoctrination by you hardly hurts at all . . ."

11

A Very Revealing May Day

:::

WHAT AN AMAZING DAY THIS WAS supposed to be in Castletownbere and on nearby Bere Island.

It was May Day, and I'd been promised all kinds of great events for the Festival of Bealtaine. It would be hard to fit all the exciting diversions into a single day, I was told. Although regrettably, there was nothing of a truly pagan nature to look forward to. Still, plenty of other diversions were in store, so everyone insisted.

And, in fact, it was remarkably easy to accomplish my tight schedule, because in the end I accomplished absolutely nothing of my original itinerary.

First, I was to meet an elderly gentleman of great learned veracity—"a sumptuous repository of all that is historical and hysterical about Bere Island," or so I'd been informed by one of my most reliable informants. Unfortunately, he called to say that, because of a "mighty matter in the way of family affairs, d' y' understand?" he'd be leaving the island about the same time I'd planned to arrive following the fifteen-minute ferry ride across from Castletownbere. Maybe we could wave at each other, he suggested humorously, but that was about all that was possible for the time being.

But I still had plans to go to Bere Island anyway to attend a resident production of one of John B. Keane's "magnificent masterworks"— *Slive*—(according to another one of my informants. Admittedly I'd never heard of the play and, until a few days previously, was not even familiar with this much-beloved Kerryman-author. Which I hate to admit, because his reputation has the ring of righteousness and ruthless justice and anyone who admits to an ignorance of his fine literary works is likely to diminish rapidly in stature in the eyes of the locals. But as I am an honest fellow and always welcome a bit of stature-diminishment due to my overindulgent gastronomic and other tendencies—I indicated a willingness to be informed. And informed I was. Endlessly and enthusiastically.

And so, primed and pumped on the splendidly outspoken Mr. Keane and his career as both pub owner and prolific writer, I was there early to catch the ferry to Bere Island at the dock across from the church and the Supervalue supermarket. I settled down by the harbor wall and waited. And waited. And waited. After an hour had passed, there was still no sign of the ferry. Admittedly it was a small craft, particularly in comparison to the enormous hulls and superstructures of the Spanish fishing trawlers in the harbor that day, and although it was barely capable of carrying more than a couple of vehicles at a time, you couldn't really miss its cheery red paint job and its sprightly chug across the harbor. Finally I strolled across to our little supermarket and asked one of the cashiers what had happened to the boat.

"Oh, I think now they've changed the times . . ."

"Where are you going on the island?" asked another cashier.

"To see *Slive*—you know, John B. Keane's play."

She gave me an odd look. "Who?" (Ah, so I wasn't the only one here with a significant gap in my Irish Trivial Pursuit talents.)

"You'll maybe need the other ferry—up the peninsula a mile or so."

"I didn't know there was another ferry."

"Ah yes, well, that's to be expected. Many don't. It's more recent, y'see."

"So I should take that one, then?"

Trawlers at Castletownbere

"Yes, I'm thinking that would be best for you . . ."

"Well, thanks—you've saved me a wasted—"

"Except it'll not be running today . . ."

"Oh—and why's that?"

"I suppose because it's a public holiday," said the cashier, obviously perplexed by the stupidity of my question.

"But wouldn't that be the perfect time to be running a ferry?"

"Ah, yes indeed, you could be right there."

That's one of those wonderfully typical ways the Irish have of ending a discussion that seems destined to go nowhere. A pleasant acknowledgment of the pointlessness of trying to derive sense out of a senseless situation. Sounds a bit like something out of *Waiting for Godot*. Beckett would have loved such nonsensical dialogues.

It was too late anyhow now for the play on Bere Island, even if I'd had a chance of getting there, which apparently I didn't. So I wandered back home with every intention of resuming a slow-unraveling schedule later on in the evening after a cup of tea and a brief rest.

And thus later on in the evening I'm down at the Beara Bay Hotel to enjoy what I'd been told was to be an evening of Beatles music—a "greatest hits" spectacular, presumably by one of those mop-top impersonator groups that keep popping up all over the globe. Like Elvis impersonators, only usually worse. But—bear in mind—this is the Beara, and anything in the way of live entertainment is a must on my—and everyone else's—list.

However, just as with the play, this was another "not to be" event on this increasingly noneventful day.

"Eh, well, he'll not be here. Unfortunately," said the man at the desk outside the concert room (otherwise known during the week as Skipper's Bar).

"How do you mean, 'he'? I thought it was a 'they.' Y' know, the whole Beatles band. All four of 'em."

"Oh-no-no. Just the one fella. With a lot of nifty synthesizer stuff. Got quite a range. Give him a glass slide tube and a resonator guitar and he'll out-blues the great bluesman himself—Robert Johnson. Not bad with Hawaiian slack key guitar too. Pretty neat act . . ."

"But we won't be having his nifty act tonight, then?"

"No, no-no-no. We won't. Regrettably he's stuck somewhere between Waterford and Cork. Something wrong with his truck."

"Well, that's a shame, then."

"Yes, yes. 'Tis, 'tis."

"Well—so I guess that just leaves the old set dancing at Twomey's." (I was intending to enjoy them both, but one would have to suffice now.)

"Ah, well, no."

"Sorry?"

"No, that's not on, either. It's been canceled because of our show."

"You mean the show you're not going to have now because the Beatle man is stuck between Waterford and Cork."

"Yeah, that just about sums it up nicely."

"So there's nothing going on tonight, then? Anywhere?"

"Yeah . . . guess so—well, except for our show . . .'

"You just said your show was canceled . . ."

"Oh, no-no-no—I'm talking about the other show. The late show. At eleven-thirty P.M. *Euro-Centerfolds*. Very . . . what you might call . . . exotic."

I don't think I've ever heard of anything on the Beara being described as "exotic," with the possible exception of those tumultuously tropical Garinish Gardens at Glengarriff, and the sumptuous Derreen Garden at Lauragh . . . but I soon got the point as he grinned a lascivious grin and indicated a lurid poster at the side of the door. In prose and photos that left little to the imagination, it advertised a late evening of sensual delights featuring extraordinarily large-chested ladies dressed in leather belts and thongs and little else, prancing across the stage with whips and other pernicious instruments of sadomasochistic application and a sign saying YOUR EVERY PLEASURE GUARANTEED. And all this in our little Castletownbere!

Well, maybe I was wrong then about the lack of pagan festivities for Bealtaine. Apparently here they all were for the delight and titillation of the tanked-up, testosterone-crazed youths and not-so-youths of my normally quiet—or relatively so—little town.

"So—you think you'll be coming then?" asked the hotel barman, still smirking lasciviously.

"Well . . ."

"Should be an even bigger show than last night . . . ," said the man with a widening sneer.

"Last night?! What the heck did I miss last night?!"

"*You*! Well, *you* missed nothing. But the ladies had a great time. All these guys—Chippendale types, y'know—big bodies, bulging muscles out to here . . . They put on a real great bling-bling bada-bing show . . ."

"*Full Monty* stuff, eh?"

"Oh, yeah. *Full Monty* . . . and beyond. Let's just say, a very, very good time was had by one and all—kinda harmless high school debaucher level, y'know. But tonight should be even better . . . I mean, you only get this kind of show once a year, y' know . . . on crazy May Day . . ."

Well, I'd hoped for a belt of Bealtaine, although I was thinking of something a little more ancient and ritualistic with more sublimated libidinal energies, maybe up on the high flanks of Hungry Hill among the old standing stones and neolithic circles. Instead we get simulated in flagrante delicto sex orgies down by the docks in celebration of fertility and fecundity, and tantalizing *Flashdance* acrobatics all fired up in an alcohol-fueled blitzkrieg of ribald voyeurism.

Ah well . . . when in Castletownbere I guess you just zig and zag with the prevailing zeitgeist. . . .

And as I said, even though I accomplished absolutely none of my intentions, it was nevertheless a most revealing May Day in every sense of the word.

12

Beara Healers

∷

I FEEL HEIGHTENED BY HEALERS. Once I allowed the old cynical nay-saying morass of my brain-biases to fall away, I began to enjoy and value the company of some remarkable individuals on Beara.

Why so many healers, clairvoyants, philosophers, facilitators, and practitioners in the holistic arts have gathered here on the tip end of this relatively unknown peninsula is a fascinating question.

"It must be all our crystal," said Donogh O'Kelly, a local journalist. "There's massive veins of quartzite crystal running the length of the land here. Y' see it spurting out in great shiny white ribbons along the cliffs and coves and particularly around the Allihies copper mines. And—well, when you've got crystal, you've got some mighty powerful forces floating about, wouldn't y' say?"

"I'm not sure . . . ," I replied hesitantly. "I've always felt a bit of a *Twilight Zone* aura around crystal enthusiasts and the like. I'm suspicious of canned hokum, I guess, and sudsy platitudes."

"Sure, sure, 'tis normal y'are. Many feel the same. And doubtless there'll always be cranks and shylocks around offering wonderful fake crystal cures . . . at a cost, of course. But . . . well, you'll have to make your own mind up. Most of our healers and alternative medicine people here seem pretty genuine to me . . . and modest. It's hard to get any of them to claim anything except being like some kind of channel for self-healing . . . y'know, a link or something to unfamiliar powers you already possess but don't use. But maybe I'm biased. I like most of 'em . . . and maybe you will too, when y' get to meet them."

My first meeting—accidental, coincidental, and possibly inevitable—was with Dr. Michael Murphy. I didn't expect such a great bear of a man. Not at all. The way people on Beara spoke of Michael, in subdued terms of respect, humility, and deep affection in most cases, led me to picture him as one of those cuddly, warm, and fuzzy therapist types, always ready with a few encouraging aphorisms to stimulate the release of underused human potentials. And there's definitely that side to Michael. His voice is gentle with a pleasurable reassuring "bedside manner" burr to it, and a pin-drop vérité ambience. The accent, reflecting his Anglo-Irish/American heritage, is I suppose some kind of mellow mid-Atlantic mélange. Certainly, despite his long Irish ancestry, I rarely noticed anything of the local Beara brogue. His humor is generous and gleeful—he smiles and laughs easily, openly, and as far as any learned, ever-analyzing psychotherapist can be, he seems very much at peace with himself. His large and all-enveloping self.

Before I met him, a friend showed me something Michael had written about the importance of Beara and his great love for the land and its people:

> I wrote these lines recently and all those who love Ireland
> and the Beara in particular will know exactly what I mean:
>
> > Ireland
> > Is the place that I have lived in
> > And the place that has lived in me
>
> I rediscovered my Celtic roots on the Beara Peninsula in
> Ireland a handful of miles from where my father was born in
> 1888. Beara is a spectacular speck on our planet where the

*wild masculine spirit of nature is so much in evidence and
the earthy feminine soulful welcome of the place is so Irish.
I've lived on and off here in recent years and have found the
life-enhancing balance of the Soul and the Spirit of nature is
nowhere more palatable and breathtaking. Ireland and the
Irish people are magnets that draw others from many parts of
the world where Soul and Spirit may seem to be in shorter
supply. Here on Beara there is softness and wetness in the
bogs between the rocks and the sea invites us to dive deep,
for the depths of the sea and the depths of the Soul contain
the essence of love. The Soul of nature here beckons us to join
her. The Spirit of the place is often wildly exuberant, with
frequent gale-force winds churning up the sea; many fishermen from the towns here have been lost in storms at sea.
Sometimes the clouds seem alive as they dash across the sky
and sometimes they breeze gently by like a blessing . . . It
is so easy to gaze at all this natural beauty, and in those
moments when I am open, I feel the Soul and Spirit of nature
gazing back at me.*

I relished Michael's receptivity to the power and essence of Beara
and was rapidly learning to share his love—his transcendental
empathy—for this remarkable corner of Ireland. Many sense personal possibilities in its power—possibilities for reinvented lives, for
solace and protection from mind-wrecking burdens, for releasing the
huge healing potentials of love and forgiveness and for learning to
live on after traumas and losses. Such possibilities attract both seekers and healers, and Beara has an abundance of both.

Michael picked a segment from Oscar Wilde's *De Profundis* to
describe the needs of many "pilgrims" to Beara:

*Society, as we have constituted it, will have no place for me,
has none so to offer; but Nature, whose sweet rains fall on
unjust and just alike, will have clefts in the rocks where I
may hide, and the secret valleys in whose silence I may weep*

*undisturbed. She will hang the night and stars so that I may
walk abroad in the darkness without stumbling, and send
the wind over my footprints so that none may track me to my
hurt; she will cleanse me in great waters and with bitter
herbs make me whole.*

(Later on I discovered how literal the "bitter herbs" are to many of
the lotions and potions created here by Beara's healers and holistic
counselors.)

Michael's life and career seem to have many elements right out
of *A Course in Miracles.* The accolades for his own book, *The
Wisdom of Dying: Practices for Living,* and his famous workshops
on love, loss and forgiveness, from such prominent individuals as
Elisabeth Kübler-Ross, Thomas Moore (*Care of the Soul*), James Hill-
man, Paulo Coelho, and many others, are mightily impressive.
Michael is particularly proud of Matthew Fox's foreword to his latest
book in progress, *Secrets of Love, Loss and Forgiveness—A Drug-Free
Prescription for the Loving Life*:

> *I welcome this book, this bard, this storyteller, this healer
> who speaks not just his own thoughts, but the stories of so
> many he witnessed in his workshops . . . [The book]
> holds many treasures and while they parallel the teachings
> of many of our greatest mystics ranging from Lao Tzu and
> Buddha to Meister Eckhart and Jesus, they emerge from a
> Celtic soul that is very Twenty-first Century, very busy
> waking people up who have quite fallen asleep. And for that
> reason it is applicable to all of us.*

A number of our newfound friends on Beara had participated in
Michael's week-long workshops. Without exception they spoke of
him in the warmest of terms and insisted that Anne and I meet him.
"He's a very gentle soul," one woman told us, "but his workshops
are not for the faint of heart. It's a grueling, cleansing process—he

Dr. Michael Murphy
by Celia Teichman

warned us about embracing dark shadows and gale-force winds of change, and he was dead right. Fortunately he's got a laughing Irish soul and a wonderful smile too, so it helped us through the rough passages—those revelations you hadn't expected or wanted. But at the end of it all after it's shaken your bones and transformed all your dreams—you get a new lease on life and, most important, on love."

So finally we met—at an idyllic cottage Michael rents at the western edge of Castletownbere. It sits coyly on a rise above fields that slope down to the black ragged surf-whipped rocks along Bere Island Channel. And as Anne and I were admiring the vistas, the door opened and out stepped this tall, burly, platinum-haired man with a grin that wrapped around his face and a chuckle that, as Anne said later, "has real sunshine in it!"

Conversation flowed on crests of easy conviviality. Despite an amazingly wattled and grooved career as a general practitioner in London, a psychotherapist in Boston, and cofounder of one of the first hospices in the USA at St. Peter's Hospital in Albany, New York, there was no complacency in Michael's manner. Rather he exuded an almost boyish enthusiasm for his work, his books, and his hundreds of workshops given around the world in the USA, Belgium, Holland, Germany, France, Canada, Romania, and Ireland. And that smile of his filled the room, even when he left it to make us a cup of tea.

Unfortunately we were never able to attend one of his workshops on Beara, but our friendship with Michael grew as we began to understand more and more about the spiritual depths of his philosophy.

"It's really quite simple—if sad," he once told us over dinner at our cottage looking across that beautiful white sand beach at Allihies. We were sitting outside on the patio, the sun was sinking over the Skelligs, and that gorgeous evening light that we so loved bathed the whole landscape once again in a sheen of platinum-gold.

"At the workshop I tell a rather long tale of the Celtic Trinity, which in essence says that today we are much too overconcerned with our mortal 'shell.' All our efforts to reinforce it from the dangers and insecurities of life through the accumulation of 'things' and possessions and ego boosters eventually end up with us losing touch with Soul and Spirit. They begin to atrophy and fester in chaos. However, the link can be reestablished by a bridge—we call it the bridge of forgiveness and love. But in order to cross this delicate bridge, you must surrender up all those burdens and trauma stories of your life—betrayals, abuse, loneliness, loss, and rage—and cross as lightly as possible to reestablish the Trinity of mortal Self, Soul, and Spirit that is your true state in life—and in death."

"And that's it?" I asked, surprised by the apparent simplicity of the process.

"Yep—that's it." Michael laughed. "Sounds simple, but believe me, it can take a lifetime to get it right!"

"Just what you'd expect a psychiatrist would say!"

"Yes—and unfortunately, many do. And they make sure it does!"

■ ■ ■

ONE OF THE MOST moving miniadventures with Michael occurred when, on a beautiful evening, he asked me if I'd like to see where he takes his workshop participants to "throw off their burdens."

We drove to the western tip of Beara to a small harbor at Garnish, a little to the north of Dursey Island and the cable car across its churning sound. The sun was just beginning its long slow descent over the Skelligs as we climbed up steep moorland slopes and across the rock-pocked plateaus of spiky marsh grass and peat bogs. Finally, through a narrow defile in the strata we suddenly emerged on the edge of jagged cliffs with a sixty-foot drop into the churning surf below. Gulls hung above us, floating on the vigorous updrafts, the seaweedy smell of the ocean filled our nostrils, and the sea spray fell like delicate dew on our heads.

"Now what?" I said, a little puffed by the climb.

"Well—I can explain what we do . . . or you can do it."

"S'long as it doesn't involve me leaping off these cliffs, I'll do it!"

"Okay," said Michael, laughing. "Try to imagine one of the most burdensome memories or losses or hurts you carry around somewhere inside . . ."

"I'm not sure I . . ."

"Just try. There's no rush . . . Remember—if you want to live deeply, live slowly . . ."

So I tried, but nothing seemed to be clamoring for attention. I was reluctant to say this to Michael but . . . and then, wham! A memory so vivid and painful rammed itself up from somewhere deep down in that forgotten zone way below everyday consciousness. It came with such force that it actually felt like a physical blow inside my head—and my heart.

"Ah . . . I saw you get that one!" said Michael quietly. "That's a biggie."

I didn't know what to say. The memory of the incident was now so tangible that I felt almost disconnected from time and space.

Michael seemed to understand exactly what was happening. "Okay—take it easy, and when you're ready, just go look around for a rock—something about the size and weight of that trauma that's in your head and then bring it back to the edge of the cliff here."

So I walked off slowly among the peat bogs until I saw one particular rock—a nasty, jagged, broken shard about three feet long and extremely malicious-looking. I lifted it. It was very heavy and seemed reluctant to be pried out of its mud hole. But eventually with a wet sigh and vigorous peaty squirts, I managed to ease it up and carry it back to where Michael stood at the cliff edge.

"Wow! That's a beauty!" He chuckled.

"Yeah. And it's damned heavy. What's next?"

"Well, very simple. You're now going to toss the stone away down into the surf, and as you toss it, you'll release the trauma it represents, you'll forgive yourself and forgive others, if that's part of the story, and you'll be relieved of that burden forever . . ."

"Can I add in a couple more I've just thought of?"

"Add as many as you like—it's your life you're cleaning up."

I think I managed to cram in about four other somewhat less prominent burdens before the weight of the stone began to cut into my hands. And then, with all my strength, I tossed it over the cliff.

And immediately—and in all honesty—a great wave of peace flowed over me. Until that point I must admit to having a healthy dose of skepticism about this whole procedure. But the sensations that followed the release of my rock convinced me that something had changed. I felt lighter—buoyant, almost. There was even, for a fleeting moment, a temptation to step off the cliff edge and allow myself to float with the gulls, circling over the surf far below on the updrafts of cool, spray-filled air currents.

Michael was bemused. Doubtless he'd seen similar reactions from many other workshop participants. "Better stand back a bit there, David," he said.

I nodded. What I had released at that cliff edge was a memory—long buried—over a particularly sad event in my life and the life of my father. Except it wasn't his life that was the memory—it was his death. A death that came far too abruptly at a time when Anne and I were away on one of our world wanderings, but also at a time when those years upon years of noncommunication with my father were finally being bridged. Conversation was still a little difficult, but at least we'd had a few enjoyable times together—sketching and talking—followed by lunches in local pubs and a little more tentative outreach on both our parts. And then, just when it looked as if we might be able to open up a whole new relationship, I left to complete a travel book. And then he left shortly afterward—by dying.

Guilt pursued me for months, maybe years. But finally I thought the matter had been put to rest—until this particular evening with Michael. Now I knew it could truly rest—that Dad and I had finally forgiven each other, reaffirmed Spirit and Soul, and reconciled love and loss.

I thanked Michael for his being there and for guiding me. "Listen, you might as well come back to the cottage and join us for dinner. One good turn, etc., etc."

"Well, that's a lovely idea. And of course one good turn also deserves one good tale. Y'wanna hear one—it's actually part of something that's going on right now . . . ?"

"I love your tales. Michael, but hold it till we get back so Anne can enjoy it."

HALF AN HOUR LATER with cocktails rampant on the patio and a soft, milky twilight descending, Michael began his tale.

"Okay—well, this is about a guy who actually . . . as we speak . . . is thinking about making a movie on these workshops I do and got in touch with me just a few weeks ago from New York. It's years since he came to one of them. But it must have moved him, and he's sort of kept in touch . . . He's one of the great people I've met . . . young fellow who lived in New York State and he had very little of what you might call 'goods and chattels.' Now he said he wanted to repeat the workshop, so I sent him all the preinstructions and one new thing I was trying was a gifting process whereby each participant brings something of significant material or personal value and then, in a sort of chance situation game, gifts it to another participant and eventually receives a reciprocal gift. And each gift comes with a story so that the recipient will understand the value of the item being given . . .

"So . . . he got the instruction that said 'Please bring something of personal value to the workshop.' He told me he'd spent days thinking about this and decided he'd only got one real possession of any true value and he brought it with him. And . . . it was a penknife. A very swanky penknife with every kind of gadget—like one of those Swiss Army knives. Very expensive. Very desirable. And the story he told about the penknife when he gifted it to another one of the workshop participants moved everyone. Apparently, when he went to college, he arrived at his dorm the first day and walked past somebody's door, and on this somebody's door was a pasted note saying: 'Only sailing and mountain climbing spoken here.' And it just so happened that sailing and mountain climbing were two of this guy's favorite hobbies. So he knocked at the door, and they became fast friends. And eventually they climbed everywhere—in South America, the Himalayas, in Alaska . . . this other fellow came from Alaska— and it was a very firm friendship. At one time they were in Alaska (the father was wealthy and had plenty of ranch acreage up there), they cut down some trees and prepared the wood and put it aside, saying that 'one day we're going to build a boat.' And they had the capacity to do this . . . they both knew how. 'And all that either one of us has to do is to write to the other and say, It's time to build that boat . . .' and when that time came, they agreed they'd drop everything and build the boat and sail around the world together.

"So this was the guy who came to my workshop. He was in New York at the time . . . He was quite a well-known photographer, and he was also starting to make movies. Anyway, he'd been working in the city for three or four years and decided he needed a change. So he wrote to his friend and told him he thought it was time to build that boat for their world-sail odyssey. And he told me that it was just ten days later that he got a call, and he was certain that it was his friend speaking. But it was actually his friend's father. And his friend's father said, 'On the very day you wrote that letter, we had word that our son was killed in Nicaragua . . . in the troubles out there . . .' and he said they were going to have a private funeral. But then he said, 'As one of his closest friends, we'd like you to come '

"So—they had the funeral, and it was a very moving affair. And the father then said to the photographer, 'You and I have got to do a memorial sail for my son.' They weren't going to go around the world, but they were going to go to the Aleutian Islands. The father had his own boat all ready. So they were vittling the boat for the trip and they went to get final supplies and whatnot, and when they were on the father's boat, he saw this knife—this beautiful, multifunction knife. And he must have made some kind of remark . . . what a wonderful knife it was or something like that . . . Anyway, they moved on, got the stuff, got on the boat, and left the harbor. Pretty soon . . . it was totally amazing, actually . . . they soon got into a heavy swell on the sea. The boat really was moving around a whole lot. And what he told me happened was a bottle of champagne that they'd brought with them to drink a toast to his friend who was killed . . . it opened all by itself. They didn't open it. He said it was very eerie. The two of them just stood and stared . . . The bottle was there open and the cork was on the other side of the galley. And they both sensed that he was there with them in that boat. So they drank the toast to him and the father wanted to give my friend a memorial gift. He'd seen how much he'd admired the knife, so he said, 'You were my son's best friend and this was his favorite knife . . .' So the father gave him the knife—and that was the very knife he gave away at my workshop."

Michael paused to let the images sink in. There was a thoughtful silence. Then Anne smiled. "Lovely story," she said.

Michael nodded: "Yeah . . . yeah, it is. But it's not quite over yet. Y'see—what happened at the workshop was equally wonderful. Because, who should receive the knife, but a woman. My friend had told his tale, and there was hardly a dry eye in the room. And they passed by chance . . . we do this kind of musical chairs chance ritual when it comes to who gets which of the gifts. Anyway, this woman, a striking, mature but troubled lady, got the knife, and she held it for a long time, stroking it. And then she spoke. Quietly but with a strength she'd not shown before at the workshop, she said: 'I couldn't have had anything more appropriate for me at this moment in my life than this knife. I'm in a shitty relationship and I need to cut my way out of it. And this knife is going to give me the courage to do what I have to do—and I shall always be grateful. Your generosity will help me release myself . . .'"

More silence. We sat with Michael, not saying anything. Then: "It's always a magical process," said Michael. "The spirit of releasing something you value and seeing it bring meaning and value to someone else . . . the true gift that keeps on giving . . . yeah, I know that's some inane advertising jingle for . . . something or other . . ."

"Diamonds, I think," said Anne.

"Right. Quite possibly." Michael nodded. "But in these sessions, these exchanges, it really means something . . . What's the point of accumulating stuff, especially when others can benefit. David—what was that zany country song you were singing the other day?"

"Oh, that . . . ," I said, not quite able to remember the words. "How's it go? Something like: 'La dee da, la dee da, la dee da . . . / Where I'm going, I won't be comin' back/And I've never seen a hearse/With a luggage rack,' or at least I think that's the gist of it."

"Yeah, I guess that just about sums it all up!" Michael laughed.

"No luggage racks. So—share yourself and give away as much as you can before someone else ends up doing it for you when you're gone!"

OUR FRIENDSHIP WITH MICHAEL continued to grow over the months on Beara, culminating one amazing evening when he invited Anne and me and some of our friends, newly arrived from America, to celebrate the finale of one of his week-long workshops . . . as will be revealed later . . .

Michael also told us of other healers and therapists and counselors living on Beara. Some had attended his workshops, others he'd met socially. Their range of practices varied enormously, from massage therapy, homeopathy, and reflexology to art therapy, craniosacral, color, crystal, and aroma therapies and various forms of meditation including the more "down-to-earth," nonmystical Vipassana and Metta traditions. Yet despite all these different approaches, the purpose of these "healing" techniques seemed to be to help enhance sound holistic foundations for our poor confused human spirits—spirits often broken, distorted, or abandoned in the welter of worries and stresses and traumas in the world beyond Beara. Souls distorted in a solipsistic confusion of endless consumption of things not needed and virtual reality living that eliminates the true, the tangible, the "now" of a simple existence. People in despair and suffering, even in the most idyllic of places and circumstances, thinking themselves unworthy of true happiness. Others fluttering around the edges of their own lives, unable to see how all the apparently unrelated coincidences dotted along the path of their existences were actually benevolent stepping-stones to a potentially joyous future.

MARJÓ OOSTERHOFF SUMMED UP her purpose in offering various meditation instructions at her small Passaddhi Center high on the

Caha flanks between Hungry Hill and Sugar Loaf Mountain and overlooking Bere Island and Bantry Bay. *"Vipassana* means 'clear seeing,'" she told me with a beguiling smile and a slight Dutch accent. Her silver hair moved slightly in breezes that rolled up through the hedge-bound pastures below and wafted through the huge open windows into the main meditation room. A plump, furry, three-legged cat came and sat itself on my knee. Marjó laughed—a youthful laugh, full of honesty, and a furrowless face bathed in what I can only call a "giving" spirit. She was one of those rare individuals you know you're going to like almost before anything is said.

Once the cat had snuggled its way into a ball on my lap, Marjó continued. "This kind of 'clear seeing' helps us touch and understand our mental, physical, and emotional processes. We begin to see patterns and habits more clearly, and we can undertake journeys of pragmatic self-discovery. It's not about getting mystical experiences. We don't do levitation here! Very verboten! It's simply about emerging from living on automatic pilot, from being only half awake, and learning to live life more fully—more open-minded and open-hearted—with a lot less fear and clinging to things. And this process can be reinforced with Metta or 'loving kindness' meditation. This helps us make friends with our minds and release ourselves from our cunning chronic little critic who's always trying to sabotage our natural ability to wake up and love ourselves and thus truly love others and live fully. We remove unnecessary boundaries that we often create for ourselves, eliminate fears and blocks, and come to see the inherent interconnectedness of things."

Marjó has been offering many of her short and long (ten-day) retreats for up to ten people on a donation basis since 1999. "It gets harder each year to do things that way, but it still feels right . . . and somehow we get by. I spend time in Burma most years on retreats and—wow! When you see what those people have to put up with over there, it makes our challenges—our lives here—seem so very easy. I'm constantly amazed by their grace and peace in the midst of so much disease and poverty and hunger—and overt injustice. What I learn from them—which increases each time I'm there—I try to share with others here . . . and I think it's helped quite a lot of people. At least"—Marjó chuck_ed—"that's what they tell me . . . I try to explain how quickly and eerily tragedy can enter our lives and change everything in an instant. I emphasize how vital love is—there's no time to waste on arguing or unloving behavior. A simple message, but you'd be amazed how people react—like sudden transformations!"

"YES, I DEAL WITH that quite a lot too," said Alan Hughes with a strong rugby player's laugh. "Although when most people come here they have no idea at all what the heck my craniosacral therapy is. Do you know?"

"Well, Alan, I must be honest, I suppose I cheated a bit," I said. "I picked up one of your brochures in the Supervalue supermarket down the street and got a bit of background. I know it's called a 'gentle, hands-on therapy,' although it started to lose me with all those references to cerebrospinal fluids and craniosacral congestions and restrictions. But what did fascinate me was that one of our friends here said you had 'magical ghost hands' that applied no pressure on a body at all and merely floated over sensitive points and yet she felt as if they were relaxing, easing, a dozen places at once. She said 'I could see Alan's hands over my legs but I could swear I was actually feeling them up around my shoulders and my head where he'd been a few minutes before!' "

Alan laughed. He was a lean, good-looking (rugby-playing) man in his late forties with blinkless—almost hypnotic—blue eyes. His office was next to the enormous church in Castletownbere across the road from Jack Patrick's, our favorite local butcher. Alan had spent his youth in South Africa and then zigzagged through a "mélange-career" in photography, computer programming, store management, water sports, and more recently "serious gardening"

and African drumming with a Beara drumming circle. His fascination with different forms of healing began with a visit to Beara in
1997 and then a series of intensive courses in Indian head massage
and Reiki, Thai, and Hawaiian massage, aura-soma color therapy,
sound therapy, and craniosacral therapy.

"Why Beara?" I asked.

"Well—I have some 'Irish roots.' My grandfather was from Limerick. But I discovered the peninsula by accident. I was traveling—
'rooting'—around, trying to avoid the tourist crowds on Dingle and
the Ring of Kerry. And I found Beara and I sensed it was one of those
unique places—a sort of real genuine power point. You could feel it
in the air and the land. I'd seen Deirdre Purcell's *Falling for a Dancer*
movie—it was filmed in and around Eyeries here where I live now—
and it was like *Wuthering Heights*, you could just sense that vast
natural power of the cliffs, the islands, the ocean, the whole wild
tone of the place!"

"And how does this craniosacral therapy work?"

Alan laughed again. His blue eyes glinted but, as from the start
of our chat, hardly ever blinked. I felt if I looked too closely I really
would be hypnotized. "Well—fast version—at the core of our bodies
is the cerebrospinal fluid, which cushions and bathes the brain and
the spinal cord in sort of wavelike ebb-and-flow movements. The
other pieces—bones, organs, and whatnot—each follows its own particular pattern of movement. So with the hands of a trained therapist, these movements can be perceived and manipulated, especially
to relieve strains and stresses stored up in the body and mind, which
can restrict overall holistic functioning. It's a strange process and
hard to explain, but I use my hands to identify 'congestions and
blockages' and then reflect them back into the body to remove them.
One analogy is a mirror. If I hold a mirror in front of you, you may
see in the reflection that you're frowning and then, if you decide
you'd prefer not to be frowning, you'd relax your eyebrows and smile.
And—poof!—the frown is gone . . ."

"And that's it?"

"Well, it took me almost three years of hard slog to get a diploma in this, so it's obviously a bit more complex. But, in essence, that's what I end up doing. Helping unblock blocks. The point is that, in most cases, the 'health' of the body is there. You just need to release it. You can never control everything—life's a random crapshoot. The Creator's got all the aces! But we can help enhance the edges—that old saying—'Life throws you curves so you learn how to swerve.' So—I suppose that's my main job. Teaching physiological and psychological driving skills!"

MARY PADWICK—ONE OF Beara's leading reflexologists—giggled when I quoted Alan's job description. She was an attractively vibrant woman living with her photographer-husband, Neil, and immensely proud of her son Matt, whom we'd met and who directs all the administrative complexities at Dzogchen Beara.

"But Alan's right. That's really the essence of all these healing practices here. I remember way back when we lived in England, Neil treated me to a health farm weekend for my birthday once, and boy!—they had the lot! Yoga in a dozen different forms, acupuncture, reflexology, Reiki, massages, tai chi, hot stones, dancing circles, crystals—you name it. It seemed a bit wacky at first, but wonderful in a way. A whole new world for me. And I asked—what's it really all about? And one of the therapists told me 'It's very simple—the body is a mass of energy pathways and channels, and some get blocked and need help in opening up again. After that, the body usually has ample capacities to restore its own equilibrium. All you have to do is work with the body—but don't get in the way of allowing its own healthy generating powers to do their job.'"

"Everyone here, all the healers I've met, seem to make their roles appear very simple and obvious," I suggested, staring out of the windows of their home overlooking the vast panorama of Bantry Bay and thinking, You could heal anything and anyone in a setting like this.

Mary laughed. "Well, it is simple. I always knew I had a gift for listening to and helping people. The key I find to my way of reflexology is to open up to each person and allow them to trust you while you're working on the foot exercises. Once they sense you're truly focusing on them, they allow themselves to improve and to heal. In the end—no matter how sophisticated the techniques you use—it's their choices about themselves that really make the true difference."

There was warmth and translucence in the way she expressed herself—definitely the kind of therapist I'd seek out if I ever needed one.

Mary's husband, Neil, had been working quietly with his photographs in a corner of the living room, only moving when he spotted spare slices of Mary's amazing homemade ginger cake. ("It's Delia Smith's recipe. Not mine," she said modestly.) But he'd obviously been listening to our conversation and finally added his own opinion. "I honestly think that one of our main problems today is that we limit ourselves by the false and very incomplete logic of scientific knowledge when all the major forces and energies are infinitely powerful and way beyond any kind of logic."

That seemed to sum up what Mary was saying, so we spent most of the rest of the time admiring Neil's remarkable high-resolution landscape shots of Beara. "This peninsula is just full of these vast panoramas," he said enthusiastically, "and I'm starting to produce a whole series of cards to sell locally—plus some very expensive mega-blowups for affluent blow-ins. They seem to love them and find them 'very relaxing'—so I guess it's my small contribution to all these healing activities on Beara!"

"I wouldn't call them affluent—most of the blow-ins I meet here are carrying backpacks and eating day-old sandwiches," said Julie

Aldridge, founder of Soul Ray. The sign on the door next to the supermarket was a little frayed at the edges, but there was a pamphlet
pinned to the hallway wall inside explaining that Soul Ray offered a
variety of services, including art therapy: "A unique approach to
emotional and psychological problems . . . enabling access to your
deeper understanding as well as strengthening your imaginative and
creative potentials." And it also mentioned something about "flower
remedies."

"What in the world are flower remedies?" asked Anne.

"Never heard of them," I said. "I thought I'd seen just about
every kind of therapy there was offered on that notice board in the
supermarket—I even found some new ones today like shiatsu,
ayurveda body massage and acupressure, pulsating magnetic fields
therapy, asana, *pranayama*, trance-dancing, hyperthermic chamber
therapy, timeline therapy, mora and hydro-colon therapies, chakra
and regression therapies—oh! and kinesiology and iridology. And all
this in and around little Castletownbere. If they had someone doing
Kabbala training, we'd just about have the lot."

"You're forgetting angel channeling," said Anne with a grin.

"What?"

"Angel channeling. Using the power of your own guardian angel,
or something like that. There was someone talking about it on Irish
TV last week . . ."

"Okay—if you say so, although I haven't seen that offered here
yet! But 'flower remedies' . . . I'm stuck!"

"Actually," said Anne, "it says 'Peralandra and Bach Flower
Remedies—offering gentle support during times of difficulty, stress
or crisis.'"

"So—let's go and ask this Julie Aldridge what she's really doing."

We climbed two long flights of stairs, and just as we reached the
door to the Soul Ray office, out stepped this very tall bundle of
energy, high spirits, and infectious laughter.

"Oh, hello," she said (with that very infectious laugh). "I'm

Julie—are you coming to see me? I was just leaving . . ."

"Well, we'll come back—" Anne started to say.

"Oh, no no—come on in. I'm not going anywhere special. I just needed a break. Fancy a cup of tea?"

And that was it. We were smitten. She was lovely, lively, and seemed to float about on a little cushion of joy and giggles—all topped off with a dainty

Julie Aldridge by Celia Teichman

broad-rimmed bonnet sprouting ribbons and feathers. "It takes me forever to put this thing on, so—if you don't mind I'll leave it on. I'm trying it out for a wedding next week." Ah—zaniness personified. I sensed we had found a potential new friend. Anne was laughing a lot too, along with Julie—always a sign of instant- bonding. And as it turned out, there was actually some serious and very valuable bonding to be done with Julie in our future on Beara.

It began almost immediately in her cozy counseling room overlooking Castletownbere harbor. We were talking about the peninsula and its ability to lure people into its mysteries and magic. Julie grinned. "Well, first it's the landscape, I think. There's a kind of gateway here at Glengarriff. The town itself can be touristy in the summer with its weirdly humid Gulf Stream climate, those two fancy botanical gardens, and the gorgeous hidden valleys back in the forest there. You've got to explore those. It's another world. But if you turn west, and pass through that invisible gateway, you're into a different form of energy altogether. Some people can't stay here on Beara for long. Others find it very hard to leave. Must be because—like everyone tells you—we're sitting on this enormous crystal bedrock here! It also all depends really where you are in your own evolution. If you need to go deeper or find space for your own creativity—Beara's very conducive for doing work on yourself. Expanding your artistic eye, writing that novel, opening up new channels of health and happiness for yourself and for those you love too."

"Well—you certainly look happy enough!" said Anne. "Beara obviously works for you."

Another enticing laugh from Julie. "Yes but it's not for everyone. Certainly not the way we—Jim, my partner, and I—live . . . a tiny cottage near Eyeries up on the mountainside, no running water, no electricity, no TV . . . oh, and no car!"

"No car?! How do you get around?" asked Anne.

"Walk . . . or get lifts."

"That's a heck of a walk—over the top from here to Eyeries. What is it—six miles? Maybe more?" I asked.

"Almost seven. But it's a lovely experience. Except in the winter. That can be a bit nippy! Sometimes I think we're crazy. I'm originally from Sheffield in Yorkshire—the *Full Monty* city. That's a strong place too, but I never really learned to love it like Beara. The landscape is so powerful here. It works on you whether you know it or not. It's like a purification process just living here. That's why we've got our little cold, damp cottage—we're living intentionally at a pretty primitive level. But it's real. I've never felt so connected to anyplace before—at all levels. When we first came to Ireland we traveled around with a tent for five months looking for . . . something. And then we found Beara, and we were, well—transfixed and transformed! It was like we'd entered one of our own fantasy dreams. We couldn't leave. Even now if I have to nip over to England to see family or whatever, I always feel the land trying to hold me back. And that's after years of living here!"

"How did you get into therapies and counseling?" asked Anne.

"I suppose it just sort of came—but of course it was possibly already cosmically preordained! I thought I'd be doing some painting. Trying to sell a few canvases to make ends meet. And I must admit, that side of things is working out pretty well. I've just had an exhibition at Anam Cara, and some galleries are now interested. Jim was planning to do some computer work—teaching, programming, and whatnot. It was all very vague, but we both sensed that we only have this one life and time seems to be relatively short and there was an awful lot we wanted to do without distractions and without wasting energy going after material things we really didn't want or need. So, as we opened up to the place, the place sort of opened up to us too. In the most natural and gentle of ways. It showed us—reminded us—that the human being is so much more complex than most of us imagine. We often end up barely scratching the surface of our own lives. But when you do release different facets of yourself, you're on an incredible learning curve. You start to love yourself and all those new facets of yourself more and more. Then you find yourself opening up to similar kind of facets in other people. You see things—into things—much more. It's like, the deeper you go inside yourself, the wider you can spread your understanding . . . your empathy and love."

"And out of that . . . empathy . . . comes an ability to heal?" Anne asked.

"Yeah—eventually it can. If you direct it that way. But not all at once. I can't say suddenly you become some kind of mystical guru—because I'm not mystical at all really, and I'm certainly not a blinking guru! I'm really quite pragmatic. I think, to a large extent, we're all capable and in charge of our own healing. All that's needed usually is someone to listen, to really hear, and to suggest where the paths to recovery might be. How they might be used through—well, all kinds of resources—imagery, art, and art therapy; I teach a course in that at Cork University now—and all the various holistic processes. They're all different, but their potentials and benefits are similar and all mutually reinforcing."

"And then there's your 'flower remedies' . . . what are they?" asked Anne.

Julie laughed once again. We were learning to love that laugh. "Ah . . . ," she began, "oh, heck—look. I'm finished here for the day. I was going to set off home when you arrived . . ."

"Walking?" I asked.

"Right—walking. Or getting a lift . . . whatever. People know me and stop. I usually don't need my thumb! And in this blinkin' bonnet I'll get a lift in no time flat! So why don't you come back to the cottage. See how we really live in the rough on Beara. We can walk or . . ."

"We've got a car outside. So why don't we . . ."

". . . Go by car. Lovely idea. Let's went!"

It was a beautiful evening. The air was crisp and the lowering sun bathed the Caha hills in a soft golden light. And when we arrived on the northern slopes of the peninsula, the cottage hidden in a thicket of tangled trees down a narrow unpaved lane, looked like something out of one of those syrupy sweet Kinkade paintings. It was outrageously romantic, unbelievably cute and cozy, with its whitewashed walls highlighted with Greek blue trim, and explosions of flowers all around the windows and doors. At the side was a small, neatly sheep-cropped lawn shaded by trees. Beyond the end of the cottage, fields and hedgerows fell gently down the flanks of the hills to a curling series of coves along Kenmare Bay and the purpling massifs of Macgillycuddy's Reeks on the Ring of Kerry.

"Absolutely perfect! We'll take it!" gasped Anne.

Julie smiled. "Our reactions precisely when we found it eons back. Despite no plumbing, no water, no electricity, no heating except for the peat fires . . ."

"No problem!" Anne chuckled. "We've lived and roamed the

globe in very small motor homes—writing travel books—so we've had some experience of basic living—but this place is just . . . gorgeous!"

And the mood of cozy country living continued inside the cottage. The furniture in the living room arced around a glowing peat fire and looked comfortable and well used. Mouthwatering aromas wafted out of a small kitchen at the side. "That's Jim's bread. He must have been baking this afternoon. He's out tonight, but there should be a couple of loaves waiting . . . yes, they're here! Fat, brown, and beautiful. So—you might as well stay for a bit of supper, if you want. Won't be too much—thick homemade soup and fresh-baked bread. Sound okay?"

We both nodded. Whatever Julie offered was fine with us. And she was laughing again as she led us along a narrow hallway to "my art studio, actually the old cowshed that can still smell a bit you-know-what on warm days."

"They say it's a healthy smell," I said.

"Who does?"

"Well—my grandmother did, I think. 'Course she never actually lived in the country, so she didn't really spend too much time with cows!"

"Lucky her. We've got a dairy farm just down the lane here, and believe me, I can think of far healthier smells. Thank the Lord for aromatherapy!"

Julie pulled aside white coverall sheets to reveal some of her latest paintings. "I'm doing almost all landscapes and seascapes now. Very ethereal . . ."

They were amazing. Even in the fading dusk light, the gentle turquoises, lemons, and soft scarlets she'd chosen for the canvases glowed like Caribbean beaches. And she'd very delicately run threads of gold leaf across them, like sunlight on slow surf wavelets—you could almost hear their ocean rhythms and sounds rippling sloppily across blond beach sands.

"Beautiful—absolutely beautiful!" said Anne.

"Is that what you teach in art therapy—this kind of evocative mood?" I asked.

"Oh, no!" said Julie. "No—this is very much my own work. Therapy art's entirely different. You're trying to get people to dig out traumas, stresses, hidden fears—to help them release all these and transform them into new, more positive healing perceptions and energies. Their canvases can get pretty brutal at times—they paint out their problems. Big and colorful and violent as they want. But the changes can be really amazing—I've seen dramatic transformations right here in this little room. I can't talk about it too much because the clients need total privacy—I promise them that. But it certainly works . . ."

I nodded in agreement. "And near-deaths can do that too. Anne and I have had a few traumas in that area. And each time it's like you, as you say, feel utterly transformed—given a new life. It's an amazing sensation! And an amazing opportunity to reinvent your whole future . . ."

Julie laughed. "Yes, I've seen so many new lives emerge . . ."

"Is it mainly blow-ins you work with?" Anne asked.

"Actually, it's about fifty-fifty—locals and blow-ins And I've learned so much from my Beara clients. At first I was staggered at how much pain and suffering lay behind that patina—that surface thing of all the Irish friendliness and charm. You can't look at anything here in isolation—it's all part of interwoven continuances—the individual, the family the clan, the land. A whole complex matrix of interrelationships. That's why the healing process can be so layered and challenging. We understood these linkages once—intuitively. We tapped into energies—earth energies like ley lines—through standing stones and circles and all that ancient stuff. But we've forgotten all that—lost the powers. Partly because there's been so much suffering here—the terrible famines, the poison in the land, and the horrific memories of the people about the wars, the Troubles, the slaughters, the hard-slog marriages, the layers and layers of guilt in-jected by the priests—it's all still lurking here, if you dig deep enough . . . and in order to heal, you need to dig deep!"

"And flower remedies can help with all this?" asked Anne.

"Actually I was talking more about art therapy," said Julie. But then she proceeded to give us a condensed summary of the princi-ples and purposes of flower remedies. I lost track of some of the de-tails. Anne said it involved using tarot cards and other methods to discover each individual's needs—physically, mentally, and spiritu-ally. Then Julie blends various flower essences she buys in tiny bot-tles from the USA into customized sipping fluids primarily to help restore balance in bodily systems and "blown circuits"! It all sounded harmless enough. I assumed a lot of the "healing" would come through simple belief or faith in the process itself—the driving force throughout so much of the holistic world.

On the way home to Allihies after a truly superb supper of a thick soup, made from homegrown vegetables, and Jim's crunchy wheaten loaves, we were comparing notes on Julie and all her ideas and ac-tivities. Then, without any preamble, Anne said quietly: "I'm going to go and see her next week."

"Oh, that's great," I said. "There are a few more things I'd like to know, especially about her art therapy."

"No," said Anne. "This is different. I'm going to see if she can help me with my FMS."

There was a long silence. For many years Anne had lived with this pernicious muscle condition known as fibromyalgia syndrome (FMS). Essentially, in her case, it caused tremendous fatigue and de-bilitating pain throughout her body. Many doctors rejected this and other similar disorders, such as chronic fatigue syndrome, as "hys-terical ailments" or "women's problems." Fortunately, enough evi-dence has since been generated to prove beyond any doubt that these are indeed potentially serious life-changing conditions. In Anne's case, as the problem worsened, she had to cut back on her consultancy work and her work with AWARE (a nonprofit organization she'd founded to serve adults who are blind or have low vision); and to resign from her position as a university professor in Japan. That was particularly disheartening, as we both loved our four years there on Kyushu Island and had managed to effectively combine her teaching and our journeys in Europe for the *Seasons* series of books.

Her FMS was now in its eighth year. She had tried every cure in the catalog, all to no avail. In the past, I know she wouldn't have paid much attention to "nontraditional" cures, but as the traditional remedies had all proven to be utterly useless, I could sense a definite change in her attitude. Julie had apparently spotted something was amiss when she and Anne were chatting together in the kitchen.

Rather than go into any more detail about holistic processes that neither of us truly understand, I'll merely summarize the outcome of this strange experiment in "flower remedies" as—utterly transformational! Within a short time of taking a few of these little drops of flower essence fluid every day, Anne suddenly found the pain and fatigue diminishing for the first time in all those eight long years. A month later there was virtually none. I felt my wife had been "returned" to me—with her previous high energy, enthusiasm, and celebratory lust for life. And today, almost two years later—there has never been a single recurrence . . .

And to add to Julie's accolades, three other friends who visited us during the ensuing months from the USA were captivated by her laughter and uplifting spirit. Each in turn revealed their challenges to her, from mild depression and family concerns to postcancer stress. And Julie dutifully developed customized flower fluids and even sent requested refills to the USA after they'd returned home. Gratitude and gushing thanks rolled in from across the Atlantic. And she smiled and laughed and sent notes of encouragement to our "recovered" friends who still talk about our "lovely, laughing healer" with admiration and awe. Julie, of course, who is one of the most modest "healers" we met on Beara, always emphasized that the process is primarily one of self-healing. She never seemed to accept direct credit for any of her cures. We had the odd sense that while she knew she was tapping into little understood but apparently effective forces and energies, she preferred not to analyze them too deeply. And Anne, whose work in vision rehabilitation has always focused so much on the inherent inner strength of self-help, obviously agrees. But yet, the amazingly rapid pace of her FMS healing occasionally makes us both wonder . . .

And I also certainly know that the somewhat cynical naysayer described at the beginning of this chapter (me) has now matured a little. And while maybe not yet a total convert to the mysteries of nontraditional healing, I'm certainly a far more enthusiastic supporter of these unusual people on Beara who offer their knowledge, wisdom, and lives to help others in a wealth of holistic ways.

Thank you—and more power to you all.

13

Leaving Beara for the First Time

.
.
.

WE REALLY DON'T WANT TO LEAVE. Particularly on a day like this. After almost a week of miserable gray glop, our last morning of the spring season on Beara, and the dawn is crisp-clear. Within an hour, the sky is pigeon-egg blue dappled with tiny white curlicues of cloud. The Skelligs are there too, no longer playing hide-and-seek in the sea hazes, but bold and proud as galleons—seemingly close enough to us to stroke their razored, almost reptilian ridges.

The tall grasses along the stream are swaying in the faintest of breezes, the buttercups beaming with a gilded sheen, and the daisies virginal white and nodding like a happy host of behatted schoolgirls. (Forgive the overindulgent imagery, but I was feeling rather Wordsworthian that morning.) Behind us are the rugged remnants of the tin mines, the chimneys and stone-walled engine houses, broken and black against the brittle summits and strangely eroded flanks of the hills.

Over a fold in the half-moor of abandoned fields with their collapsing walls peeps the gaudy strip of houses, pubs, and shops of Allihies. The carnival cacophony of colors seems almost too blushingly self-conscious, especially as across the rest of the sweeping landscape bound by high ridges, most of the cottages and farms are demurely white or, at their most flamboyant, a delicate shade of lemony cream. This is a color echoed in the broad sweep of our sand beach, that unexpected bonus of copper ore tailings once washed down to the sea from the mines up on the hill. And then—of course—come the greens of the fields and pastures and inbye plots in a patch-work quilt of fervent late spring fertility. You could spend a year painting these and still not exhaust the patterned permutations of green in every imaginable tone and hue.

And as the sun begins its daily arc, the land seems to change shape constantly. The slowly moving shadows expose a welter of bumps and lumps that could be—and in most instances actually are—anything from ancient neolithic ring forts or stone circles to more recent ruins of the old "famine-era" houses, tumbled in tirades of wrath by avaricious eviction-lusting landlords or merely long col-lapsed through structural fatigue and the ever-increasing weight of sodden, mold-ridden thatch.

One thing is obvious from all these shadowy presences—this has been an active, well-used land, far more populous than today. And when the mists float across these bumps and lumps here and when the twilight blurs edges and diffuses things, you can often sense the soft sussurus, the eerie echoes of layered existences.

And we shall miss them—all of them. And we shall miss even the gray glop days when those proud Skelligs vanish and the unshorn sheep look like bags of rags scattered among the gorse and marsh grass. We shall miss our Beara. Very much.

And talking of the Skelligs—we shall also miss all those inter-ludes and characters that brought so much depth, resonance, and humor to our daily adventures. For it was the Skelligs that were the key focus of our reunion with Seamus Gleason, whom we'd met in Dublin shortly after our first arrival in Ireland. He was a swarthy, bearded man somewhere "on the top side of forty—make that forty-five," so he told us. He was also a fine raconteur with a rich brogue, and he promised to look us up when he made one of his occasional visits to the southwest. When he arrived on his first of two trips we

O'Neill's—Allihies

happened to take him up to O'Neill's in Allihies for lunch and a bit of sunshine on the pub's outdoor tables, which crowded the roadside. By chance we were sitting next to a group of rather rowdy punk-haired youths from the north of England, and Seamus, with a sly grin, whispered to us: "Watch me stir this little lot up a bit . . ."

He cleared his throat, winked at us, and started speaking with a distinctly bombastic bellow. "So that's how the story of the Irish saving civilization emerged: the Irish—we Irish—saved your whole bloody world, y'know!" said Seamus with a menacing laugh, inviting rebuttals.

There was a silence that was indeed pregnant at the punks' table. But it was obviously one of those premature pregnancies—quickly followed by a gush of sprayed Guinness and a series of full ejaculatory exclamations.

"You bloody *what*!"

"Flippin' stupid sod!"

"Crawl back to y' bog, y'old Celtic clod!" (And other random pleasantries.)

Then silence. Until someone—presumably seeking to cast a little more fuel on this fire of furor—piped up: "Oh, well—pray, tell us more, Mr. Philosopher."

I was expecting Seamus to raise a two-fingered gesture of dismissal and adjourn to a friendlier environment. But he didn't. Instead he smiled an inscrutable smile and continued. "Yes, I will. I will indeed. When you gentlemen have piped down and shown yourselves capable of listening to a little common sense and a modicum of undisputed history. Not philosophy. But fact. Granite hard facts!"

More silence.

"Okay," said someone else. "Cool it, lads. Let the man have his say."

And his say was indeed worth saying. At least, Anne and I thought so. And the others certainly remained silent and semi-respectful throughout Seamus's intriguing discourse.

"No one, I don't think, would ever link the word *civilization* with fifth-century Ireland . . . ," he began.

Nods and grunts all around.

"But if it hadna been for our little colonies of monastic scribes inspired by our St. Patrick, carrying the Gospel of Jesus Christ to this pagan wilderness in the fifth century and beyond, it's likely that all the thinking and writing that had been collected in Rome from their empire, the early Judeo-Christians and the Greeks and the Egyptians and the Etruscans and many other wonderful cultures—all of it would have been torched and decimated by the barbarian hordes that sacked the Roman Empire and most other parts of Europe and Asia . . . and all would have been lost forever."

Seamus paused for a long swig of his porter and then smiled slyly at his (apparently) captivated, or maybe just confused, audience. "And all because these few righteous men could write and could copy and could then start to spread all these wonderful words and thoughts back to a broken, burnt-out Europe . . . and you'd know the kind of place that these remarkable men lived in . . . ? D'y'know?" ("Behind

Paddy O'Shea's Pub on Limerick Street in Dublin!" said one wise-acre, but nobody even so much as sniggered. Seamus seemed to have this rowdy bunch in his hand.) "Where they lived was places like Skellig Michael off the Iveragh Peninsula—the Ring of Kerry. Go down the road here and you'll see the island. A terrible broken pyramid of rock twenty miles off in the Atlantic. Seven hundred feet high where they had to climb seven hundred steps to their tiny little beehive huts—their *clochans*—made of dry-laid stones. And there they led lives of absolute asceticism, and for most of their relatively short and hard existences, scribbled copies of these books rescued from the pillaging and plunder of the barbarians . . ."

Silence. Until someone finally felt he had to challenge the adamant Seamus.

"Clochans" on Skellig Michael

"So, you're saying these little guys—these monks or whatever—stuck up on this rock and other places around Ireland 'saved civilization'?"

"Well done!" said Seamus. "That's precisely what I said. You're obviously listening."

"And so everything we see around today—books, libraries, universities, churches . . . all these things—they're here because of these scribbling guys stuck on mountaintops and whatnot?"

"Yes—everything!" said Seamus. "Everything."

"Makes y' think," said one young man, obviously impressed by Seamus's ideas.

"Makes y' thirsty too," said another. "Whose round is it now?"

"*Saol fada chugat!* Long life to you all!" said Seamus with a wide grin.

"An' now I suppose you'll be expectin' a pint too after all that history stuff," said one of the punks with something like a smile.

"A splendid idea indeed, my friend—*Bail ó Dhia is Muir duit.*"

"An' I bet that's something really rude . . ."

"On the contrary—I am asking God and Holy Mary to bless you for your spontaneous generosity!"

AND THUS WISDOM AND insight is passed—or not—on your typical Friday-evening get-togethers at the local in Allihies. But Seamus had opened a little door of perception and insight in my head, and I decided to do some research of my own, starting with Thomas Cahill's delightful book *How the Irish Saved Civilization.* And what I found was utterly intriguing and for the most part, reinforcing of Seamus's basic premises. It seemed that tiny Ireland had indeed saved civilization as we know it. Cahill writes:

> Had the destruction been complete—had every library been
> disassembled and every book burned—we would have lost

> *Homer and Virgil and all of classical poetry, Herodotus and*
> *Tacitus and all classical history, Demosthenes and Cicero*
> *and all of the classical orators, Plato and Aristotle and the*
> *Greek philosophers and Plotinus and Porphyry and all*
> *subsequent commentaries. We would have lost the taste and*
> *smell of twelve centuries of civilization . . . All of Latin and*
> *Greek literature would almost surely have vanished without*
> *the Irish, and illiterate Europe would hardly have developed*
> *its great national libraries without the example of Irish, the*
> *first vernacular language to be written down . . The weight*
> *of Irish influence on the continent [of Europe] is incalculable.*

Cahill describes how, as the Irish monks and missionaries moved eastward from their lonely Eire outposts, proselytizing the Catholic faith, they also carried copies of "the great books." In 870 Heiric of Auxerre, France, recorded that "almost all of Ireland, despising the sea, is migrating to our shores with a herd of philosophers." Wherever they went, the Irish brought with them these books, many of them never seen in Europe for centuries . . . They reestablished libraries and breathed new life into the exhausted, virtually extinguished literary culture of Europe. "And that," concludes Mr. Cahill, "is how the Irish saved civilization as we know it today."

WE'RE GOING TO MISS these kinds of spontaneously bizarre episodes, but God willing and fate being fortuitous—we shall return in a few weeks, once the rush and crush of summer has faded. Of course we should emphasize that our beautiful, secluded peninsula bears few of the touristic burdens and the hullabaloo of holiday hordes that descend on Killarney and the Ring of Kerry the next peninsula north. And the one after that too, the Dingle, which has increased dramatically in popularity in the last two decades. But even here—while our roads are far too narrow to permit the scourge of bumper-to-bumper tourist buses that plague the Ring of Kerry in particular—Beara seems to be attracting more and more discerning "backroading" travelers. So—we decided to share the bounty of our peninsula with others and offered our little cottage to them for a while. So they could enjoy the briny breezes, the infinite greens in our sheltered nook, and sunsets splashed like scarlet fire on the surrounding crags and ridges. We'll come back when they leave—hopefully calmed and nurtured by this amazing place. Just as we have been.

SUMMER

The Season of Beltaine
("Bright Fire")

FINALLY, SUMMER SURGES IN. GREEN AS only Ireland can be. Iridescent greens that sting the eyes with their brilliance. So many greens that a painter could go mad trying to capture their permutations. And humid-hot too. Particularly in the southwest and Beara, where the Gulf Stream nurtures palms and hosts of exotic species once planted by eccentric, decadently rich "intruders." (Lands given away to the English elite by Oliver Cromwell back in the seventeenth century are still indignantly decried by some indigenous locals.)

In this season the sap races faster and smoother than stout and porter from the pulls in the pubs. It's a time of increasing abundance—stacks of fresh-cut peat turf (although far less than in the past), vast catches of seafood, sweet "salt-meadow" lamb, a furious surging of vegetables "in the sod," a surfeit of praties (potatoes), and the searing sheen of newly golden grain fields.

By this time, the menacing midges of May are being forgotten, festivals are being organized, the Garda (police) are preparing themselves for controlling "excessive displays of exuberance," and villages are being repainted and dolled up with hanging flower baskets for the Tidy Towns Competition. Eyeries is invariably the odds-on favorite. Allihies is pretty colorful too—particularly the bloodred walls of O'Neill's pub (now with a fancy new restaurant upstairs)—but Eyeries has gone all-out rainbow. This tiny community seems to be determined to match the abundance of colors in the landscape all around—golden gorse, brilliant green ferns, explosions of fuchsia and honeysuckle, carpets of cornflowers, and the sprawls of moor-hugging purple heather.

Butterflies are everywhere—Red Admirals, Tortoiseshells, Speck-led Woods, and the ubiquitous (but still virginally dainty) Cabbage Whites. That beautiful blond beach of ours at Allihies entices us once again to abandon projects and productivity and go flop down by gently lapping, lolling wavelets and thank whomever we normally thank for the soothing pace of summer, the glories of golden-honey days, and the sepulchral silences of those long velvety evenings.

Although—and we hate to break this flow of hedonistic images—summer is not always so. Our summer was punctuated with a return to England to celebrate Anne's father's ninety-fourth birthday. Although his health was not good, his Yorkshire humor and determination to enjoy each day was an inspiration to us all. And for those who were on Beara in the summer of 2007, we can only empathize with their perseverance through "one of the worst wet summers in living memory." And the old Irish adage about "if you don't like the weather here, just wait five minutes" didn't quite reflect the reality of day after day of downpours, mud, and murk.

But—eternally optimistic—our Beara friends assured us that next summer would be superb, and, anyway, there was still the mel-low autumn to come . . .

14

Days with Carey Conrad

■
■
■

CAREY CONRAD IS A GLORIOUSLY EXTROVERTED blow-in (with distinctly introvert tendencies too, but she keeps these under wraps) who brought great energy and insight to our lives on Beara. And Carey's voice is not one that goes unnoticed in the librarylike quietude of the Internet store across the square from MacCarthy's Bar in Castletownbere. Invariably there's a somnolent silence in here. The owner whispers into his phone behind the counter (either conducting complex counterintelligence campaigns or plotting nefarious number-crunching business schemes—we never knew which, although his tales encompassed both possibilities). And users of the dozen or so computers gaze raptly at their screens, mesmerized by their scrolling downloads.

But then this buoyant ball of energy rolls in, her blond hair piled up into a loose bun, her long coat flapping around her ankles like a hyperactive bat, and her face flushed with her perpetual aura of vivacious enthusiasm.

"Hi . . . ," she calls out, oblivious to the owner's intense phone conversation, and then, as heads stir and lift from flickering screens around the room, she issues another, more generally collective "Hi!" to the huddled customers. There's a kind of grunty mumbling of responses, which seems enough to keep Carey's smile bright and buoyant. Then she spots the two of us snuggled together in a corner, crouched over a computer and trying to frantically compose e-mails to resolve a number of issues that need to be dealt with urgently back at our home in New York.

Why is it that traumas always seem to occur there when we're not? At home, that is. In the USA. Why is it, for example, that our refrigerator has chosen this particular week, after over sixteen loyal years of uninterrupted service, to suddenly die and spill its lifeblood of minilakes of de-iced water and less savory fluids all over the kitchen floor. Fortunately our dear friend Celia, guardian of our domestic affairs and just about everything else during our absences, was around to do the mopping up and to add a few more unwelcome but, alas, necessary warnings about our gas stove ("I think there's a bit of a leak there somewhere . . ."), our deck ("It may be just me, but I think it's starting to look a little lopsided . . ."), and our car ("I tried starting it up, but it didn't seem to want to cooperate . . ."). Poor Celia. She hates giving out bad news and she knows how helpless we feel three thousand miles out here in the Atlantic with normally not a care in the world and no decisions of any import to be made except which pub to grace with our lunchtime presences.

"I know who you two are!" cried this woman as she pointed to us with the certainty of a witness at a criminal suspect lineup. We were right in the middle of deciding which domestic trauma we should attend to first, and suddenly, here was this strident lady, obviously very American in attitude and ambience, rushing toward us with an outstretched finger, determined to tell us and everyone else in the room exactly who we were and what we were doing here on Beara.

And the odd thing was that she got most of it right. I suppose we could have done the British thing and become all huffy and puffy about such an unexpected invasion of our privacy. But she was obviously the kind of individual who wouldn't even notice such an Anglophilic rebuff. So we laughed instead, invited her to sit down and tell us how she had managed to accumulate her remarkably accurate data.

And that was the beginning of a most entertaining and valued friendship. Carey's long love of Beara, her second home now for over sixteen years, and her extensive knowledge of the people here was intriguing, particularly when it encompassed reclusive celebrities who sought safe havens in and around Beara.

Later on in our relationship she even tried to arrange interviews for us with such notable "locals" as Maureen O'Hara (star of *The Quiet Man*, that classic Irish film with John Wayne), who still lives up in Glengarriff; Julia Roberts; the filmmaker Neil Jordan; and a little farther beyond Bantry, Jeremy Irons in his ancient castle, which on some odd whim he painted a joyous pink. In the end, and for a bizarre range of reasons, none of the interviews materialized, but Carey's other bulwarks of knowledge of local history, folklore, and all the rest of the Celtic-Gaelic-Gothic fantasy world here provided a sound foundation for a mutually enduring relationship.

A couple of days after our first meeting at the Internet center, she invited us to her seashore home in Adrigole, a few miles from Beara's infamous Hungry Hill. Over tea and homemade cookies, she regaled us with tales of how she and a friend had created this enticingly intimate and richly handcrafted retreat. Carey's talents and enthusiasm

Hungry Hill

seemed boundless. She was particularly enamored by "our wonderful local characters here—Old Peg at the store, and Jim, the shoemaker. Real Beara people." And then she set about telling us her life story. It certainly seemed that our new friend had enjoyed a vividly kaleidoscopic kind of existence encompassing a multiself array of interests, from real estate and property refurbishment, ceramics, jewelry making, and art, to Buddhist meditation (yes, the Dzogchen Center again), spiritual healing, architectural design, and occasional bouts of "amateurish" (her expression) writing.

Rather than put her vivid life story into my own words, it's possibly best merely to offer a partial transcript of the tape that we made of her colorful summary:

"I was born in Ashland, Wisconsin. And I was born rear end first . . . I always felt that was significant, as I seem to like to look at the ending of books first and then start reading from the beginning. My mom saw her dead father the moment I was born. Must have been the drugs . . . Leaping ahead, I graduated from Sun Prairie High School in 1969. I decided to become an X-ray technician and studied at the University of Wisconsin and practiced at the University Hospital in Madison. I learned quickly how to deal with death, and how to live with it.

"My husband and I got married like my mother and father did. During a war period—Vietnam—in a hurry and without really knowing one another. We were friends originally. We would have been better off if we'd stayed friends too. But then again, that's not really true because my beautiful daughter, Melissa Marie, came from that union. She I would never give back.

"After Brian and I got divorced, I moved to Milwaukee, Wisconsin. I went to hock my wedding ring when I met this jeweler who was selling his store and had an inventory to get rid of. I told him that maybe we could do some business together. So that's when I started selling jewelry in bars. I'd hit nine bars a night, and soon the word spread and women would gather around me when I came into a place to see what new jewelry I had out. It was the 1980s and everyone loved flash and sparkle and bling! Lots of ba-roque 'n' roll stuff. They called me 'The Jewelry Lady from the East Side,' and my following grew. An article in the *Milwaukee Journal* about me brought some notoriety, and soon I had a line of people waiting to see me in a little office I was renting. Word of mouth is great in Milwaukee, and a couple who acted as agents booking major acts into the city started hiring me to make jewelry thank-you gifts for the visiting stars. I was commissioned to make Eric Clapton a tiny guitar that had strings you could pluck. Also Sammy Hagar, Mario Andretti, Paul Newman, Air Supply, the Moody Blues, Cher, Gladys Knight, Lou Rawls, even Liberace, and especially Tom Jones, who I kissed onstage. I made for him a little charm of a bra-and-panties tie tack.

"It was a great time. I met Ladysmith Black Mambazo with Paul Simon after they'd made their fabulous album *Graceland.* I made a pendant that symbolized how their music had spanned the globe, bringing awareness of the horrors of apartheid.

"Then things changed. My mother died in 1991 of ovarian cancer. Immediately afterward I got a phone call from a friend. She'd moved to Ireland but was returning to the States and asked me to come and help her pack. I needed a break, so I flew into Dublin in midwinter for a two-week stay. When I got there I found out that my friend could not get off work for longer than three days. So we worked hard together packing all her stuff, and after she left I decided to just drive wherever I felt like driving. I took my map and just set off. And as I worked my way down the coast, I was overwhelmed by the beauty of the land. Finally I drove into Bantry, and there was a market going on. I bought some old lace and some jewelry and heard a voice in my head saying, *You could live here.* So I decided to explore the Beara Peninsula, and as I drove, it just got more and more beautiful. I stopped for toothpaste in Glengarriff at the drugstore and saw a sign that said HARRINGTON'S PUB AND AUCTIONEERS. I knew 'auctioneers' meant real estate over here, so it suddenly hit me to go in and ask how much oceanfront property was going for in those days.

"Bernard Harrington was behind the bar, and I asked him, 'Is this a real estate office or a pub?' 'A little bit o' both' was his answer. And when I asked about oceanfront property for sale, he took me out to one of the most beautiful places I've ever seen. A valley carved out of the side of a mountain with lovely green fields and the ocean crashing in on huge rocks. I took one look and knew I was gonna change my life and live there.

"It was one of the best decisions I ever made. And I quickly learned so much about healing in this place where there are so many wonderful healers who've come to this enchanted land. And I needed them. My body was a bit of a mess. I feel in my heart it's because the land is so ancient and untouched in so many places. There's still a pure energy here that's not compromised by industry or overpopulation. The light, the rain, the rainbows, and the quick wit of the people embrace me here. I've discovered so many beautiful places at the end of small dirt roads. The sea was so close to me that every day I looked out of my window to see seals, birds, and swans. It was, and still is, a place of incredible beauty. And I've known a happiness here that I don't think could be replicated anywhere else in the world."

CAREY'S CONTAGIOUS SPIRIT OF urgency and energy energized us, and when she started to plan a series of exploratory expeditions for us to her favorite "secret spots" around Beara, we found ourselves unable to resist and decided just to go with the flow. Her flow, of course.

And quite a flow—and show—she provided over subsequent weeks. She had a deeply empathetic understanding of the Irish instinct for the mysteries of religious faith, for the supernatural, and for the long storyteller epics combining real and mystical events, which still form such a vital part of the fabric of the national psyche here.

In typical American fashion, Carey quickly opened her heart and spirit. "I try to find a kind of balance—six months here on Beara and six months back in the USA. But the trouble is, it's so hard to leave this place. I just love being here."

We mentioned to her that we'd both been impressed by Julie Aldridge and her spiritual healing activities at Soul Ray. Carey laughed and clapped her hands. "Ah, yes—Julie! She's the best! Her art therapy is amazing. You know, she teaches that at Cork University every week. Her approach seems so simple the way she describes it—she says, 'Your soul will talk to you through your drawing, and if you have someone to work through the process with you—a kind of interpreter—you start to see what you're trying to unravel in your life—patterns of hurt, abuse, whatever.' She knew I'd been through some traumas earlier in my own life and she said, 'Look at your family and you'll see patterns that keep repeating themselves. It can be depression, early pregnancies, divorce, illnesses—all sorts of things. Emotional patterns, physical patterns—when you start recognizing and acknowledging the patterns, you can stop them from reemerging in your and your children's lives. Otherwise you'll just keep on continually repeating them.'"

"Yes," said Anne. "And all this apparently can be revealed through art. That's what she was explaining to David and me. We were up there with her last week, and we saw her studio in the old cow byre at the back of their cottage. She kept most of her own artwork there—big ethereal canvases of oceanscapes and cloudscapes. Beautiful glowing colors. Sometimes she used gold leaf to emphasize horizons and reflections."

Carey nodded vigorously. "Yeah, wonderful pieces. So energetic and yet . . . peaceful too. I tell you—this whole peninsula is a real hotbed of artistry and healing. There's a new generation of people here with amazing powers . . . I really feel blessed that I found this place. In some ways I think, well, like it kind of 'saved' me. I was a bit of a mess when I first came and a lot of stuff I'd heard sounded a bit too mumbo jumbo for my tastes—for my needs. But you know, as time went on and I met more people and got involved in handcrafting this house, things began to make much more sense. They lost that dodgy 'New Age' image and became . . . well, I guess you'd say . . . much more pragmatic . . . eminently sensible and focused."

Then Carey suddenly stopped and chuckled. "I'm wondering . . . are you two open to a spot of eminently unsensible spontaneity? Right now?"

"Always," we answered in unison.

"Well . . . why don't we take a little drive into the mountains. There's so much to see out there. We've got two hundred and fourteen official prehistoric sites on Beara and countless others that aren't even on the formal record—stone circles, dolmens, souterrains, standing stones, the lot! And there are special places—really special. Julie helped me find my own 'mother earth place' . . . I'd love to show it to you . . ."

You don't turn down offers of this kind, and of course, even if you tried to, Carey would somehow carry you off anyway in a surge of effervescent energy.

Which is precisely what she did.

Looking back, I remember a magical jumble of images and stories as we drove on rough back roads deeper and deeper into the mountainous heart of this wild peninsula. The scale of the place is utterly confusing. From the map we knew that Beara at its widest point was barely eight miles across from Bantry Bay in the south to the Kenmare River and the hazy hills of the Ring of Kerry to the north. And yet it seemed with Carey as our guide that we wriggled and romped for hours and never appeared to get close to either coast. And it didn't matter. We had no particular destination in mind, and we were happy just to bounce and float through this secret hinterland, listening to Carey's tales and seeing the landscape through her

eyes. Eyes that brought the land to life as she pointed to a huge up-
surge of broken strata that tore through the turf and towered a good
thirty feet into the chill moorland air.

"That's Mass Rock—one of a number of places where the Catholics would gather to worship, away from the prying eyes and terrible
punishments of the British Protestant overlords a couple of centuries back."

She pointed to a nearby broken capstone of an enormous neolithic dolmen, two small stone circles half hidden in thick brush,
one very prominent standing stone over ten feet high, and a host of
shadowy lumps and bumps in the earth that she insisted were the
remains of human settlements over three thousand years old.

Then we descended rapidly in a series of sudden twists and curls
through a rumpus of tumbling hillocks down into a lush valley of
alders, dwarf beech, green meadows, and remnants of ancient peat
beds close to a winding stream.

"People around here still treasure their 'turf rights.' They're written into the house and farm deeds and were once very jealously
guarded. There's not so much cutting going on nowadays—you can
still see a couple of stacks up there." Carey pointed up the valley,
where a small waterfall tumbled lacelike off a rocky precipice. "But
once it was your lifeblood for the winter. If you didn't cut enough
turf and dry it properly on the moor before carrying it back to your
house in your wicker creel basket—some could weigh a hundred and
fifty pounds when they were full—then woe beside your winter
nights. It's not so much ice and snow and the like. We never got
much of that because of the Gulf Stream. It's more the damp chill,
which can eat into your bones like acid. And I know! I've got arthri-
tis, which is why I usually go back to the States during the winter. I
could hardly move about if I stayed here!"

At that very moment, as she conjured up the gray glop of winter,
a shaft of brilliant light shot through the clouds and bathed the central part of the valley in a golden sheen. It was almost Edenic in its

haloed intensity, reminding me of one of my favorite Dylan Thomas snippets: "And so it must have been after the birth of the simple light in that first spinning space . . ."

Carey seemed so delighted in our delight at her secret places that she may have been a little carried away at times. As, for example, when she described bizarre theories about a vast network of underground souterrain communities that once existed across these wild moors. She also told us of a tendency toward cat worship in ancient temples here, as reflected in stones carved with feline faces; the Celtic acknowledgment of "ancient feminine energies"; a theory that pre-Celtic settlers here were of Far Eastern origin; and a great national fear of fairies and their penchant for stealing babies and leaving behind nefarious "changelings," which still persists today and explains the deposits of "little gifts" for the fairies, particularly around May Day and Halloween.

"You might well laugh," said Carey (I was only smiling benevolently, I thought), "but there are still many places here that people are nervous about." She stopped suddenly at the far edge of the valley with the peat beds. Ahead of us rose an enormous rampart of bare rock hundreds of feet high. A great gash filled with dense scrub split the hillside from top to bottom. "Y'see that place ahead of us?" asked Carey with a sinister tone in her voice. "That's where the Witch of the Red Door lives. Y'see just to the right of that big split in the rock there's an area that looks darker than the rest . . . sort of blood-red . . ."

We were a little unsure we could see anything red but nodded anyway.

"Well—it seems there was once a tribe living here in this valley, and they were starving. The crops had failed and people were dying, so the chief went high up into this cleft, and for three days he prayed to the gods for water and sustenance. And on the fourth day that area of rock—now called the Red Door—opened and out came this beautiful young woman carrying two enormous baskets of food. She walked down toward the people in the valley, and they cheered and grabbed the food from her baskets. And as fast as they grabbed and ate, the baskets would refill themselves. But when the chief saw what was happening he rushed down from the cleft. He was immediately jealous of the power of this woman but also doubted if she was indeed 'a gift from the gods' and declared her to be an evil presence. She smiled and approached him, but he turned his back. She approached again, but he cursed her and her 'evil fairy ways,' so she dropped the baskets on the ground, walked back into the hillside, and disappeared And as she vanished, so did the baskets and all the food, and a sheen of red, like a huge spilling of blood, covered the place where she had vanished. And immediately the chief fell dead and all his tribe was left to starve horribly . . ."

Carey paused dramatically. "And they say this is still a cursed place and that you must never go anywhere near the Red Door over there . . . They say people have disappeared . . ."

I love the silence that follows an eerie fairy tale and the little tinges of terror, or certainly trepidation, that scamper up and down your spine.

"And if you like that tale, then I've got a real special place I want to take you . . . I'd like you to meet my favorite person on the whole peninsula . . . The Hag of Beara."

"A hag?! You mean an old woman—a witch?" asked Anne, slightly bemused.

Carey chuckled. "Well—in essence, yes. A very ancient woman . . . a mythical figure . . . the Cailleach Bhearra. You've always got to be careful when you visit . . . You should take a gift— flowers, ribbons, coins, or something shiny—and when you leave, you have to give a bit of yourself as a sign of respect. The locals usually spit on the ground, like they do when they enter cemeteries. They spit and say, 'God bless all of you.' Or you can cut off a bit of hair—anything to acknowledge her and the fact you're pleased to visit her and meet her."

"Sounds fascinating," said Anne. "Is she close by?"

"Not far—just out of Eyeries on the Kenmare road. Past that very ancient Ballycrovane ogham stone marked with a unique script that looks like knife cuts. One of the world's earliest written languages, so they say. Up past Kilcatherine church—or what's left of it. She's high on a hillside looking out across Inishfarnard island to Kenmare Bay and the Skelligs."

"Sounds a great spot. Let's go, and you can tell us the tale on the way," I said.

"Oh God, no! That's an ancient terror of a tale. Dozens of different tellings . . . dozens of different names for her."

"Yes, but from what I understand, she's such a vital part of not just Beara folklore, but also the whole of Ireland," I suggested.

There was a pause. I knew Carey wanted to tell the tale. She was a natural *seanachai*, but something was holding her back, and it wasn't coyness or modesty. I wondered if it was the old bardic fear that, if a tale was told inaccurately or any of the subtle nuances were missing, dire consequences could befall the unfortunate tale teller.

Eventually she capitulated. "Okay—but mind you, I know various versions based on all kinds of different tales. They're not gospel or anything. Lots of people will tell you different stories. But this one is about as simple a way as I can tell it—it's based on Julie's version of the legend. Some say the Hag's real name is Boi—wife of Lugh, the Celtic god of light, and one of the original great land goddesses. Y'know, the Great Mother—Magna Mater, source of all fertility, female power, corn goddess, protector of wild nature, symbol of enduring longevity, and all that kind of thing. And she lived on Innes Boi at the tip of Beara. We call it Dursey Island today—a focal point of Ireland's 'other world' of the dead and mysterious beings. There's a great poem-lament about her written, so they say, around AD 900. She's the mythical, some think sinister, 'old woman' of so many Irish legends. I'm not sure if I can remember all of it, but it goes something like this:

'The old woman of Beara am I
Who once was beautiful
Now all I know is how to die
I do it well

'Look at my skin
Stretched taught across my bones
Where kings have placed their lips
Ah the pain, the pain

'I do not hate men
Who swore truth rested in their lies
But one thing I do hate
Is woman's eyes

'I drank the great wine with kings
They rested their loving eyes on my hair
Now among stinking old hags
I chew the cud of prayer

'Time was broad as the sea
And brought kings like slaves to me
But now I fear the face of God
And crabs crawl through my blood

'The sea—ah the sea—grows distant now
Away, away it goes
And I lie here when the foam dries
On this deserted land
Dry as my shrunken limbs
As the tongue that presses my lips
As the veins that break through my hands' "

There was silence. Carey seemed to be trying to remember more, but then she smiled. "I think that's where it ends . . ."

"Fantastic—well done!" said Anne, patting her shoulder. "Amazing images—kings as slaves, hating women's eyes, crabs crawling in her blood, veins breaking through her hands . . ."

"Yeah," nodded Carey. "Wild stuff, eh? They could really write in the ninth and tenth centuries."

"Yes, they could but . . . I hesitate to ask. What does it all mean?"

"Well—once again, it depends who's telling it. She's been a key part of Celtic-Gaelic tales for so long. You also find talk of her in Scottish legends . . . but she shape-shifts, depending on the age of the story and the source. The earliest one shows her as the corn goddess, possessor of all the secrets of seed sowing and harvesting, destroyer of male reapers who fail to equal her reaping prowess. Then she becomes kind of a legend for longevity who seemed to live 'the seven ages of womanhood,' constantly and simultaneously breeding 'all peoples and all races.' And I suppose she was a giantess, because tales of her footprints all over Beara and Dursey Island are well known."

"Y'know—Julie told us a long complex tale about her great leaps," I said. "There was one in particular where she'd soared from a rock near Eyeries across Coulagh Bay to Kilcatherine, leaving behind two huge indentations, which we could actually see in the rock and touch—definitely a size twenty-four in boots, she was!"

"Well, that sounds like a mixed-up version of another tale where the Hag punished a woman near Hungry Hill for stealing butter. She transformed her into a giant cock, and it left footprints all over Cuaileach and other parts around here. But there's all kinds of versions, from Yeatsian reverie to gothic horror! Some say she changed herself into a rock on that hillside to guard Ireland's shores and await the return of her husband, Mannan, Lord of the Sea. Others say that the Hag—as Mother Earth—got into a fight with Mannan. She became so angry that she turned into molten lava and Mannan overwhelmed her. And, as happens to lava when it hits the ocean, she became a solid lump of rock. And—ironically—that rock is claimed to be the only piece of lava on the whole of our peninsula! Another says that this is the form she took in perpetual humility to God when she rejected her pagan origins and became a Christianized nun. A fourth suggests pretty much the opposite—that she transformed herself—or was transformed—into stone because of her hatred of the Christianizing impact on ancient pagan gods. A lesser theme was her being turned into stone by an angry priest from whom she'd stolen a Mass book."

"What an incredible kaleidoscope of epics!" said Anne.

"Ah boy, yes—endless! Some call her 'Our Irish Mary Magdalene.' Others see her as being symbolic of the Irish and European purge of female witches. Some of the old gods like Dna, the mother of Irish gods, became St. Brigid, whose annual festival celebrates the beginning of spring. In some ways they could have been forgotten as the Catholic church became supreme, but there seems to be a new level of interest in these ancient, powerful, and pagan forces today. Maybe we see great wisdom in their awareness of the interconnectedness of all things and the balancing of male and female forces. Things we're still trying to work out ourselves right now!"

"I hadn't thought of that," I said. "The old values resonating once again in all our current chaos of global decimation and disaster!"

"Story of life really, isn't it?" said Carey. "In the tough times, we dig back to the simpler, clearer beliefs. Yesterday I heard of a woman in town . . . someone called her 'as ancient as the Cailleach Bhearra.' She's still a feared—but also very respected—Hag. In fact her code for a healthy life is still listened to today:

> 'I never let the top of my head see the air
> I never let the sole of my foot ever touch the ground
> I never ate food but when I was hungry
> I never went to sleep but when I would be sleepy
> I never throw out dirty water until I've taken in the clean.' "

"So the spirit of the Hag is still alive and well," I suggested.

Carey laughed. "Sometimes a bit more alive than seems sensible or safe! You talk to some of those folks who come over all the way from Belgium or Germany to visit The Hag rock and leave gifts and whatnot and you worry a bit about where their heads are at!"

I worried about our heads too. But we steadfastly decided to honor the required rituals, and all in all, it was a unique and pleasant experience.

We left the car at the roadside and entered the moor by a small gate. The sun was bright, and a refreshing briny breeze scampered up the hillside from the small bay below us. A mussel farm and a couple of modest fishing boats (the old kind—nothing like the mega-monsters now in Casteltownbere harbor) occupied the landward side

The Hag of Beara

of the bay. In the hazy distance, purpled and jaggedly mysterious, were the two Skelligs, so strangely similar in profile, like enormous schooners on the horizon.

A narrow, muddy path led us around the flank of the hill. For some bizarre reason, rather than avoiding all the bogs and peaty patches, it seemed to delight in taking us straight through them and soaking us up to our calves.

"What is this—some kind of endurance test?" I asked, annoyed to see my new hiking boots obliterated in thick black mud.

Carey gave me a warning frown and whispered (she actually *whispered*), "Best to be quiet now. We're almost there. She's just around the bend . . ."

And Carey as usual was correct. As we shuffled in soggy single

file along the path, an oddly shaped rock rose up just ahead. Compared to all the bulky "standing stones" and stone circles on Beara this was a very modest-sized rock, barely five feet high. But it did possess a definite animate presence. In silhouette it was like a large figure sitting on the ground wrapped in a broad blanket with a small head perched on wide shoulders. And, as we got closer, we realized that, just as we'd been told, the rock was covered with and surrounded by the most bizarre types of "personal gifts"—buttons, coins, cheap rings, bracelets, necklaces, and even pens, ribbons, and a number of those popular rubber wristbands proclaiming support for worthy causes.

We stood in silence for a while. Maybe even a little awe crept in. It was obvious that scores of people had made their way here over the months, trekking through the peaty glop, to pay their respects and sit or stand silently in The Hag's presence. She seemed to induce that kind of respect. Stupid really that a bit of odd-shaped boulder set on a lonely hillside in a very remote part of Ireland should engender so much veneration. And who knows, maybe even a little fear too. Hags to many people are obviously not harmless. Especially Hags that may be tangible links to the greatest female goddesses of all—the ones with the real powers for earthly fertility and life-continuity.

Eventually Carey broke the silence and said quietly. "This is my favorite place—here with her. When you think of all those prayers and wishes and all those people over the ages who've left imprints of energy here, it kind of cloaks you in a mystery when you touch her. After all, she is Mother Nature in solid form. And across this small bay here is that giant ogham stone—a huge masculine symbol of energy. The two of them facing each other, watching one another, seeking to maintain balance and harmony . . . makes me just want to sit and be a little part of all that . . ."

I reached out and stroked The Hag. The rock was rough with dry lichen and felt pretty much as a rock normally feels. But as I moved my fingers slowly across its surfaces I sensed two odd sensations—a distinct warmth in the rock despite the fact it was a rather gray and chilly day, and sudden faint tingles of energy, like low-voltage electricity that radiated up my arm . . .

OVER THE MONTHS WE returned to The Hag a number of times, bearing our small gifts and leaving our spit as gestures of respectful farewells. Invariably we brought our American friends with us—Robby, Celia, Danny, Theo, Lizbeth, Kathleen, and others, and in every instance, each one sensed the power and impact of this strange, beguiling entity. I can't say we actually came to love The Hag, but we were certainly proud she was here with us on Beara. And—in an odd way—I guess this book is a kind of homage not only to this magnificent peninsula but also to the earth-nurturing spirit that resides here, centered on places like this wild hillside.

And while I'm in this homage mode, I'll also acknowledge other friends of ours—the magnificent O'Reilly family. Two of them, James and Sean, creators of the Travelers' Tales publishing company in San Francisco, came over for an enormous family reunion near Killarney (forty plus children and grandchildren reflecting a "fine Catholic family!"). While we never managed to lure them over Moll's Gap to Beara, we visited them and were treated to a personal tour of an enormous ruined castle they'd recently purchased. It was a most impressive if very broken pile, set high on a wooden hilltop overlooking the Macgillycuddy's Reeks range. And they had absolutely no idea what to do with it. We suggested that a visit to our powerful Hag and a few questing prayers might help resolve the matter . . .

IT WAS FASCINATING TO watch the different impacts Beara had upon our friends. Each one had gone to a considerable amount of trouble to reach our tiny wild corner of southwest Ireland. Some had landed in

200 + At the Edge of Ireland

Dublin, some in Shannon, and all had to fight the horrors of the rental car rip-off when they realized that Ireland was one of only three nations on earth not recognized by USA insurance and credit card policies (the others being Israel and Jamaica!).

But finally they arrived, each one bearing lurid tales of crazy drivers, horrendously narrow roads, gorgeous little rainbow-colored villages, the oddly brain-numbing porridgy impact of a *céilí* hang-over, the gargantuan breakfasts particularly following a night of *craic* and overconsumption . . . ("How can anyone start the morning with one of those cholesterol-dripping platters of bacon, sausage, black pudding, white pudding, fried tomatoes, fried mushrooms, fried bread, eggs, and baked beans and still hope to stay upright for the rest of the day?!") Others less inclined to the juice of the barley thought they were some of the best breakfasts they'd every eaten.

We sympathized, empathized, and finally itemized for our poor overburdened guests, all the joys of Beara and beyond. And they—god bless 'em, each and every one—smiled and sank into receptive mode for the rest of their visits. And, of course, respectful trips to The Hag helped consolidate their fun and good fortune.

So thanks once again, Cailleach Bhearra—and Carey too, for first introducing us to her and to so many other delights in this wild and spirit-nurturing place.

15

Cookies with Cormac and Rachael

∷

"WELL, I MEAN, JUST LOOK AT all . . . this . . ." Cormac Boydell, one of Ireland's foremost ceramic artists, laughs and flings his arms wide. "You can't possibly be dishonest, can you? . . . Untrue to yourself . . . your creative self—in a place like this . . ."

And what a place it is. Just past an amazing geological tangle of scalloped rocks and "curled strata" constantly being carved out by furious ocean surf, we'd found this modest cottage tucked away at the end of a narrow rocky boreen off the Allihies-to-Eyeries Road. It was virtually invisible and set in a rocky cleft filled with a tumultuous tropical riot of bamboo, palms, huge explosions of rhubarb-like Gunnera with leaves as big as elephant ears and nine-foot-high clusters of something strangely giraffelike. Add to this Edenic environment a chuckling but barely visible stream, a constant chorus of birds, soft ocean breezes that make the brittle palm fronds chatter together, and deep shadowy enclaves behind the huge plants. Then you begin to understand the broad smile that appears on Cormac's lean face when he watches our reaction to his hidden haven of peace and creativity.

"I don't really encourage visitors," he said almost apologetically, as if guilty at having this amazing place all to himself and his artist wife, Rachael Parry. "It's not that I'm antisocial or anything, but I get so easily distracted and time just seems to leak away. And I honestly prefer the selling and whatnot to take place in the galleries—not here. After all, I'm not making mugs with people's names on them. I need all the focus and quietude I can get just for the creative work . . ."

Rachael emerged from the house bearing a tray of tea and home-made ginger biscuits (some of the best we've ever tasted). She was a small, lean woman with an aquiline face and large, melt-your-heart eyes that made me immediately want to pick up a pen and sketch her. She'd heard Cormac's comments and laughed softly. "Oh yes—he certainly needs all that. And he gets it too! Have you seen his little hotbed of creativity yet . . . ?"

"Yes," said Anne. "We snuck into his studio for a peep on the way up from the car. Powerful stuff in there!"

"Curved Strata" near Allihies

Cormac smiled bashfully and pulled his Aussie outback canvas hat tighter over his wild mop of sandy hair. The hat was a throwback to an early life as a geologist in Australia long before he met Rachael at a transcendental meditation workshop in Ireland in the 1970s.

"That poor little shed. It's been around for decades. Hardly enough room to swing a cat. But at least I'm going to get it insulated. I'm too old now for the winter cold. Rachael's got her own shed"—Cormac pointed to the rocky crest of the cleft—"and hers has views."

"When did you actually move here?" I asked.

"After Australia. In 1972. Pursuing the self-sufficient life, which actually turned out to be harder than we planned. But eventually we got things in focus. Rachael and our two children were wonderful. And my father too—Brian Boydell. His life was always an example to me. He also gave up geology for his real love—music. Became a pretty celebrated composer and professor of music at Trinity College in Dublin. And my mother, Mary, is a prominent authority on Irish glass. That's her real love. So in 1983 I decided it was time to pursue my own real love of—clay! Our gorgeous, rich, chocolaty Irish Wexford clay. Using my hands as my only tools . . . and, well, I guess I was lucky. Very lucky. Galleries started to feature my work almost from the very start! I expected I'd have to go through the standard 'starving artist' gauntlet, but somehow I managed to skip that challenge, and doors opened and lo—I was an 'Artist'! People started buying all my colorful creations."

"Similar to what we saw in the shed?" I asked. "All those wonderfully primeval slabs of fired clay painted in brilliant wild Fauvist colors . . ."

"Similar. Maybe not quite so bold and carefree as now . . . and maybe not so tongue-in-cheek and humorous. But sometimes I'm surprised by the consistency because . . . well, I'm very fluid in the way I work. I don't really know what I'm going to create with each piece until I knead the clay in my hands—like baker's dough . . . letting the work lead me to new possibilities and forms I didn't know

I wanted to make. I'm usually inspired by prehistoric and tribal art and the New York abstracts of the 1950s and I guess all the incidental abstraction that surrounds us. Particularly in a place as powerful as Beara. You sense a great spiritual centering here. Magic in the mystic misty silences. And then the colors—well, that's my latent geologist reemerging. I mix my own colors mainly from minerals and whatnot. You get some pretty unique shades and textures. And it doesn't all happen at once. I know they might look simple—even primitive—but each piece goes through a complex series of color layerings and firings . . ."

"I love their brightness—their vibrancy," said Anne.

Cormac smiled, bashfully again and rubbed his fingers together, as if slowly mixing soft clay. "Well—I blame that on where we are." He flung his arms out again to encompass the surging tsunamis of vegetation around us. Pieces of his sculpture peeked out from the greenery. "I mean, look at this corner of Beara—beautiful rocks, the ocean just down the track, this jungle of a garden, the light, the sky, the colors all around . . . Then I combine all that with memories of wonderful bold images I've seen—Minoan sculpture, cave art . . . anything and everything!"

"And then on a couple of plate-forms, I saw a cartoonlike portrait of Van Gogh . . . and the two Skellig islands on another," I said.

"Yeah, odd, isn't it. I never really know what will appear. But whatever comes seems to sell. I think the humor in some of the pieces appeals—the enjoyment and play of art as a medium of communication. Also the sense of authenticity in the basic clay material and, well, I suppose what you might call an aura of primitive spirituality without overanalyzing . . . Also, I've never really cared that much about money . . . or celebrity. I'm honestly happiest just being here, working by myself and with Rachael. We work on multimedia pieces together—and I'm happy if my work just makes people feel happy. That's success to me. If you're driven by money concerns and desires, then you're setting yourself up for failure. Your work becomes dictated by these elements—and you end up more concerned about what'll sell and you start producing strings of sausages or objects that don't particularly enhance your own life—or anyone else's. So what's the point? You project bad karma . . ."

"Ah, another Beara Buddhist!" said Anne with a laugh.

Cormac chuckled. "Actually, you're right. I'm very involved with the center. Have been for years. Ever since I met Peter Cornish, the founder, and his late wife, Harriet. And before that Rachael and I were teaching transcendental meditation workshops. So I guess art and Buddhism play a large part in our lives—they're interchangeable really. I guess the Buddhist way of looking at things influences my art too . . . unconsciously. Being 'present' and 'mindful' can produce a kind of immediacy and freshness in what I try to do. Meditation is important to me too, primarily for pragmatic reasons. It helps eliminate distractions and keeps me in the 'now,' to use that much overused—and misused—word. It's very contrary to our normal habits and scattered minds, so it's something you have to work on . . ."

"And karma . . . you mentioned karma," asked Anne.

"Well . . . I certainly understand the concept of karma . . . everything you do has an effect on the universe. But it's also another very misused—and misunderstood—word . . ."

"And reincarnation?" I asked.

"Ah, well, that's . . . well, let's just say . . . I'm still working on that concept!"

Rachael's fabulous ginger cookies were almost gone from the tea tray now, and she gave us all a forgiving smile and went back in the house to bring more. Silence settled, and a cool breeze tumbled over the lip of the deep cleft in which we, the house, the shed-studios, and the riotous vegetation were all cozily cocooned. I smiled as the air brought momentary relief to the warm sunshine, and then I realized we were all smiling together. Rachael laughed as she rejoined us (with another brimming cookie plate). "You all look as if you've just finished off a whole bottle of sherry together!"

Bees buzzed about; the birds were still chattering away; the stream chittered down over the rocks in the deep shadows behind the big tropical leaves; another cool breeze slipped over into our cleft. And we all smiled again. Together.

And I began to understand some of the many influences floating behind the works of Cormac Boydell.

EVENTUALLY—WHEN THE SECOND plate of Rachael's ginger cookies had been devoured—Cormac excused himself and retreated down through the dense foliage to his reclusive cavelike studio. We wondered if we should leave too, but we were curious about Rachael and her own creative work.

"Oh well—he's the famous one in the family . . . ," she said with a wry grin. "Compared to Cormac, my work's more like a hobby—I don't even have a permanent gallery yet."

"Yes, but you've had a load of shows, according to something I read in our local paper," said Anne. "They were very complimentary. And they mentioned your studio here—something about it feeling like being in a floating balloon!"

Rachael chuckled. "You want to take a peep?"

"We'd love to!" (in unison).

And so we left the craggy confines of the garden and the "jungle" deep in the rocky cleft and climbed up a series of steep steps to a high ridge. Suddenly the still, moist air around the house was replaced by the invigorating thwack of sprightly sea breezes redolent with the briny bouquet of ocean spray.

And there it was—Rachael's small, compact studio perched resolutely atop the ridge with vast vistas of seascapes, cliffs, and the mountainous spine of Beara retreating eastward into a golden afternoon haze.

"Beautiful!" gushed Anne.

"Fantastic!" I said. "I want it!"

Rachael laughed. "Well, maybe you want it now. But on stormy days when the wind's trying to tear this little place apart and you wish you'd roped the thing down as you kept promising yourself you would, or when that deep winter chill really sets in and you just can't get the place warmed up . . . you may not be quite so enthusiastic!"

"Oh I guess I'd learn to cope," I said. "Beara seems to teach you that—the power and beauty of places like this seem to overwhelm all the hardships and inconveniences. We've met quite a few people here living in old cottages without any running water, using clapped-out generators for electricity, peat for fire fuel . . . just like the last century, except that the livestock, if they have any, now at least they have their own accommodations! No more pigs under the beds and fighting the family cow for a space by the fire . . ."

"Oh, that's so true. You should have seen our place when we first moved in. It's a palace today compared to how it was . . . But, even now it's still pretty basic . . ."

"Well, this place certainly isn't," I said, admiring the meticulously organized appearance of her small studio. There was everything an artist would need to generate, intensify, and satisfy almost every creative urge. I particularly admired her eclectic collection of CDs—Tibetan Buddhist chants, Modern Jazz Quartet, Monty Python, Tracy Chapman . . .

"Ah well, they're all a part of me, y'see," Rachael said softly. Then she started to pull out a series of drawers filled with a bizarre miscellany of objects to be used one day in her works—poppy seed heads, bleached skeletal bits and pieces from animals and birds, chunks of copper ore rock from the nearby mines, clusters of sharp, dark hedgehog's spines, knots of ancient "bog oak," pieces of dried fish skin, whole bird wings with hundreds of meticulously colored feathers, bunches of wizened red chili peppers . . .

Rachael was watching our amazed faces as we wondered how she intended to use these remarkable repositories of nature in her creations.

"I told you—all parts of me." She chuckled. Her comment reminded me of one of Kofi Annan's sayings: "We all have multiple identities." "Maybe you should read this first before I start showing you some of the actual pieces." She pointed to something she'd written herself pinned up on the wall:

> *I make things that symbolically denote a special act, rite of passage, or shared human experience. My choice and use of materials are intrinsic to the work. Often the work is about my life and my friends' lives, but I also use images from stories—especially mythology and other "teaching stories"—which have potent universal themes.*

I nodded. "Well, it's not the usual gobbledygook you get at many art exhibitions. Tom Wolfe ridiculed all that esoteric arty verbiage that nobody really understands in his biting little book *The Painted Word*."

Rachael laughed. "Yeah—there's far too much mumbo jumbo surrounding art. You can instill depth and resonance in what you create without having to make it exclusionary—elitist. I mean, people may not always know precisely what I'm trying to say in some of my works, but they're often so intrigued by the actual objects themselves—their uniqueness and strangeness—that they invent their own stories. And that's just fine. It's all about perception and interpretation—the more interpretations a piece stimulates, the more successful I think it is . . ."

"Well—I guess it's time we saw some of the actual objects," said Anne, although both of us had been sneaking glances at the potpourri of strange and seductive works around the studio, some complete in meticulously crafted boxes, others still at an initial assembly phase. One major piece, displayed in a series of carefully shaped containers in the shape of a rib cage—a "healing chest"—possessed a variety of tiny hearts fashioned from such diverse and bizarre materials as hedgehog spines, baby thrush feathers, turf ash, and glass—all reminders of tenderness, vulnerability, and "the extinction of passion." Despite the work's strangeness, it possessed an aura of silent healing.

"Pieces like this—I think—emerge from a fantastic trip I once took in a camper van all around New Mexico," Rachael told us, her sharp, bird-bright eyes flashing as memories flooded in. "One place in particular—the old adobe church in Chimayo—was a real center for spiritual healing. The place was full of votive offerings, symbolic gifts of thanks, and a wall full of abandoned crutches no longer needed after successful healings had taken place. Oh! and a sacred 'sand room' for deep prayer. You had a feeling that people who came here seeking recovery and renewal were tapping into really deep and ancient forces. They used objects—especially natural objects of wood or rock or feathers or seeds—as tokens. Ways to enter the spirit world and use its healing powers. Ways of linking themselves to ancient myths, folk beliefs, and rituals that for eons of time have offered solutions to all the ailments we have to deal with throughout our lives."

I smiled as she described this remarkable place. I had spent a couple of days there a few years back while writing my "Hidden America" series of articles for *National Geographic Traveler*. The power and ethos of healing and gratitude there were almost tangible. I still have a small vial of "blessed sand," which I regard as a protective token (so far—so good!).

It was not easy to absorb all the rich symbolism of Rachel's creations, but their diversity and uniqueness were unforgettable: amusing "creatures" created from meldings of birds' feathers and wings, skeletal heads, and snakeskin legs; one alarming kneeling figure with a huge ejaculation of wire wool "fire" from his huge mouth; a series of "clothes for the spirit," including the lacy delicacy of a pair of gloves made from fish skins; "fire shoes" made from dried chili peppers and desert berries delicately sewn together; and an "earth hat" constructed of translucent skins shed by snakes and bound with handmade paper.

Her skills in glass and metal casting, weaving, spinning, and sewing permeated her creations. But perhaps the most amazing—the one that made both of us gasp in admiration—was Rachael's "Veil."

It was a masterwork requiring a definite "suspension of disbelief." Made entirely out of spindled threads of spiderwebs arduously collected by Rachael from the rafters, windows, and doors of barns on the Beara Peninsula, "The Veil" was meticulously spun and woven into a heavy, platinum-colored headdress. Like most of her works, it possessed a powerful potpourri of symbols—a thick, impenetrable "female" veil, but crafted in such a dense manner that it also resembled a warrior's chain mail helmet. One review pinned to the studio wall suggested that "its interconnected, yet separate components, represent a possible healing between the male and female psyches . . . The importance Rachael Parry attaches to the mythical, the personal, and the metaphysical, particularly where women and their relationships with themselves and others are concerned, is clear in all her works."

Anne was obviously moved by the power and symbolism of Rachael's creations: "I think it's a combination of the loving, empathetic female spirit with a harder, more perceptive, less forgiving energy . . . Even your softer, more sensual objects have a little sting in the tail . . ."

Rachael laughed. Her finely faceted face sparkled. "Actually, that's the exact idea I've been playing with recently—the 'sting in the tail' idea. Softness with a sear of pain. The eternal dichotomy . . ."

"You can't have one without the other," suggested Anne.

"Well, I suppose you could—but wouldn't life be boring? Far less colorful."

"Ah!" I said. "So that explains the explosive vibrancy of all Cormac's plates and bowls. You keep life colorful—dichotomous—for him!"

"I'm not sure he'd describe it that way . . ." Rachael laughed.

"Well—I'm sure he's in good and loving hands. I mean, look at what this reviewer writes," I said, pointing to a clip pinned to a wall by her CD collection. 'Her work is imbued with a desire to promote healing.' "

"Well yes—that's true right enough, but sometimes it's a matter of 'healer, heal thyself' too . . . Look, let me show you something I'm working on. It's still incomplete, but when our daughter, Molly, left home recently, I recognized a sort of ending of motherhood by casting my own breasts. Then I structured them, using ground-up turf

Cormac Boydell

on the outside and soft white gannet feathers on the inside as a lining—a symbolic kind of relining of my 'breast nest' . . ."

It was a delicately entrancing work with, once again, a striking dichotomy between the rough earth turf exterior and the softness of the interior couched in the gentle shapes of female breasts.

We stayed talking with Rachael a lot longer than we'd intended. In fact we were there until Cormac finally rejoined us (surprised to see us still hanging around) and insisted it was time for more of her ginger cookies. And so we stayed even longer . . .

16

The Creators

■
■
■

AFTER THOSE INTRIGUING INTERLUDES WITH COFMAC and Rachael, we thought things were pretty much over for a while in terms of meeting prominent "creators" on the peninsula. But on Beara, as we learned over and over again, things are rarely over. Connections spawn connections, insights reveal more insights, friends create new friends, and the magic of spontaneous synergisms and synchronicities flourishes.

Rachael was strolling with us down through her Edenic garden to our car. "Oh, by the way, you'll have met Tim, right?" she asked. "Tim Goulding?"

"No," we said in unison.

"Oh—ah!—well. That'll be a nice surprise for you. He's a lovely man—artist, composer, onetime rock musician—and another 'cleft-dweller' like us. Lives just up the road. Go to where it turns sharply to climb over the pass to Eyeries and take the rough track on the left. You go up a very narrow rocky valley—the house is painted blue and the garden is even wilder than ours . . . but it's worth the journey."

And so it goes. The serendipitous linking of creative spirits here who enjoy mutual nurture and nourishment on this wonderfully wild Irish finger of land.

Tim was home and didn't seem at all surprised or irritated by our impromptu visit. Rachael had indeed been right. Here was another hand-built home secreted away in a deeply incised cleft in the strata and guarded by enormous upthrusting bulwarks of dark rock. And so dense was the junglelike profusion of small tiered gardens that the house and its outbuildings revealed themselves only gradually in coy surprises.

"And all this," suggested Anne, "all this gorgeous exuberance, I imagine, gives you what Cormac and Rachael have found in their cleft—that sense of being utterly immersed in nature and inspired by it. From these tiny scatters of wildflowers and your enormous subtropical specimens to the sheer power of those bare rock precipices towering over everything."

Tim laughed. "So, you know my work? My paintings?"

Anne was honest. "Actually, no. Sorry. In fact, I didn't know of you at all until earlier on today when Rachael suggested we visit you."

Maybe a little too honest, I wondered. But Tim was a man of grace, charm—and good humor. His face lit up in a huge smile and his long blond hair shook as he chuckled. "Great! Then I can brainwash you without fear of you quoting snide critics' comments at me."

"We are open books—scribble away upon our psyches!" I said.

So he did. We toured his remarkable home, admiring his airy studio and other spaces that seemed to appear as if by magic. Rooms flowed liquidlike into other rooms, and we had a sense of literally floating past large windows with dramatic images of Tim's cleft-and-jungle topography and white-painted walls filled with a vast array of his own vibrant oils and acrylics.

Then in the corner of his studio I noticed a John Cage quote written on an index card and pinned to the wall. It read: "I can't understand why people are frightened of new ideas. I'm frightened of the old ones."

Tim saw me reading the card. "That's great, isn't it . . . such a waste of possibilities and joys," he said, "the joys of endless discoveries of all the amazing creative and other selves we possess. Why would anyone not want to reach out and grab them all! What was it Bob Dylan once said—something like 'a real artist has to be in a constant state of becoming.' Great phase, that! Great reminder not to get too stuck!"

"Rachael told me you'd think something like that—and it reminds me of that other saying, can't think who said it: 'Creation is born of passion and reshaped anew in passion,'" I said. "She seems to see you as a true restless Renaissance man pushing out the edges in so many different ways . . ."

"Ah, Rachael and Cormac. Great, great friends. And constant inspirations. And I need that. I've always had a dread of getting stuck in a rut. It's happened with some of my paintings. If I get into a new series and people enjoy them, then I'm offered these deadly commissions—you know, 'Can you do me one just like that, but a . . . a little bluer to match my carpet!' If you're not careful you can become a sausage machine. Cormac fights the same battle with his ceramics."

It was interesting to learn the coincidental parallels between Tim and Cormac. Both in their sixties, both living on Beara for over thirty years, both with prominent parents who gained fame and some notoriety from passionately pursuing their own unique lives. In the case of Tim, who was born in Dublin in 1946, his father was the noted businessman and art collector Sir Basil Goulding. "He was certainly what you might call a rather unorthodox figure," said Tim. "On the one hand, a no-nonsense and nontraditional chairman of his own major business—he was also an avid and celebrated gardener, a great athlete, and a fanatical fast car driver. He and Valerie, my mother, gave me and my two brothers a wonderful upbringing by the River Dargle, which rolls out of the northern Wicklow Mountains. But—poor old Dad—he must have felt really let down when none of us wanted to take over the family firm. And especially with me—who kind of just disappeared into my own self-taught world of art and music. Although I think he would have sort of liked to live my kind of life—particularly the art part—so I guess I gave him a bit of a vicarious lift. Maybe!"

"What kind of music?" I asked.

"Oh, all kinds of weird stuff. I formed this group in the late 1960s—Dr. Strangely Strange. We had quite a bit of zany success for a couple of years. We still get together on occasion and create new stuff. I even did my own album in 2005—*Midnight Fry*. Remind me. I'll give you a copy. It's a real mishmash—a little bluesy, lots of dance-based loops, some great world-music-type multitracking. It's best listened to with top-class headphones—takes you to another level . . . another wacko planet! C'mon, I'll show you my recording studio . . ."

"You've got your own studio?" said Anne.

"Sure. I don't use it as much as I should—but it's great fun."

Tim exuded a spirit of constant bemusement with himself, with everything around him, and the serendipity of the world in general. It was a contagious characteristic, and we found ourselves following him from surprise to surprise with permanent grins on our faces.

And there it was, another surprise, a small shed hidden atop a series of slippery, moss-coated steps up through the "jungle" and crammed with guitars, keyboards, speakers, and amplifiers, and a huge 140-track digital recording board.

"This looks like very serious stuff," I said.

"Well—the art world has been good to me so . . . Oh, listen. Let me play you the first track of *Midnight Fry*—'On the Fly.' See what you think."

Within seconds the tiny recording "shed" was shaking with a rich multitracked cacophony of sound. It was like being inside a gigantic stadium speaker. Incessant bongo beats merged with staccato loops in eerie echoing Philip Glass–type synthesizer sounds followed by Ry Cooder–type slide guitar infills. Tim passed me the CD box and it read:

*Recipe for Midnight Fry: Stunning vocals, ambient sound-
scapes, chill-out interludes, cutting edge samples—all
prepared in a bowl of World and Celtic spices by Ireland's
finest contemporary musicians.*

"Can't argue with any of that!" I shouted to Tim over the scream-
ing speakers. He laughed and handed me a new copy. "Try the rest at
home."

"And what's this other building higher up the garden?" asked
Anne when the track ended and the little studio seemed eerily
silent.

"Oh, that's another recent project, a special studio for Georgina.
My wife. Well—second wife, actually. My first lives just down the
road. We're still great friends. Georgina's into aromatherapy and
'essences.' All rather mysterious at the moment—it's a new
business—but it smells so lovely in there."

"Any other building projects?" Anne asked.

"Well—I'm tempted to expand my art studio a little more, but I
guess I'd just be getting a bit too greedy. My mother had a great phi-
lanthropist's spirit, so I get a little self-conscious about overly indul-
gent antics. She founded a clinic in Dublin for the physically disabled
in the 1950s after that terrible polio epidemic. It's a huge operation
now. Twenty-five hundred people. And she was a fabulous fund-
raiser, always putting on concerts in our home and having these
great overnight guests—people like Grace Kelly, Albert Einstein,
Peter Ustinov, Orson Welles. On and on. I never knew who I'd see
wandering around in pajamas or who'd be joining us for breakfast. I
even got a private lesson from Henry Moore once when I was just
starting to paint. He advised me how to tackle three pots standing
on a windowsill. I kinda got into this semirealistic, semiabstract,
straddling-the-fence kind of mode. A way to express and appreciate a
single image in different ways simultaneously, and it sort of stuck.
One of my earliest series was *Earth Fire*. Very intense dramatic

canvases inspired by the colors and ferocity of our ritual gorse burning in the fields and on the moors every year. C'mon, I'll show you some of my stuff back in the house."

And what a show it turned out to be. The gorse-burning works seemed to possess almost demonic energy as huge scarlet flames writhed up from the black earth into a black sky. Others portrayed the powerfully bold and broken landscape around the Allihies hills and the old tin mines. "There's so much inspiration right here—in this fantastic place. Huge rock massings, vast ocean and skyscapes, islands, pounding storms, platinum sunsets, the wild loneliness of the moors. Then you come right down to the fantastic miniature worlds of lichen patterns on worn strata, the primordial darkness of the old mining tunnels, the timelessness of our standing stones, circles and souterrains—it's all pure magic. And always with that underlayer of mystery . . . that sense that there's so much more to see and understand. I mean, I've learned so much since 1969 when I bought this clapped-out cottage for virtually pennies, but there's so much more now, so much . . ."

"But after all that time can you still see all this?" asked Anne, pointing to the vast vista outside one of Tim's huge picture windows.

"Oh, yes! Oh, my God, yes! I mean, there are times when familiarity can drift in like a fog, but it soon lifts—burns off—and it's all fresh and full of meaning again. It's not all positive, though—the reality of this hard place. I mean if I wrote what I know—truly know—about Beara or even just this one tiny part, I don't think I'd be able to live here anymore. There are still feuds and vendettas here going back decades—centuries! Depression is a scourge too, and the occasional suicide. Deirdre Purcell caught some of that in her famous book *Falling for a Dancer*. They filmed that for TV just over the top in Eyeries village. If you go to Caskey's pub, you'll see photos of the production. And Deirdre's such a fine person. Lives some of the year just outside Eyeries on the Kenmare road. She's a great lover of Beara—told me once she thought it was 'one of the last places in Europe where everything is possible—and in a very relaxed and mellow way.' I like that idea. It reminded me of the old man who lived in that tiny stone cottage just down the cliff here. He had this magnificent view over Allihies and the whole bay and out to the Skelligs and he'd spend hours on an old chair by his door, sheltered from the winds. He'd just sit and look and sit and look . . . closest thing to a true Zen monk we had on this tiny corner of the peninsula, although he'd have no idea what a Zen monk was! I think his silence and utter peace inspired me—and it sort of crept into some of my work . . ."

"But not into your music, I don't think!" I said. My ears were still ringing from the traumatic barrage of Tim's music mix in the studio.

He laughed. "No, I guess not. That's another universe. It was a collective thing. Everyone wanted to be on the tracks, and there were over twenty-six musicians involved at one time or another. In fact I have a guy coming over tomorrow night—a wandering monk—he plays the Apache flute. Made from cedar—very unique sound. He's laying down a track for a new piece I'm pulling together—stop by if you want. Oh, and while I'm thinking, don't forget that just down the road toward Eyeries you've got Leanne O'Sullivan, one of Ireland's very best young poets. Beautiful girl. You both should meet her. And then there's John Kingerlee farther on. House near Deirdre Purcell's place. Has a reputation for . . . shall we say . . . bluntness, but he's a very talented guy. I'll call them if you like. Let them know you're floating about . . ."

AND SO WE FLOATED about—buoyed by the spirit of great active creativity on this amazing little hideaway peninsula.

And Leanne was, indeed, a beautiful young woman. We found her a few days later at her family home overlooking Eyeries and the

great mountain mass of Carraun-
tuohill rising high over Macgillycuddy's Reeks and the Ring
of Kerry. At that first meeting it was the colors I remember most of all. The
bright lemon of the
O'Sullivans' large house,
the vibrant intensity of
the green fields drop-
ping down the long,
slow slope of the land
from brittle ridge sum-
mits to the surfy reefs
and bays of the coast.
Then came the almost
red-golden richness of Leanne's long hair, her soft but
intensely luminous blue-green eyes,

Leanne O'Sullivan

sprays of ginger freckles on her face and arms, and her pale, almost
translucent skin. Dante Gabriel Rossetti or John Millais would have
whisked her off to their pre-Raphaelite studios in the mid-1800s
and immortalized her in one of their highly mannered, laconically
moody, meticulously detailed masterworks. (I merely managed a
scribbled sketch.)

Today, while only in her early twenties, Leanne has become ac-
customed to her celebrity as a gifted young Irish poet. "It began so
early on, I couldn't really get serious about it. I was only a child
when the English teacher brought this well-known Cork poet,
Thomas MacCarthy, to our class. He read some of his works and
then asked if anyone would like to share one of their own poems.
And there was this deathly hush. Everyone sitting there like stone
statues, hoping they wouldn't be picked out. So the teacher turned

to me, and I could have fainted. But I'd been writing quite a few poems around that time, so I got up—knees all quivery—and recited one. And it seemed to go down all right. The class gave me a bit of applause, and then Mr. MacCarthy was very sweet and asked, 'Did y' ever think about gettin' y'self published?' I sort of looked at him like he might be a little crazy and I said, 'I'm only twelve!'

"But I guess the idea stuck—the idea of getting some of the poems published. Much later I got involved with Sue Booth-Forbes at Anam Cara—her center for writers and artists just down the hill from here. She's a beautiful altruistic person—a real creative catalyst—always helping others. My mum—Maureen—works with her, organizing workshops and special events. I'll be doing a reading there in a couple of weeks—come if you both have time. Sue would love that. Anyway, I was only sixteen or so and working on new poetry and I got one published in *Poetry*. Then I started entering all these various regional and national competitions and winning quite a few awards. Part of me couldn't take it all in. Things were happening too fast, and I was still just this skinny teenager. In fact, I was very skinny—actualy anorexic. So—well . . . here . . . this is a copy of my first book published a couple of years ago when I was twenty-one. It sort of gives you an idea of where I was at that very strange time . . ."

Leanne handed us a copy of a small paperback with a very black cover and a photo of a girl half-naked in a hospital gown with her back to the camera sitting on a heavy wooden chair with a strange ghoulish mask propped up against one of its legs. The title of the book was *Waiting for My Clothes*. Anne and I read the summary and reviews on the back cover together.

Leanne O'Sullivan was born in 1983 in Cork and is currently studying English at the University College Cork. Her poems have been published or given many national awards when no one knew her age . . . Waiting for My Clothes *traces a deeply*

personal journey, from the traumas of eating disorders and
low self-esteem to the saving powers of love and positive
awareness. [Leanne summarized the essence of her poems:]
"I was writing down the reasons I should live for and then
became addicted to looking at things to find beauty in
them."

Billy Collins, the celebrated American poet laureate, was full of adulation: "Of course she's far too young to be so good! She dares to write about exactly what it is to be young. A teenage Virgil, she guides us down some of the more hellish corridors of adolescence with a voice that is strong and true."

And Selina Guinness, who celebrated Leanne in her 2004 *The New Irish Poets* book, wrote: "This voice seeks its own history in the most difficult terrains of the psyche; anorexia, sexuality, the loss of innocence; but resurfaces to discover afresh a world new and strange in images of startling perspicacity."

One reviewer suggested that Leanne "writes with a visceral frankness about what it is like to be young in Celtic Tiger Ireland. The unabashed eroticism of her new work reestablishes a continuity with an earlier phase in Irish literature stretching way back to the pre-Christian sages."

Another reviewer sought to place Leanne in a modern-day societal context: "The social revolution which has occurred in Ireland in the last two decades has made the youngest generation feel as if their immediate predecessors were raised on a different planet . . . Irish poets are today easily influenced by poets from elsewhere, in a way that is even more invigorating in this globalized world than it was in the '60s and '70s."

Anne handed the book back.

"No, no—it's yours," said Leanne. "Please, keep it. I'll sign it, if you like."

"Thank you so much," said Anne. Then she became very quiet as she scanned the first two poems in the book. Finally she smiled:

"Leanne—this is going to be a rich experience reading this book. You seem to love to . . . to 'zoom.' A line like—'I see myself in the well of her pupil'—that's a wonderful image!"

Leanne giggled. "Is that what that is—a 'zoom'?"

Anne laughed. "Well, that's what David calls it when he suddenly goes from a typical wide-angle view of things when he's writing to a tiny image or microcosm, just like a camera zoom lens."

"Great word." Leanne chuckled. "I'll use that!"

"So, what's the current project? Another book of poetry?" I asked.

"Oh, yeah! So many things. Beara is still a very important element in our family lives. This is my father's family home here. I'm always discovering new things. For example, just up a track there behind the house is a secret place—an unsigned secret sad place. It's a place of unsanctified ground where they used to bury babies who died at childbirth or before they were baptized. According to the Catholic church, they went to limbo, where they'd never ever see the face of God. Little tiny innocent babies buried, unrecorded in any book—only in the hearts of their families—with only small rocks for gravestones in a cold cruel field called a *Ceallunach*. It's such a horrible idea—although, thank the Lord, they've stopped it now. The new pope has declared that there's no such thing as limbo anymore! But Beara is full of secret places like that. The Hag used to be a secret too. You know, that rock just outside Eyeries? It's become a bit of a pilgrim site now and the folktales are getting all jumbled up. But I love anything with links to the ancient pagan power sources—fertility, harvests, mortality, and of course, immortality—the tales that once made the poetic oral traditions of Ireland so renowned in the Celtic world. Poets were regarded as seers, magicians, healers, second-sighters—sometimes the equal of bishops and even kings. We've got some of that in our own family—the ability of second sight. We don't talk about it much, though. You've got to be careful. The old superstitions and fears are still floating about. Some have been Christianized a bit and some of the old power's gone out of them—the things you read about in *The Book of Cailleach* and *Gearoid O'Crualaoich*. But I'm working on a set of new poems now about The Hag of Beara, and I find, even as I write, there are unfamiliar and powerful energies flowing through me.

"Yeah, I know it sounds a little odd, although—like I said, I do tend to be a sucker for superstitions and these ancient stories. But certainly I find the feminine in me is strengthened—made prouder—the more I seek out the power and the links between the tough women of Beara and the mighty female goddess inside The Hag. The church has tried to play all this down—but the older Beara women know how to weave a Celtic knot pattern of these stories. Especially about Bui—another name for The Hag, but also for The Cow—symbol of everlasting life."

Our conversation grew increasingly fascinating. Both Anne and I could sense a different mood in the house, in the room, where we sat overlooking Kenmare Bay. And then Leanne began, without any fanfare, to read some of her new and soon-to-be-published Hag poems in a quiet voice full of restrained energy and fire. We just sat silently. Leanne had told us that her mother had problems listening to these poems—they made her blither (weep). One of them seemed to be having that same impact on Anne. But we still sat there and sensed The Hag almost as a tangible presence around us.

It's only an old and not very big chunk of rock on an empty hillside, my skeptical, pragmatic self declared.

No, no. It's the ultimate soul of Irish folklore—the indomitable feminine, the very essence of fertility, the underlying strength of the land and of the soil, my ancient Celtic self insisted. *And this young woman, this walking-talking pre-Raphaelite portrait of beauty and insight, will be the one to reconnect all these ancient forces with modern-day mores and perceptions.*

We left Leanne, wishing her that traditional Irish good

night—*oíche mhaith duit*—to which she laughingly gave the traditional response *gurab amhlaidh duit*. Anne thanked her again, and I noticed she was clutching her book very tightly against her chest like a totem.

JOHN KINGERLEE LIVED IN a cottage of interlocking rooms and spaces. It was located at the side of the road to Kenmare—almost in the road—but buffered by a tall thick hedge that blocked the fine vista across Kenmare Bay. The place was artistically chaotic—books everywhere, scattered canvases, newspapers, things piled up in corners. And John was a different kind of individual altogether from any other artist I met on the peninsula—zanily irascible, opinionated, bloody-minded, rude, even a little crude, but gloriously honest and open.

Our meeting began with an initial request. "Hi—take your shoes off, please," and I found myself looking at a small wiry individual, someone who seemed like he could throw a pretty mean punch and you'd never see it coming. His face was long and wolfish. Within seconds of our exchange of hellos I sensed a distinct aura of pent-up fury in the man—or at least a hefty dose of frustration—that might explode like a land mine if an unsuspecting stranger happened to step in the wrong place. His eyes were like little dark hard pebbles that darkened even more when he flung out one particular remark at me—fast as a throwing knife—after I thought we were having a pretty amenable let's-get-to-know-one-another kind of chitchat.

"Quite frankly, David—I don't think I agree with a single thing you've said so far . . ."

"Oh—sorry about that," was about the only inane response I could come with at that particular moment.

". . . although I certainly do envy you your certainty . . ."

I couldn't suppress a chuckle. Most people, friends included, tend to accuse me of constant devil's advocacy. Always testing out new ideas and trying to see things from different points of view. This accusation of certainty and implied dogmatism was altogether new to me. I have difficulty making up my mind finally about anything. Playing with options is invariably far more intriguing—and fun.

"I'm gonna take that as a kind of backhanded compliment and . . ."

"You can take it any way you bloody—"

"Yes, yes—I'm sure. So that's what I'll do as you tell me the story of your life. In a nutshell. So to speak."

"In a nutshell?"

"Or anything else that's small, compact . . . and with edges!"

"With edges?!"

"Yeah—edges."

Kingerlee looked at me again with those oh-so-dark, almost feral eyes. He was either about to explode—or laugh. Thankfully, he laughed. "In a nutshell. Okay. Here we go. Born Birmingham, England. Spent time in London. Dad a manager of some kind of poker club. Started painting at three (me, not my dad). My Auntie Anna looked after me—her boyfriend was Douglas Fairbanks Jr. Went to a very Catholic boarding school. Did odd writing and poetry projects and learned to paint in the furnished bedsit where I lived. The place drove me nuts, so I painted like mad and began to find patrons and buyers. Christy Moore, the famous Irish folksinger, bought a lot of my stuff in those days and that helped. Got deeply into Jung. In the 1960s lived in Ibiza and Cornwall and then dumped all that eventually and lived in Morocco, Fez, and Tangiers—and became Sufi. Changed my life completely, inside out and upside down. Now I live here part of the year since 1982. My main patron is a fine guy—Larry Powell—who buys most of my work. He helped me publish a very fancy retrospective book—big coffee-table format—on my art."

"And how would you describe your art?" I'd seen an odd mix of his pieces since my arrival. Some were scattered across a table between piles of art books. Some were framed on the walls. Others were in various stages of completion—strange collages of images, haunted multilayered portraits thick with still-moist paint . . . These did not appear to be happy works. Apparently I was right.

"My portraits are layered alienations . . . I particularly watch the faces of politicians and so-called world leaders. Maybe that's where some of my portraits get their sense of cynical presence from. One of my favorite works is a canvas that got partly chewed up by a cow. She gave it real texture and a sort of unique 3-D tactile energy!

Farm near Eyeries

I don't know why these portraits are popular—maybe it's that they're kind of iconic. But also very human. Some have taken over a couple of years to complete—a slow accumulation, layer upon layer of paint, but each one quick and spontaneous. And most are not people I know—except the self-portraits. Even Christy Moore said he recognized me from those portraits. But then I'm into the 'squares' paintings—kind of restrained classical grids and little tiny abstracts. There's a whole mix of stuff—some are very extrovert and flamboyant."

I'd done some homework on Kingerlee before my visit. Anne is a whiz with the Internet, and the Internet is a whiz with instant information. So all I have to do is say something along the lines of "Darling, I wonder if you could just tap out a nice fat ream of stuff on . . ." and she'll smile her bewitching kind of smile and the stuff would pour out in nanoseconds. Kingerlee has obviously garnered a host of admirers around him and his works. One critic compared him (favorably) with Mark Rothko; another claimed his thick, stratified landscapes, with sometimes up to a hundred overlayers of paint, as "a richness beyond compare." Art critic John Benington gushed that "he re-creates spaces that we could enter mentally and visually in a way that seems to have no parallel in contemporary art . . . His work literally frizzles with energy as if seen through the eyes of a child . . . creating a unique cosmic world."

One writer suggested that Ezra Pound, Paul Klee, Jean Dubuffet, and Jean-Michel Basquiat were key influences on his work and that "anyone privileged enough to watch him paint is struck by an analogy with gardening—He tends the grounds of his pictures with the same devotion as a gardener." Apparently his key implements are palette knives (often one in each hand) and large decorator painting brushes.

Unfortunately I was not "privileged enough" to see the man in action, but there were other things I was curious about—most notably what I tend to label as "The Vivaldi" approach to creativity, where similar themes and arrangements recur again and again in a string of different works.

"Did Sufism lead to any changes in your art?" Ever since John had mentioned his sudden conversion, I'd sensed he'd wanted to tell me more.

"Oh boy, yes—although it's hard to be specific. In fact, it's difficult, actually, to recall what I was like before I became Sufi. But I'm very much involved in their world—their explanation of our mutual integration in a web, a vast web of connections. If I suffer from anything now, it's me as a Muslim in a non-Muslim world. I'm particularly skeptical, as you may have gathered, of paternal institutions like the World Bank, the IMF, and the mindless damage they do and the corruption and horror stories they generate. I'm also very skeptical of 'New Age Business' in general. It can be so insular and greedy. It needs to be 'cleansed.' [Ironically his words were highly predictive of the financial calamities that arose round the world a year or so later!] Proponents of it should celebrate the month of Ramadan instead—you lose some of that glib civilized veneer, and by your daily fasting, you learn—you're reminded—what it's like to be poor every day of the year. When you remove the prestige of food and drink, you become much more humble and vulnerable. You also begin to recognize that *you* don't really exist, and neither do I. It's a long explanation . . . but, well, on the Night of Power toward the end of Ramadan—for those who are open to it—your identity becomes like a wave of light, and you hardly exist at all. It's as though the heavens open and Allah sends down his messengers and his knowledge."

It would be impossible to recollect all the meanderings and abrupt direction-shifts of our long and wide-ranging conversation. Fortunately, however, my loyal little tape recorder whirled and whirred away in my pocket, and I picked up a remarkable range of Kingerlee-isms over the course of our first two-hour meeting. I include a random selection:

- "I'm seventy and I've been vagabonding most of my life, but on Beara I found myself in the footsteps of the Celtic revival artists and everything changed."
- "I want fewer and fewer things and an ever-enlarging life."
- "I'm really only interested in people who are trying to promote tolerance, empathy and understanding."
- "The World Bank and the IMF and a lot of the 'do-good' organizations are ironically great stiflers of compassion. They kill millions of people a year with their financial structures and terrible burdens of usury. I've lost a lot of friends arguing about all this." [His argument reminded me of Ezra Pound's outrages at the scourges of bankers and "international finance."]
- "The more 'good' things you do, the more 'bad' things you end up creating. You know, that old chestnut 'No good deed ever goes unpunished'! Or that other one: 'Every action creates an equal and opposite reaction.'"
- "Poor old USA. It's damned if it does and damned if it doesn't. The world always turns to the USA in any crisis—and then sits back and sneers and criticizes while the USA tries to respond—which it normally does pretty badly."
- "Amateur 'artists' wait for inspiration. The rest of us rise up every morning, splash our bodies, and get down to hard work."
- "Picasso was a great rediscoverer. Sometimes I think I'd like to 'reinvent myself every day,' like he suggested all artists should do. But I also like boundaries. Limitlessness can lead to insanity. But so can success! Picasso also said 'Of all the things God sends you—poverty, injustice, hunger, lack of recognition—fame is the hardest to deal with'!"
- "The best joy of life is spontaneity—to be a slave to the second!"
- "Some of us can go back mentally—believe it or not—to their

very first feast on the rich milk from their mother's breast . . .
You get an amazing sense of where we all come from when
that happens."

As with Tim and Leanne, I left John Kingerlee much later than I
intended. It had been a remarkable few hours. At times I felt we had
skirted the edges of malicious minefields and the possibility of actual physical confrontation over economic and social issues. But
then there were moments of great warmth, and the whole experience ended almost blissfully. It reminded me of a paraphrase quote
of Kurt Vonnegut's—"There's only one rule I know of here on
earth—Goddamn it, we've just got to be kind to one another."

John was even gracious about one of my earlier books—*Seasons
on Harris*. I brought a copy to show him what I hoped to produce on
Beara. He studied the book and its illustrations very intently, and I
was preparing myself for another of his verbal assaults. But instead
he looked at me, smiled a truly genuine smile, and said, "David,
I'm envious. I couldn't do what you've done here. The artwork is particularly beautiful."

That, I thought, deserved a handshake and a hug and I reached
out to grab him. He suddenly looked startled—almost afraid. Then
he explained. "So sorry—it's Ramadan. I can't . . .'

"Oh," I said. "I'm sorry too. I didn't know."

"Don't worry, even my wife, Mo, can't touch me during Ramadan. But I owe you one when it's over next week."

I haven't had that hug . . . yet.

17

The Enumerator Cometh

.

IT WAS A BALMY SUMMER EVENING. Anne and I were enjoying our 6 P.M. glasses of wine at the patio table overlooking the bay, and all seemed at peace with the world until . . .

"Hello? Hello?" (with a very heavy emphasis on the *H*s.) "Can I . . . in?"

We turned. A young lady with a long cascade of black hair framing her rather gaunt face stood at our garden gate and seemed reluctant to open it. Across her shoulders was a large canvas bag—something like a mailman might carry. But the mailman had already been. Hours ago.

"Sure, come on in," Anne said, beaming her usual welcoming smile.

"Ah, zank you, zank you." The young lady seemed a little nervous. I stood up and offered my seat, but she seemed to prefer standing as she reached deep into her overlarge bag.

"I am your enum . . . enumer . . . enum . . ." She was obviously having problems explaining who she was, but as whatever word she tried to pronounce was unfamiliar to us, we couldn't do much more than smile encouragingly and wait. Eventually she found the correct sequence of syllables.

"Enum-er-ator. Enumerator . . . yes . . . I am your enumerator. I am sorry. I am not from Ireland. I am from the Poland," she finally explained and stood waiting for our reaction. Which—beyond a questioning expression—was not forthcoming. We had no idea what an enumerator said or did, so we waited for her to continue. We were, however, familiar with Poland and wondered if that might ultimately be a fruitful line of chat.

"You know about big national census?" she asked hopefully.

"Census?" I said. "No, we know nothing about any census."

"But it has been on the TV . . . on the radio . . . for many weeks. All about it . . . big census. For all country . . ."

We looked at each other and shrugged.

"No, never heard of it," I said. "But we haven't been here very long. We don't live here. We're just visiting . . . we're not Irish . . ."

"That is not matter," said the Polish lady with emphasis. Now she sounded more certain of herself and her ability to deal with the minutiae of bureaucratic legalities. Her voice took on a more strident tone. "No, it is not matter at all. This form is for you. Please take."

"But we don't live here—we're British, and we live in America. We're just here for a few weeks . . ."

"Pliss," the lady said. "Is law. Everybody must fill form. Everyone in Ireland . . ."

I thought I'd try one more time. "I'm sorry, but we are not Irish, we're renting this place, so we shouldn't be filling out any census forms. Otherwise your numbers will include hundreds, maybe thousands, of foreign tourists and travelers. It would be a very strange census!"

But our lady enumerator would have none of this. She had a job to do and seemed to relish her little arena of newfound authority.

"No!" she said again with a definite degree of determination. "It is law that if you do not fill in you will be punish. Very much . . ."

"Punished?" I asked.

"With a fine of twenty-five thousand euro and maybe—imprisonment. It is law!"

I was slowly moving toward the region of blood-pressure territory. "I've never heard of anything so bloody stupid in . . ."

Anne could see my patience was running out in this increasing
cacophony of miscommunication, so she jumped in with her "let's
all calm down" demeanor, which she invariably demonstrates to
great effect wherever we go and whenever I'm approaching the bal-
listic "rockets-away" stage.

So I left Anne to accept the form on our behalf and make some
complimentary comments about its extensive content. And a few
less complimentary suggestions, such as:

"This is a rather odd question here, number eleven. How many
children have you given birth to . . . ?"

"Yes, I see it," said the enumerator. "There is problem?"

"Because then it says underneath 'This question is for women
only.' "

Our enumerator remained unamused.

"And there are some interesting choices for 'ethnic or cultural
background,' " said Anne. "For example, what is an 'Irish traveler'—is
that like the old tinker gypsies? Romanies? Or 'Black Irish'—that
sounds like a term Queen Victoria might have used . . ."

Again, no reaction. Just a rather grim-faced look from our Polish
lady, who we felt must really be missing the good old days of Polish
communism, when a mere nod from a loyal informer could have
sent the two of us into Warsaw's deepest dungeons.

It was my turn. I scanned the form. "Here's an interesting
question—'Can you speak Irish—answer if age three or over.' First,
what does 'speak Irish' mean? I imagine every Irishman has some
smattering of Gaelic in his vocabulary. But the age-three thing is
curious. I'd have thought that anyone younger than three who was
speaking fluent Irish would be of far more interest than the older
ones. Just think—you'd be able to identify all your child prodigies in
a flash . . ."

It was hopeless. The enumerator was determined not to be

amused or distracted from her mission. Even when I pointed out that the whole form was legally invalid, as it guaranteed total privacy and anonymity and yet required names, addresses, phone numbers, and signatures.

"Okay," said Anne. "Why don't you leave the forms with us and we'll have a look at them."

Not good enough. Our enumerator was now determined to assert her authority. "I am come back here early Monday. Please have census forms ready for me . . ."

"We'll be out on Monday," I said.

"Well, please leave under mat outside. If not here, then it will be penalty. Twenty-five thousand euro."

"Good-bye," I said.

"I not making laws . . . I just doing job."

I was about to remind her that such a remark has often been used throughout history (and particularly in Poland!) to justify the most heinous of crimes when one of my other selves—the far more gentle and empathetic self—suddenly popped out and he decided to take another approach.

"Listen"—big sigh of surrender here—"you look like you've been going all day and it can't be an easy job. How about a cup of tea?" (Ah—the British solution to all adversities.) "Why don't you sit down and take a break for a while . . ."

The enumerator looked as surprised as I was by this unexpected shift of mood, but she remained suspicious. "I sorry—I don't have time . . ."

"Just five minutes . . . you'll feel a lot better . . ."

More hesitancy. And then, like the shaft of sudden sunshine through gloomy clouds, she smiled a truly warm smile. "Thank you. This is so very kind . . ."

And so we all sat around the patio table together and talked about Poland. Anne had spent an extensive period in that country teaching alongside her Polish colleagues and preparing graduate students to provide services to visually impaired adults. She'd enjoyed her time spent in Warsaw, so the two of them compared notes on their favorite haunts and restaurants in the city. It was obvious our enumerator missed her family in Poland. But when she left she was still smiling. And we did complete the census form, and we did leave it under the mat on Monday.

Sometimes it's better just to go along with a wink, a nod, and a smile.

18

Luka Bloom
(and Christy Moore)

∎
∎
∎

I LIKED LUKA BLOOM EVEN BEFORE I met him. And not just because his real name is Barry Moore and he's the younger brother of Christy Moore, one of Ireland's best loved and most notorious folksingers. And not just because I once missed by a week one of his folk club performances in Yorkshire, England. Luka appeared with Christy when he was barely fourteen and I, at around twenty or so, was still occasionally performing in folk clubs with my sister Lynne (she with the Joan Baez–like voice—at least in my opinion). And not just because a few years ago he'd toured the States playing with one of my favorite female country groups, the Dixie Chicks. And not just because he was coming to Beara specifically to perform a benefit concert for the emerging spiritual care hospice at the Dzogchen Center and we'd managed to finagle a couple of grab-'em-fast tickets from the owner of the whole foods store in Castletownbere.

I think one of the primary reasons for my liking this man, whom I'd never met before, was the occasional snippet of his songs on the local radio—some from his *Before Sleep Comes* album, which he describes as "nine soft songs for insomniacs," and others from his latest and strangely powerful *Innocence* album. The DJ had asked him in an interview about the odd mix of themes, from gentle songs of love and forgiveness to strident antiwar and antidiscrimination ballads to roaring chorus songs of immigration and emigration. Luka chuckled and answered very softly that they all came from his own grab bag of personal experiences and then added: "See, life's really an endless stream of challenges, and for this singer at least, the most important ingredient to hang on to is innocence and our wonder at the whole world."

Immediately I heard that I was back in the heady 1960s, immersed in that enticing world of folk music, during which time I even made a record with my sister (no—it was never a best seller, in fact it was never released). And although I've never used that word *innocence* before to describe the era, I knew Luka had captured its essence perfectly. We were indeed "innocent." Even the big names in the British and American folk field—Martin Carthy, Ewen MacColl, Peggy Seeger, Pete Seeger, and all the Irish groups too, most of whom had ample opportunity to pursue lives of hedonistic rock star excess (yes, even folksingers had "groupies")—were mostly modest, soft-spoken, even self-effacing individuals who truly believed in their troubadour tales of courageous battles and deep romance and chivalrously noble behavior.

There were notable exceptions, of course, and occasional over-indulgences of free-flowing beer and other more exotic stimulants, but for the most part we were a good-natured, earnest, well-intentioned lot. Which I guess could explain moments of outrage when the order of things in our little world was disturbed—when, for example, Scottish-born Donovan tried to copycat Bob Dylan; when there were rumors that not all of Alan Lomax's "authentic" Appalachian folk songs were truly authentic; when there was confusion over how really pro-Communist Pete Seeger was—and oh! of course, the tirade of disgust when Bob Dylan shifted from solo acoustic guitar and harmonica to full-amp-blasting, Fender Stratocaster–screeching, drum-thumping rock band renditions of "Maggie's Farm," "Mr. Tambourine Man," and "How Many Roads." How our indignation boiled over at such a betrayal!

Similar indignation greeted Christy Moore when he left Ireland's

most popular traditional folk group, Planxty, which combined singing with Irish dance music on Liam Og O'Floinn's uilleann pipes
backed by acoustic guitar and bazouki, to form Moving Hearts in
1981. People still remember the shock they had when they first heard
this new hybrid folk-jazz-rock fusion featuring saxophones, solid
guitar and bass, synthesizer keyboard, and other exotic electronics.
And even though their first album was a top-all-the-charts hit in
Ireland and many of their songs had strident antiestablishment messages so beloved by the younger liberal-minded generation, Christy
decided it was all getting far too political and propaganda-doctrinaire.
So he returned once again to his folk roots and solo career, and until
recent illnesses limited his performances, he played on—fiery and
focused as ever for almost twenty more years.

"When I sing on a stage to an audience, I go into a place which is
very special," he said recently. "I am locked into a white space that
is seldom penetrated. Nothing is quite like it and I am thankful for
the key to whatever it is."

Christy had that knack—that key—for getting to the heart of the
matter, a wide range of matters. You feel—in fact, if you've read his
song-laced autobiography, *One Voice—My Life in Song*, you'll know
how his own hard experiences in life (many self-inflicted, this man
was never a saint) have shaped his strident views. For example,
Christy's take on materialism: "There's a great emptiness in those
lives dedicated to the acquisition of wealth and power."

On the church:

> The concept of sin and sinning was daily thrust into my face;
> everlasting hell and limbo, purgatory, a mere end of the
> world away. But none of these poor sisters, brothers or fathers
> ever showed us the Love of God—all they drummed into us
> was fear and loathing and burning and suffering . . . When
> my vision of the Church crumbled into dust, I was left
> godless, and for many years I walked the dark, cold path of
> disbelief.

On political protest:

> *In 1977 I became involved with Revolutionary Struggle and*
> *a small group of very active and political people . . . I*
> *campaigned and did benefit gigs in many towns . . . It was*
> *my first time to become directly involved in a political*
> *campaign . . . It opened my eyes to the potential of people*
> *power and what can be done when we come together to effect*
> *change.*

And finally comes a tribute to his younger brother—Barry Moore, aka Luka Bloom:

> *We worked together on a number of recordings both his and*
> *mine. Occasionally we still play together on stage and when*
> *it happens it's always spontaneous and I always feel really*
> *good doing it.*

"Well—I guess it's a case of define 'very successfully,'" said Luka Bloom with a deep chuckle. Unlike his brother's burly bulldoglike appearance, Luka has a long, sensitive face, large open eyes, and just the hint of a perpetual grin around his mouth.

We'd met by pure happenstance in the kitchen of the center. I'd left it a bit late to sneak out to the bathroom before the opening act, and when I came back, a young female folksinger with a Judy Collins–style voice and maybe just a touch of Sheryl Crow had begun, and I was asked to slip in the back way through the kitchen when her song was complete and the applause started.

I nodded and smiled, remembering the days when Lynne and I sang together and there was nothing more off-putting in the middle of a song than when people started talking or moving around for drinks or bathroom trips. We liked our audiences serious and sensitive. And of course, here at the center, seriousness and sensitivity were the orders of the day. In everything.

So I crept quietly into the kitchen and went to stand by the door to the concert room, which was actually the meditation room with its spectacular cliff and ocean vistas we'd enjoyed so many times before. The applause seemed a long time coming. And then I heard this most discordant sound echoing out from the shadows of the kitchen back by the huge stove. I turned and saw someone apparently trying to tune a guitar.

"Oh, hi," I said. "You playing tonight?"

A faint chuckle was followed by: "Well—I hope so. Otherwise I've come an awful long way for nothing . . ."

"Ah—so you're with Luka Bloom?" Sometimes I can be a little slow on the uptake.

Another soft chuckle. "Well—not exactly." More strange tuning sounds that made me wonder if this guy could even play a guitar. "I *am* Luka Bloom."

"Oh . . . I, ah . . . er . . . Sorry. I didn't recognize you. Probably because I don't even know what you look like!"

"Oh, I'm nothing much special really in the looks department . . ."

"Well . . . ," I said, wondering if I was about to make another faux pas, "good to meet you. Big fan of your brother."

"Yeah—so are most people over here . . ."

"Not that . . . I mean . . . actually, I've only heard a few . . . But

Luka Bloom

by the look of the crowd in there, you've got a heck of a following too . . ."

Finally he stepped out of the shadows and I was able to see him, stop rambling on, and shake his hand. And after that, our conversation flowed a little less erratically. It was all about Christy at first, of course, and the soft-spoken Luka was remarkably open and honest.

"M'brother's hard to quantify because well—he's not . . . when you meet him he doesn't really appear to be very . . . what you might call, charismatic. He's very ordinary, y'see—very quiet and he really likes to present himself to people in that way . . . One-on-one he can be quite shy . . . But once he gets on the stage, he carries the show like a real trouper . . . although there are many shows he carried that he doesn't ever remember at all. In fact, he often had to be hoisted onstage full of God knows what—booze, drugs—and then it was magic. He'd transform in a flash, becoming a different person— the real Christy—and hold his audience—galvanize them—for two, sometimes three hours solid, and then when he came off, he'd be just the way he was when he was carried on! He's an amazing man. Truly amazing. He couldn't—wouldn't—allow himself to be confined. I re-member once an interviewer said to him: 'You seem to have so many different personas.' And Christy was right back at him: 'Well—I'd feel imprisoned, locked up, if I had to live with only one of them!'"

The kitchen door was suddenly flung back and someone (very se-rious and respectful) leaned in: "Ah . . . Mr. Bloom . . . the er, stage is yours whenever you're ready . . . sir . . ."

Luka seemed particularly amused by the "sir" bit, nodded, and kept on fiddling with his guitar tuning. It all sounded very discor-dant to me.

"You doing some special kind of open tuning or what?" I asked.

"Well—I guess you could call it that. It's something I've worked up over the years . . ."

He continued twiddling and then, having pronounced himself happy with what still sounded to me like some kind of Arabic quarter-tone disharmonic, shook my hand again, said, "Let's talk some more after the show," and walked out of the kitchen and down the aisle to the stage.

The applause was sudden, deafening, and long. This was obviously a well-informed audience packed into every corner and crevice of the meditation room. They were obviously proud to have such a highly respected celebrity-singer in their midst. He acknowledged his reception with a broad, happy smile and then, with little in the way of introduction, launched himself into a spectacular two-hour performance that encompassed just about every mood and subject one could imagine in contemporary folk songs, most of which he'd written himself.

The audience relished every moment and demanded encore after encore. And as if to celebrate the power of his performance, the sun slowly began to sink behind the huge floor-to-ceiling windows of the room and gave us one of the most spectacularly colorful eventides Anne and I had witnessed so far on Beara. The audience was bathed in a soft scarlet glow, and Luka sang his final song silhouetted against a golden sheen of light that seemed to make his whole body vibrate with the intensity of a mystical aura. And even after he'd finally left the stage and vanished back into the kitchen, his presence and the resonating intensity of his songs remained with us. And there was none of that mad scampering for the exits that usually characterizes the end of a concert. Instead, people seemed to be reluctant to leave. Some were looking around dreamily, as if waking from an enticing half sleep; others reached out to talk to friends quietly in nearby seats. Everywhere were smiles and hugs and expressions of deep satisfaction. It was as if we'd all experienced a mass meditation together and we didn't really want it to end.

I intended to join Luka back in the kitchen and congratulate him, but I too was having problems leaving my seat. Anne reached out and squeezed my hand and whispered—as she had done before and would do many times again on this amazing peninsula—"Magic! Absolute magic . . .'

19

At Anam Cara

:
:

AND HERE COMES MAGIC AGAIN—A place of magic cocooned in one
of the most beautiful spots on the Kerry side of Beara.

Alongside the road to Eyeries from Allihies, atop a rise above
pastures and bosky hedgerows overlooking Coulagh Bay, sits what
looks at first like a small neat bungalow. The grounds, sprawling
languorously behind high bushes, are meticulously manicured. Velvety lawns are edged with profusions of flowers. There's a fountain
and a duck pond, and it all seems a little decadently suburban. But
then if you wander as I did on my first visit to the rear of the house,
you'll find the land suddenly tumbling away down steep rocky clefts
crammed with Tolkienesque tangles of hawthorn and stunted,
twisted trees. Cascades and waterfalls have cut deep into the strata.
Narrow paths weave their way through a permanent twilight of
shadowy niches pierced by sudden laser-thin sun rays. The water
chitters and chuckles, invisible birds chirp and twitter, and there are
odd rustlings in the undergrowth. If you follow the path far enough
you'll end up on one of the bay beaches.

The abrupt contrast between the neat roadside garden at the front
of the house, and the primeval spirit of the tumbled land behind, is
of course absolutely intentional.

In fact everything is intentional here at Anam Cara, a place recognized as one of the finest retreats for artists, writers, and poets in

the whole of Ireland. And it has been a focal point of Beara's creative energies since 1998, when it was founded by one of the most altruistic and energetic "catalysts of change" on the peninsula. Her name is Susan Booth-Forbes and, following an extensive career as writer, editor, and communication director in Boston and "a significant change in marital status" (a divorce), she decided to follow her longtime dream to move to Ireland and create an environment where artists and writers could come together and "celebrate their muses." And Sue is one of those lucky individuals who not only listens and responds to dream-directed urges but also knows how to turn them into inspiring realities.

Anam Cara translates from Gaelic as "Soul Friend," and she dedicated her new "base" to John O'Donoghue, whose book on Celtic wisdom of the same name had long offered nurturing visions to Sue.

In her invitational Web site, she offers "an intimate residential retreat providing time, space, and creature comforts to support your focusing on your own projects and doing your best creative work." Susan goes on to describe herself as "part friend, part editor, part travel guide, and part mid-wife in stimulating creative rebirths and helping participants to slow down enough inside to maximize their individual capabilities." From what we'd heard locally, she'd helped many writers rediscover their muses and cease their languishing in unpublished purgatory.

When I first visited she greeted me with such mercurial warmth that I wondered if we'd known each other as friends in some past incarnation. And, as if to immediately confirm that odd sensation, she said, "You look familiar. I feel I've met you somewhere before." I mumbled some inane reply about "wishing we had" as I was being led on a guided interior tour of the retreat.

What seemed a modest bungalow-styled structure from the road morphed into an intriguing array of spaces. Some were small and intimate niches ideal for sharing the challenges and joys of the creative process. Others included a delightful sunroom complete with grape arbor, a charming dining area and kitchen for her ten or so "guests," a series of large central spaces that, on her popular "community evenings," can host up to a hundred or more visitors for lectures, poetry readings (Leanne O'Sullivan, one of our favorite "creators" on Beara, had a star billing here in 2006), artist shows, and workshops—and even the occasional hullabaloo of a music, singing, and dancing *hooley*.

In addition to ensuring "lots of quiet creative time" for her guests, Sue also organizes an array of writing workshops and art sessions, field trips to nearby Eyeries and other key places around Beara, Celtic-flavored events, and yoga periods. "And to cap it all—I do fab-

ulous breakfasts of omelets and homemade soca bread as top attractions!"

As she gave examples of literary and artistic "breakthrough moments" for which Anam Cara is apparently renowned, she projected a fascinating dual persona of enthusiasm wrapped in a cooler, gimlet-eyed, guru-tinged organizer-self. One of her recent "creative coups" was a workshop conducted by the Irish-American poet Billy Collins, once the poet laureate of the USA. Admirers of his power-packed works have described them as "full of quirky bends and heart-stopping imagery" and "like a plate of fat pancakes—lots of good stuff that will stick to your ribs for a long time."

Eyeries Village

Apparently the workshop was a roaring success, with Billy in fine fettle offering "no mollycoddling," criticizing the overuse of the thesaurus in certain works in progress, and "treating us like real poets," according to one participant, who also described him as "a Peter Pan high on Ireland—and a fantastic dancer, inside the house, outside and, on one occasion, in the duck pond!"

"Listen," said Sue as we sat sipping afternoon tea in the sunroom. "Maybe you'd like to join us next week. We're having a couple of Beara artists bring their works in and give us a talk. They're both well known here and on show at local galleries on the peninsula. It should be fun."

"Most of the artists I know seem to hate describing their work habits and paintings," I suggested, "except in the most esoteric of terms, which is usually not much fun at all!"

"Trust me. You'll love these two . . ."

And so I came and I did.

JOHN BRENNAN WAS A bald, bright-eyed, young-looking man who seemed to relish the uncertainty of the "creative process." A half-hour PowerPoint presentation of his artworks seemed to enthrall the hundred or so locals in the audience. He stirred up chuckles and giggles with his references to "hours spent just looking at a painting and wondering where to go next" and "I always try to keep a number of canvases going simultaneously so I don't get bored." He emphasized that he was talking about paintings, not people, although he admitted he had a "low threshold for tolerance of sameness." And yet—superficially at least—there seemed to be a great deal of "sameness" about his colored boxes paintings. He suggested his variations were subtle and "not always immediately apparent" and the audience seemed to agree. However, the notes he used to describe his explorations of his abstract genre helped clarify the process:

What and how to paint? Imagery. Inventing a vocabulary for
a wordless world. The process of designing and then selecting
the most appropriate image to convey a given word, an
adjective . . . There are no words, no representational imagery
to guide us toward a possible meaning . . . Do these shapes
have a certain resonance for us and does this affect how we
react . . . Would an irregular shape be more potent and also
open to wider interpretation . . . Is it really possible to
communicate "a specific feeling" or "an experience" by such
simple or abstract means . . . Unlike a writer, I do not have
a plot or outline to begin, only a starting point . . . Thus
begins a journey of discovery, elimination, and of decision-
making . . . My shapes are my characters . . . I cajole and
mold them and the shapes evolve in color and form . . . I'm
always altering the direction the painting could take and
maybe taking the road less traveled . . . until I am left in no
doubt that the shapes I select work collectively within the
confines of the canvas . . . I'm always working towards the
unknown.

What could have been a load of effetist mumbo jumbo and aes-
thetic gobbledygook became instead a courageous revelation of one
artist's tenuous search for meaning and significance in totally abstract terms using nothing but color, simple random shapes, and the
critical spaces in between. Most artists prefer not to (or maybe just
can't) explain their own creative mazes. Maybe, in many instances,
there's not that much to explain anyway. In a lot of contemporary
art, one senses an arrogant dismissive "you either get it or you don't"
or "whatever it means to you is what it means" attitude on the part
of so-called artists. But John, who had a permanent exhibition of his
work at the Mill Cove Gallery just east of Castletownbere, was open,
honest, and obviously beguiled by the vagaries and vastness of the
abstract "creative process."

Admittedly, his audience seemed more beguiled as he showed
how sometimes his abstracts morphed almost unintentionally into

semirepresentational works, most notably dramatic seascapes of churning, writhing waves with maybe just a hint of land at the far edges of the canvas.

"You can tell how living here on Beara can create this kind of response," he said, smiling. "You're surrounded by the ocean. Its sound, its fury, its ever-changing moods and its dominant power . . . They all get inside and eventually emerge in my paintings, sometimes when I least expect it . . . In my sea paintings I'm trying to combine a certain balance of realism and abstraction. I'm also looking for a sense of timelessness in the colors and forms. I don't want it to be a particular time of day. I want it to be . . . eternal . . . transcendent beyond just sea paintings into something else . . . something more enduring . . . intriguing . . . fascinating."

And it was indeed fascinating to share John's fascination. He seemed, like many fine artists, to be blending the dual capacities of standing deeply within his own mind and artistry and yet far outside the source of the stimulation—seeing it objectively almost as the Creator Him/Herself might see it. And trying to express, in James Joyce's words, "the particular in the universal" (and vice versa).

Sculpture at Mill Cove Gallery

The second artist of the evening, Jeannie Richardson, was an intriguing study in contrasts. She was frail, shy, and soft-spoken and seemed to have great difficulty with the PowerPoint system. For a moment she looked so flummoxed and uncomfortable that I thought she'd hastily apologize and flee from the stage. But she didn't. And the audience applauded her spontaneously just for staying put. And I for one was delighted that she had, because her life and art were so beguilingly different from John Brennan's. She made no references to "juxtaposed abstracts," "nonrepresentational imagery," "spatial illusions," and "unresolved states." Instead she merely showed a sequence of her highly realistic work of animals, plants, and vegetables, and Vermeer-like still-life watercolors. And while it looked as if she might be tantalizingly close at times to producing Hallmark-type illustrations, she always seemed to manipulate composition, color, and moods of great calm in such a subtle way that you sensed layerings of perceptions and meanings in even the simplest of her subjects.

Someone in the audience tried to express that feeling, but while Jeannie was obviously moved, she dismissed the remarks with a blush and an "oh no . . . I just paint what I put in front of me."

It would indeed be refreshing to hear such modesty from "artists" with far less talent and clarity of vision. But I guess "the less talent you possess, the more you've got to hawk the runty-bit of it around," as a cynical editor-friend of mine once remarked when yet one more hacked-out, Harlequin-type horror-romance, as he called them, hit the top of the fiction best-seller lists in the *New York Times*.

And Sue Booth-Forbes knows plenty about best-seller lists from her experiences "in another life," with writing, writers, editing, and publishers. We hope her intimate "Soul Friend" nexus here on the peninsula continues to nurture needy creative spirits and forces for years to come. In many ways this is a key to Beara's future and its power as a muse-releasing, spirit-nurturing, soul-healing focal point. It's either that or the dreaded Ring of Kerry–type road-widening threats and bumper-to-bumper tour buses.

And for most who live here, from long-lineage families to blissful blow-ins, that's not even an option.

20
Listening and Learning

:::

THE BAR HAD A FIREPLACE—A mean bundle of misshapen fieldstone rocks seemingly dumped in the corner of the room. But at least it had a fire in it, which was something of a welcome sight on that unusually chilly and blustery market/day evening in Bantry. Not much of a fire, though—it crackled and hissed and nudged out reluctant curlicues of smoke and halfhearted insipid-colored flames. The ones you expect to vanish any moment and be replaced by big black sighs of soot. Not that I cared really what they did. I'd come in with a "by your leave, good landlord" just to use the facilities and then make a hasty getaway before the market traffic clogged the winding road all the way back to Glengarriff.

But, of course, things didn't quite work out that way. They rarely do. The facilities were fine . . . well no, actually, that's a downright lie. The facilities were unbelievably awful and enough to put you off your corned beef and cabbage for life, but when in need, etc., etc.

I was heading back to the main door when I realized that the room with the fire in it, which I would swear was empty when I'd arrived a few minutes earlier, was now occupied by the oddest trio of gentlemen it has ever been my good fortune to meet on a Bantry market day. Or any other day in Bantry, for that matter. Or anywhere else, come to think of it.

Their appearance and demeanor, to put it mildly, were utterly contradictory to the spirit and scope of their utterances. The small one by the fire, who seemed lost in his own coal-warmed world, suddenly gave out a sonorous bellow like an angry walrus. The other two didn't seem the least surprised by either the nature or volume of the explosive outburst. Even the barman seemed unperturbed. In fact he seemed blankly glass-eyed—almost taxidermied—until someone ordered drinks. Then he merely looked up from his studious pulling of a pint of the black stuff, smiled in a slightly doleful way, winked at me, shook his balding head, and lowered it again to supervise the slow filling of the glass.

The man by the fire then gave a second, less emphatic bellow and slowly looked around the room, as if to ascertain who was emitting such odd, nonverbal utterances. The other two men ceased their whispered chatter and turned to watch the smaller man.

"Y'see—dammit—the problem is . . . NO ONE KNOWS HOW TO WRITE ANYMORE! They're either trying desperately to be different so their stuff comes out all self-conscious and self-important . . . or they're imitating other writers—or a pastiche of other writers—they become sycophants of style like they've been on one of those asinine creative writing courses . . . Couldn't tell a decent *seanachai* tale to save their . . . male appendages. Assumin' they have any . ."

"Ah, but—" started the middle gentleman, his face rosy and his whiskey nose resplendently purple.

"No, no, no!" said the third, sprawling in a small wooden chair that looked dangerously close to imminent implosion. I began to sense I had emerged into a minor maelstrom of misunderstanding.

But the grammar-garbling gentleman by the fire would not be stopped. In a voice I can liken only to that of a frenetic Yorkshire terrier on an acid trip gone wrong, and with his fingers skittering nervously like trapped mice, he ignored his companions, or at least he silenced them by loudly repeating his last phrase before the interruptions had barely begun: '. . . ASININE CREATIVE WRITING COURSES . . ."

He paused long enough to regain the attention of the other two (with not a scintilla of pleasantly congenial propinquity) and then continued: "I think it was that American writer George Kerouac . . ."

"Jack," mumbled the man in the middle.

"Beg pardon?"

"Jack . . . His name was Jack Kerouac."

"You sure?"

"Sure he's sure and so am I. Jack was his name," said the sprawling man. "What's y' point?"

"MY POINT IS"—the little man by the fire repeated his attention-grabbing, capitalized semishout—"my point is that Mr. Kerouac—Jack or George—whatever—once declared that when you write you should forget all rules, literary styles, and other pretensions and write as if you were the first person ever to live on earth!"

"He said that, did he?" said the man in the middle after the three had sat through a mutually meditative pause in the proceedings.

"Yes. He did. And I think he's definitely got a point . . ."

"Ow!" shouted the sprawling man. The middle man chuckled. The man by the fire looked at the sprawling man.

"What's wrong with you then?"

The sprawling man couldn't resist a little jesty pun: "I just got your point . . . and it hurts!" He laughed at his own wit, and the middle man joined in. The man by the fire was not amused. He glowered with an almost reptilian intensity: "Waste o' my bloody breath, w' you two. Here I am tryin' to add a little elucidation to your lives and all you can do is josh around like a couple o' bloody school kids! You're both sufferin' badly from bovine spongiform encephalopathy—otherwise known as 'mad cow disease'—otherwise known as holes in y' tiny brains!" He looked as sad as a soggy crouton in a bowl of cold, greasy soup.

The man in the middle eased forward, as if about to rise to collect another round of drinks. Then he seemed to change his mind and adopted a ruminative tone: "I assume you've heard what little

Truman Capote once said of Kerouac's fiction That's not writing—that's typing'! Anyway . . . I think many of our finest Irish writers have some of that sense . . . writing as if you were seeing things new . . . for the first time. And even Welshmen do too! People like Dylan Thomas—oh, good lord—he must have really been an Irishman with all that paddywackery poetry in his veins and that rumbly humor and that rhythm with his words . . . and that lovely chocolaty voice—I can hear him now reading from his *Under Milk Wood*. Y'remember how it goes—'It is spring, moonless night in the small town, starless and bible-black, the cobblestreets silent and the hunched courters'-and-rabbits' wood limping invisible down to the sloeblack, slow, black, crowblack, fishingboat-bobbing sea. Ah. Such lovely stuff.' "

"Oh yes . . . now that's language indeed . . . ," said the sprawling man. "Old Dylan could make changin' gloppy motor oil sound as sensual as suckin' on a fine, fat peach!"

The Three Seanachai

The mirthless man by the fire nodded slowly: "Y'see what I mean—or what George Kerouac . . ."

"Jack" (both companions, in unison).

"Okay. JACK Kerouac . . . meant . . . by sounding like you were seeing things as if you were the first person ever to live on earth."

"And despite being a Welshman too . . . ," said the middle man.

"Who? Kerouac?"

"No—Dylan Thomas."

"Yes—but he was most famous in America," said the sprawling man, whose chair seemed ready to fly apart as he leaned his huge frame back on it.

"Oh, yes, America. Land of the biggest megawattage-celebrity-bore-writers . . ."

"Oh—and pray—who might they be?" asked the man in the middle in a pseudo-sagacious tone and with an ironic disassembled grin.

"The ones with that fake display of arrogant adolescence despite the onset of early senility—and then the ones wrapped in teetering naffery with egos as big as pumpkins but as frail as quail eggs—and then the bloody smoothies . . . the ones scribbling style over substance . . . the neurotic, alcoholic, depressive, dweebish, affected, academic, self-adoring, and self-hating hedonists parading and preening in front of their own self-made mirrors and giving their creative writing tuition classes for gooey-eyed stargazers and literary groupies. All these godawful, redolently gaseous, hyper-hypocritical blobs of loopy loquaciousness and blubbery bombast . . ."

"Like?"

"Like? Well, for example, John Updike, whatshisname Cheever, Bellow, Sallinger, Irving, etc., etc."

"Ah—the Lords of Language . . . ," said the sprawling man, who had now righted himself, possibly due to the ominous warning creaks of his frail chair.

"But even the big names can have a bit of fun trashing each

other," said the man in the middle. "Salman Rushdie said he thought Updike's novel *Terrorist* was 'beyond awful' and that 'he should stay in his little parochial neighborhood and write about wife swapping' because it's all he could do. And Mailer—The Late Big Norman—now there's one who seemed to enjoy being a cantankerous human being and writer. He said Saul Bellow's style was 'self-willed and unnatural' and that James Baldwin was 'far too charming to be a major writer.' The old bugger also offended every woman writer around. He said something about there won't be any really decent female writers until hookers start telling their true tales. Or something equally crude like that . . . but it was typical Mailer. Like when he said 'piety and prudery take all the art out of true thinking.'"

"Yeah, but there was another critic," said the sprawling man, now upright, "who the heck was it, anyway. He picked on Bellow too . . . Described one of his books as 'the dark grapplings one associates with Russian-Jewish authors transported to America where they become hilarious viewed through the lens of college politics and batty girlfriends instead of peasant uprisings.' Oh, and then he said there's no really good feuds between writers like there used to be because there's no really good writing—no good stories, with a beginning, a middle, and an end—anymore! Hemingway—that great old self-promoter and chest thumper—said 'the most essential gift for a good writer is a built-in shockproof shit detector.' That's why he shot himself, I suppose . . . an old man churning out too much sh . . ."

"Good point," mumbled the man in the middle.

"All carrot and no stick . . ."

"What?"

"All carr—"

"Yeah. I heard that bit. What's your point?"

"Still bloody sharp—just like it was a minute ago—and it's obvious, I should have thought!"

"Oh, you're on a real roller tonight . . ."

The literary wrangle did indeed seem to be getting a little heavy-browed fractious among these three odd characters, and I wondered if it was indeed time for me to be rolling home. But before I could empty my glass and move on, the barman leaned over and half whispered—"So what d'y think to our three *seanachai* then?"

"These are *seanachai*—storytellers?"

"Oh yes indeed they are—three of the best. You should be here on a night when they're doing one of their *seisuins*."

But I was not to hear their stories that night. Instead, I kept exchanging the occasional knowing nod and wink with the barman while these three flamboyantly erudite pontificators and passionate eccentrics continued their lambasting of literature and writers in general. I suppose I should have moved on, but Bantry's not known for its wild nightlife, and anyhow, this impromptu show of mixed misunderstandings was just too good to miss.

autumn
The Season of Lughnasa

AND, BUOYED ON RIPPLES OF BENIGN bliss (certainly our bliss), autumn finally came—day by gloriously long golden day celebrating Lugh—the pagan god of sun and light. All leading to the great fall harvests with more pagan-tinged festivities and dances and the smell of fresh-cut hay and the game-season hunting for pheasant, snipe, mallard, and deer and fly-fishing for fat trout and salmon in the dark, peaty-edged loughs, ready to be roasted on the spot over bog wood fires and washed down with fiery "gargles" of potent potato-distilled poteen. And yes—still all this in these days when the homogenizing influences of contemporary changes and the new EU-accelerated wealth of this Celtic Tiger run rampant throughout so much of Ireland.

This is the time for seanachais to tell their tales in the pubs by warming peat fires (alas, a declining tradition); for the gatherers to plunder the pastures and woods for mushrooms, hazelnuts, acorns, sweet chestnuts, windfall apples, haws and sloes; for the frolic and froth of Halloween; for allowing the lazy lassitude of the season and the pooled warmth of golden evenings to buoy you up through to the coming chilly times.

The irony here is that springs and summers in Beara are notoriously fickle, but invariably this "season of mists and mellow fruitfulness" often offers some of the finest weather of the year—even deep into November. Keats, with his glorious "To Autumn," reminds us:

> Where are the songs of spring? Aye, where are they?
> Think not of them, thou hast thy music too . .

And full-grown lambs loud bleat from hilly bourn;
Hedge-crickets sing; and now with treble soft
The red-breast whistles from a garden croft;
And gathering swallows twitter in the skies.

*Much as I admire Keats's ability to conjure autumnal moods with
their silky sensual ghostings of silvered mists, so magically, I also pay
homage to Cork author Damien Enright's fine descriptive gifts, particularly in his enticingly evocative book:* A Place Near Heaven. *Here, for
example, he offers a true "sense of place" word-song:*

Walking abroad these [mid-October] evenings . . . flights of
curlews rise from the fields with lonely cries and mixed
groups of oystercatchers and godwits fly in small squadrons
over the sea . . . Later a soft mist rises from the fields, hazing
out the distance. Sounds hang in the air. The bay is
mirror-calm, with white birds and bright boats set in the
stillness. Smoke rises straight from the village chimneys, blue
against the tall dark trees.

And that just about captures it all . . .

Barn Door, Adrigole

21

The Ryder Cup Roars In

⋮

"This will be epic!" roared the TV ad. "A WORLD EVENT WHERE THE TITANS CLASH!"

The flurries of expectations were amazing. This world-renowned USA versus Europe golfing mega-event had been eight years in the planning, with an expected global audience of well over a billion, the attendance of three USA ex-presidents, film stars galore, the gorgeous, leggy, and almost uniformly blond wives of the American players all lined up in identical top-fashion outfits, huge ten-course banquets for fourteen hundred guests created by leading Irish chefs including the irrepressible Dermot O'Shea . . . and on and on according to the gushings of an unusually enthusiastic media.

The Aer Lingus in-flight magazine summed it all up rather neatly: "This is it! The long awaited and much anticipated Thirty-Sixth Biannual Ryder Cup arrives on Irish shores this month—September 22–24, 2006—and with it comes the cream of world professional golf and, of course, tens of thousands of visitors . . . *Céad Míle Fáilte.*" Then the writer adds with typical Irish modesty: "We're unlikely to ever get the Olympics, so let's enjoy our one moment in the international sporting limelight."

Our friends at O'Neill's in Allihies were more positively

exuberant, one emphasizing that "this is a real symbol of Ireland's growth as a major world country and a creator of spectacular mega-events that'll capture the imagination of the whole globe!" There were some raised eyebrows at such lofty sentiments, but no one had the courage to contradict the man's statement—especially as he owned the pub and could be quite choosy about his customers.

And it didn't matter a lick of a leprechaun's boot whether you were interested in golf or not. Media promotion of this world-renowned competition was a take-no-prisoners, no-quarter-given tsunami of roiling rhetoric, and as an utter neophyte at the game, I'm happy to leave most of this chapter to the competitors and their verbose commentators. Both seemed to enjoy their skirmishes immensely.

So let's begin with the *Irish Times*: "The Ryder Cup puts on its mega-rich suit and struts its stuff at the K Club outside Dublin this coming week . . . The biggest sporting event ever on Irish soil gets ready to lift off. Right now, all we can do is count the hours as we wait in a state of anticipation at what may happen when the might of two continents collides. The world is watching."

Then comes the *Sunday Tribune*: "The Ryder Cup is one of sports' ultimate experiences . . . America's line-up contains the three best players in the world in Tiger Woods, Jim Furyk, and Phil Mickelson . . . Europe comes to the table with arguably their strongest team ever including three key Irish players, Padraig Harrington, Paul McGinley and Darren Clarke."

Of course there's always some journalist ready to add a few controversial comments: "Some would have us believe that America, with their four rookies and their hang-dog expression from their humiliation of two years ago, shouldn't really bother to turn up . . . They are descending on the K Club with 'all the intimidation power of the Liechtenstein Navy!' "

Another cynic wrote: "So many politicians and government officials have tried to explain what an 'honor' it is that this little country of ours has been 'chosen' to host the Ryder Cup—the subtext being, if you're in any way less than forelock-tugging about the whole business, you're a grubby begrudger."

One particularly acerbic critic, commentating with the style and flair of A. A. Gill, one of my favorite English journalists, referred to "a wish-wash of millionaire maestos in a jingoistic, willie-waggling competition exhibiting a smarmy mix of fawning snobbery, snide smirking, chippy schadenfreude, and the smug satisfaction of being beatified in the top tier questlists."

And then comes a little backhanded slap at the government's lack of initial interest in the project by Pat McQuaid, Ireland's enthusiastic promoter of international sports events: "Our political lobbying was a struggle because the Irish government had never invested in a major international sporting event as a publicity vehicle for our country . . . It took me three years to get the Minister of Tourism to go to the Cabinet and it did indeed involve the government taking a quantum leap in terms of investment . . . But in the end, millions will now be seeing Ireland in a very positive light across the planet."

But then it's back to the hullabaloo of journalistic hype: "The hardest job for us, the fans, will be to sit through the inevitable emotional roller coaster unable to hit a single shot ourselves . . . Make sure your posture is good, your concentration fixed and you drink plenty of liquids. If the tension gets too much, watch certain shots at crucial moments from behind the settee" (aka couch).

And from the players' viewpoint:

> Could it be the ultimate test of mental strength in sport? Is the Ryder Cup just about as big as it gets in terms of pressure, anticipation and expectation? For the player who comes through this crucible of heat, there is a lifetime of accolades awaiting . . . Some seem to take their game to another level, almost as if the atmosphere lifts them onto a higher plane psychologically . . . This thing called the Ryder Cup is about match play—you against him or, in a team situation, both of

you against both of them . . . a completely different set of
circumstances and rituals to go through . . . Ideally, each
player is able, in a sense, to "get out of his own way" as he
plays with all his heart for a higher cause than merely
himself . . . It's certain to be a theater of gripping entertain-
ment watching the very best in the world going head to head
and pitting mind, body and spirit against each other.

Arnold Palmer, celebrated as always by constant applause, re-membered his reaction to the Ryder in his glory days: "It doesn't matter how many titles you've won, when you stand on the tee at a Ryder Cup match and play for your country and not just your-self, your stomach rumbles like a kid turning up for his very first tournament . . . If you excel in what you do, your efforts will be rec-ognized and rewarded by your whole nation. That is what the Ryder Cup means to each of the participant countries."

Padraig Harrington, one of the Irish "stars," whose family lives on Beara, had a different take: "I don't rely on the team. I try to build up the pressure so that everything is down to me . . . Sometimes, though, you're so overloaded that you're not conscious of doing any-thing. You're just happy if the ball gets airborne . . . I find myself somewhere between being in the zone with no awareness of pressure and being totally out of it with terror."

Golf enthusiast Eamonn Sweeney summed up the mood suc-cinctly: "Believe me—the next few hours will be some of the most exciting ever in Irish sport."

After such a deluge of hyperbole, it was only the most recalcitrant antigolfers who could resist at least a peep at this four-day celebrity extravaganza. And despite my benevolent ignorance of golf, the prob-lem with the game is that, once your eyes become glued to the slow arc of a fine fairway shot or the meticulous line of a well-gauged putt, your mind quickly follows, and before you know it, you're on the edge of your seat, hoping that good old Tiger gets yet one more ace (or, for the uninformed, a hole in one). It's hypnotic, it's full of tension in a laid-back, gentlemanly kind of way, and it can eventually become as addictive as a perfect hollandaise sauce on an eggs Benedict breakfast, which apparently is a K Club gourmet specialty.

But there's always a "spoiler factor" lurking behind the magic of these mega world events. And, of course, this being Ireland in late September, it was the weather. The forecasts were full of dire warnings, not only of "heavy to torrential downpours," but also a hefty whack from the angry remnants of a hurricane that had ripped up the East Coast of the USA a few days previously. Again the papers laid on the hyperbole: "Ireland's Ryder Cup is facing the nightmare prospect of failing to start on time and not finishing until Monday . . . With overnight rain continuing to douse the course last night, there is an increasing danger that the event may become a catastrophe . . . It was even suggested that the grand opening ceremony might have to be moved indoors, though it was unclear exactly where it would go."

And then came another one: "With winds gusting up to forty-five miles per hour after a torrential early morning downpour, morning practice was postponed for health and safety issues. Ireland has waited seventy-nine years for the Ryder Cup to come here but . . . there are forecasts for thunderstorms tomorrow and Saturday which could force organizers to suspend play altogether."

At one point the weather was the cause of a most unusual outbreak of booing by a frustrated, rain-soaked crowd who complained that American players refused to tee off on their practice round where they could be seen, but chose to start way down the fairway. "That was inconsiderate—a bad mistake," said Captain Tom Lehman apologetically in an understatement that echoed throughout the whole tournament.

So—back to the weather reports: "On Friday the course was closed between 7 A.M. and 10 A.M. because of fears someone might get hurt by a flying umbrella—or perhaps the grandstand itself."

"American journalists seemed to take the threat of Hurricane

Gordon to heart. One asked whether there were any reports of cars
being turned over or of roofs being blown off by the storm . . . 'Would
you like me to give you the far less dramatic facts or make something more colorful up?' asked the press officer."

"Weather watchers will be glad to hear that the remnants of Hurricane Gordon are now en route to Portugal. Bad news, though, is
that a low pressure storm system out of Greenland is now heading
our way!"

When Tiger Woods was asked his opinion about the inclement
conditions, he launched instead into a diatribe against the staff of
The Dubliner, who had published a "satirical" piece claiming, among
other libelous rubbish, that "most American golfers are married to
women who cannot keep their clothes on in public." This was accompanied by doctored photos of Tiger's wife's head on an essentially
nude torso. Although Tiger's storm of protest was fully justified, it
regrettably only served to give free publicity to a tasteless rag.

Anyway—back to the weather. Generally speaking, the forecast-
ers were right. By the time the whole show was over, players and the
K Club had been subjected to rambunctious demonstrations of the
fickleness of early fall weather here. Rainstorms were indeed torrential, umbrellas were wielded en masse by the loyal daily crowds of
over 40,000 spectators, and the flailing tail of the hurricane with
winds over seventy-five miles per hour did indeed hit on the second
night of the event, ripping up trees, tearing tents, destroying acres of
newly landscaped gardens, and generally making "a right feckin'
mess of the whole feckin' course," according to one extremely irate
groundskeeper.

But Irish resilience coupled with a little timely luck won the day.
By the hour of play on Friday morning, most of the hurricane's havoc
had been magically removed by scores of groundskeepers, and the
crowds entered the meticulously regroomed grounds (which included
a generous application of a seaweed and iron mix to make the greens
look greener!) as if the storm had never been.

This same combination of resilience and luck continued throughout the whole weekend. There were rainstorms, but from the smiles and fortitude of spectators and players, you'd never know it. TV highlight summaries in the evenings were inevitably full of blue skies and dulcet shadows. Umbrellas were rarely visible, and Tiger's smile was as bright as ever despite an uneasy start (his first ball landed in the middle of a pond) and those distasteful doctored images of his wife on the raunchy *Dubliner* Web site.

Nudged and booted by the constant Ryder rhetoric, Anne and I forgot our vows to watch only the national news highlights for each of the three days and instead gorged ourselves on the daily three-hour-long depictions. At first, glimpses of the unbounded luxury of the K Club facilities were hedonistically off-putting with its "Look at me, I've got a Bentley and you haven't" airs and graces. its helicopter landing pad, and the conspicuous consumption of its $250-a-head menus, $8,000 bottles of rare wine, and a panoply of visiting celebrities (supported by a hopping flea circus of cronies, personal assistants, life coaches, wardrobe mavens, and the regular revenue of ex- and next "partners") that would do justice to any Hollywood A-list. The main focus was a graceful yellow country clubhouse overlooking five hundred acres of gardens and guarded by two enormous black stone cats. Within were gorgeous oriental rugs, pink sofas, bronze sculptures of racehorses, elegantly gold-framed paintings of beautiful ladies, and a definite "to the manner born" ambience.

"It's all a bit . . . overdone, don't you think? ' asked Anne.

I nodded. It seemed that wealth and status were definitely and proudly on conspicuous exhibition here. I felt more comfortable as the camera moved on to capture vignettes of the crowd—an arc of colorful umbrellas, a cluster of logoed baseball caps and rain-splattered grins, a remarkably uniform coloration of waterproof anoraks and windcheaters, a smattering of those gorgeous befreckled, green-eyed, red-haired Irish colleens, the stone hard faces of the true connoisseurs lost in their own complex world of virtual replays, and

the good old boys from the bogs who somehow had managed to finagle tickets, knock back a generous selection of libations, and now
stood, wobbly and woozy, watching the golf superstars offer their
very best just a few feet away in front of them.

Because of a very confusing (to us) scoring system for individual
and team performances, we found it hard to know exactly who was
leading whom. But it was obvious that, in this unusual kind of competition, there was no place for the competitors to hide. In a team
environment every stroke counts, and the eyes of each of the 40,000
daily spectators were on each play as applause roared at such a deci-
bel level that even the irritating buzz of helicopters hanging over
the course like locusts looking for a hefty snack was drowned out.

In the end Irish patriotism rose to a crescendo as the European
team, with their three superb Irish players, soared ahead of the
Americans to finally win the cup for the third time in a row with an
unprecedented score of 18½–9½—a devastating defeat for the Yan-
kees, whose only excuse seemed to be that "I guess we're not too familiar with team-play golf!"

Despite a briefly forlorn American team, the final moments of
the last day brought tears to the eyes of even the most distinguished
observer: "The sobs of Darren Clarke who had lost his wife to breast
cancer only six weeks previously as he was embraced by members of
both teams; the captivating chortle of US President Clinton whose
own round on the K Club course made him remark that he'd 'better
stick to politicking for a living'; the Arnold Palmer, designer of the K
Club course, comment that this had indeed been one of the best
Ryder Cups 'anytime anywhere,' and Padraig Harrington, with his
gleeful remark that 'what I feel is wonderful relief that we have won,
and won here in Ireland!' "

Of course, once again, some media pundits couldn't resist the
odd jab at less fortunate Irish tendencies. The *Irish Examiner* used
the all-too-familiar "Rip-Off Republic" label to describe the "hundreds of thousand of euros juiced from the wallets of visitors in the

form of outrageously inflated hotel, house rental, food and taxi costs." Another media wag described golf itself as "a good walk ruined" and suggested that "the event descended into a jingoistic battle between Europe and the USA . . . Golf may be the ultimate gentleman's game but that does not stop its participants from acting like babies when things aren't going their way."

Criticism was also directed at the "overly flamboyant" opening ceremonies featuring more than four hundred performers with their mix of traditional Irish music, exuberant Riverdance-like performances, an ultramodern "Celtic history ballet," and a raucous drum extravaganza all orchestrated by the Saw Doctors' ex-drummer, Johnny Donnelly. Anne and I were so mesmerized by this two-hour extravaganza that we watched it from beginning to end. And there were definitely moments, as wonderfully sad lilts of Irish folk songs rolled on, that we sensed a gathering of salty moisture in the corners of our eyes. Then one rather cruel columnist started making fun of all the "wannabe-Irish" Hollywood celebrities here, including Robert De Niro ("I'm Irish on my father's side,"), Johnny Depp ("My mother's half Irish,"), Drew Barrymore, Ben Stiller, Matt Dillon, and Sandra Bullock ("I'm convinced I'm the rightful owner of a castle over here!"). Another grumbled about the unfair amount of attention given to "an elite rich man's game" (despite the fact that, with its 415 courses, Ireland boasts more golf holes per capita than any other nation in the world, including Japan!).

Also, around the same time, this little nation was offering such other major events as the International Plowing Championship (don't laugh—this is a mega-spectacle attracting competitors from over thirty countries) and "the biggest event of our sporting calendar [the Ryder Cup won't even register compared to this] in the form of the all-Ireland championships for our beloved national games of hurling and Gaelic football."

Perhaps most satirically critical was Tom Humphries in the *Irish Times*, who offered the following stinging observations:

> *The Ryder Cup has come to Ireland at just the right time.*
> *The last kick of the astonishingly vulgar Celtic Tiger! Crass*
> *corporate elitism meets native-genius for price-gouging and*
> *pat insincerity . . . It's hideously retrograde to make the*
> *poor golfers all dress the same way, but when you see the*
> *dubious stuff the boys are sent out in, it's understandable*
> *they would want to spread the sartorial suffering . . . The*
> *Americans have opted for a diamond-patterned look which*
> *makes them appear like Rotary Club members hoping to*
> *finish golfing in time to catch the early bird menu some-*
> *where nice.*

Maybe the accolade for ace-acerbic wit goes to Jerome Reilly of the Sunday *Independent*, who shouted:

> *Roll up, roll up, roll up to the most over-hyped, overblown,*
> *overpriced event in sport. Welcome to the K Club where*
> *grown men wear pink plaid with pride and wives of the*
> *world's wealthiest sportsmen are show ponies in an unedify-*
> *ing media circus . . . victims of perhaps the most shameful*
> *example of unrelenting male chauvinism and outrageous*
> *female bitchery ever seen in this country . . . The golf, of*
> *course, is utterly beguiling and compelling and almost made*
> *up for the bullshit, the shallowness, the sexism, the conspic-*
> *uous celebration of wealth and excess that goes with the*
> *Ryder Cup. Almost.*

Like a stern schoolmaster Dermont Gilleece in the Sunday *Independent* reminded us that we should ignore this kind of griping: "When the shadows lengthen and spectators debate the deeds of the day, it will be nice to reflect on the absence of mockery and jibes which can so cheapen a great game" Gilleece even quoted John Updike, apparently a great golfing enthusiast: "This particular devotee of the ancient windswept, dune-bound game would be saddened if more of the bad air making other professional sports hyperventilate were to be let into golf's gorgeous outdoors."

However, gripes aside, it seemed the Irish media couldn't resist congratulating itself and its golfers for a magnificent spectacle. And perhaps the best summary of all was by Carolyn O'Doherty in the *Irish Examiner*, who wrote: "In the end there was such a love-in, it felt wrong to have forced the two sides in the Ryder Cup to play each other at all. As the world's greatest golf event came to a close in a sun-baked ceremony just before six on Sunday evening, the mutual outpourings of admiration and appreciation were so torrential that the umbrellas abandoned after the climactic downpours of the morning were almost called into use again."

It sounds like the spirit of Ireland finally snuck into all the proceedings here, and a true sense of *craic* too floated like Guinness froth across all these mutual reminiscences.

But alas! The same cannot be said for the spirit of the American media, most notoriously the *New York Times*, which gave sparse commentary on the event in a dismissive summation matched only by the *Los Angeles Times*, which sighed: "Stick that Ryder Cup optimism in cold storage for two more years, shake hands and say goodbye, because this thing is pretty much out of reach for the U.S. once again."

The *Chicago Tribune* pointed out that the American players competed on a course that's "'about as Irish as matzo ball soup' . . . They may have invented golf in Europe but it's quintessentially the American game and playing it on a sodden course seems a little odd . . . And so the Cup grinds on, an utter mystery to those untouched by its charms."

Sports Illustrated was exasperated: "How do we do it? Every time, whether the matches are in the USA or Europe or on fast greens or slow greens or sloped greens, it doesn't matter! We still lose!"

Jim McCabe in the *Boston Globe* was a little more generous: "The PGA of America is trying to figure out the puzzle that is the Ryder Cup. I don't know what to say, said Phil Mickelson. Well, that's okay, the Europeans have enough spirit and passion to go around for both teams. It is their show now, and they're doing a most beautiful job with it, too."

I guess if we hadn't been in Ireland, we would have scarcely noticed the Ryder Cup, especially as we are (were) in no way golf aficionados. But watching the highlights in our little Beara cottage, we sensed something important in the players, in the courteous manners of the game itself, and indeed in Ireland herself. Something that might even one day tempt us both to take up the clubs and stroll the fairways bawling out our "fores" and recording our menageries of eagles, birdies, doglegs, drained snakes—and worm burners (you see—we did learn a few things from all that TV watching).

But in the meantime the whole event, despite all the poundings and pontifications of the press, has engendered in the two of us an even deeper love and respect for Ireland and pride in her potential future.

22

With the Fish People

I've heard most of the arguments about "the end of the fishing industry" through Draconian restrictions many times, both here and previously up in the Outer Hebrides of Scotland when Anne and I were recently staying on the island of Harris and writing our second *Seasons* book. But usually the information came through newspaper features or regional TV reports, not directly through the voices and hearts of the fishermen themselves. On this occasion, however, four of them were clustered around one of the tables in the "lower room" of O'Donoghue's. They weren't exactly what you'd call "old salts," but their young-old faces were pale, suggesting quite a long absence from the rigors of trawler voyages. I wasn't part of this group but close enough to make notes on their conversation, and most revealing it was too . .

" 'S getting worse and worse with the salmon now. Quota's down to 90,000 fish from over 250,000 five years ago How the hell do they expect us to make a living . . . and how can stocks come back if the young sprats are getting caught up as a bycatch of the mackerel?"

"Well—there's always the voluntary compensation packages. Give up y' license and y' drift nets and get a nice sack o' cash from the government. M'be start a B and B or build a guest cottage for rent . . ."

"Aw, don't y' believe all y' hear about these packages. What's to stop 'em just tightening up the quotas and letting us get driven out of business with no compensation at all?"

"And it's even worse with the cod and whiting. All but disappearing, and even if you can get a decent catch, fish prices don't keep up and sometimes it's hardly worth unloading 'em."

"Climate shift is movin' the shoals. That's what it is."

"Well, they've certainly gone from around the Aran Islands and Rosaveel. Prawn grounds on the west are still okay—but there's no mature fish left. It's all overworked. Too much intensive fishing. Stocks are ravaged—wiped out. Tows all end up the same. Undersized or nothin' at all sometimes. Hardly a sprat for all y' troubles. And all this—and the fuel going up like the very devil . . ."

"And look at the harbors. Decommissioned boats everywhere. Tied up. Useless. All over the country. Never be used again. Terrible, terrible waste of money and men. So many good lives wrecked . . ."

Fisherman's Boots

"Porcupine Bank's still good, though . . ."

"And what use is that, for God's sake? We don't have the big boats. Not like the damn French and Spanish. Been there scraping it clean for twenty years . . . We've always been decades behind . . . Never got government help . . . We were all stuck with our smaller boats . . . Couldn't compete . . ."

"Aye, that's Ireland

now, isn't that the truth—always at the back of the field, living off the scraps of all those greedy foreign buggers . . ."

"Ah, s'not that simple. We didn't see what was happenin' with the European Union. Government here gave our fishin' away in exchange for flush agricultural subsidies for the farmers. There just weren't enough of us and too many bloody farmers—and now they get all the cash—tons and tons of euros and we sit here moanin' and groanin' and doing sweet nothin'."

"Yeah—and listen, I've got this latest thing in the paper . . . this report on the fishing by Údarás na Gaeltachta . . . This'll make you moan even more . . How's this for statin' the bleedin' obvious: 'There is no doubt that a range of forces, internal and external, continue to work toward the elimination of drift net fishing in Ireland . . .' "

"Ah—now there's new news f'y' . . . bloody stupid gobshites!"

"And were they paid to write this crap too?."

"Yeah—but listen to this end bit: 'While we admit we have limited statutory remit in this sector, we acknowledge the importance of the industry, not only for local fishing communities, but for the local fish processing, tourism and restaurant sectors.' "

"And that's it?! That's all it says?!"

"Just about. They end up claimin' they support compensation for relinquishing drift net licenses . . . which is a load of old garbage we've heard again and again . . ."

"Yeah, but like Sean said, the government could just sit back and let the stocks get so low that we'll all be bankrupt . . . without any compensation!"

"M'be—and m'be what that bunch of backside-scratchin' bureaucrats needs is what those French guys gave the British Royal Navy when they boarded one of their boats a few weeks back to check out their catch . . ."

"And what was that?"

"Pot loads of toilet crap from the johns . . . all over their heads!"

"The French did that?!"

"Yeah—tough bunch. Don't like foreigners snooping around. And that's our problem too . . . too many commissions and politicians snooping around, writing reports and such like, tellin' us what we've all known for years like it was a brand-new revelation, and making stupid useless suggestions. And in the meantime, we're all stuck here in port, quotas all finished, no place to take our boats . . . and just watching the cash get pissed away . . ."

"It's a real terrible mess and no doubt on that . . ."

Fisherman with Pot

"No doubt at all . . . and no way out . . ."

Silence descended on the group, and even the pints of stout remained untouched, circled around the table like dark standing stones raised up in far-distant eras when the ancients who peopled this island believed the gods would always protect them in their times of need.

Where are those gods today? I wondered . . .

I SHARED ALL THIS fascinating new information with Anne and we decided it was time to go looking for these gods and some of their more fortunate recipients.

And despite all the ongoing moans and groans we found a few. Regular rumors abounded of enormous (if occasionally illegal) hauls here, even after a mere couple of days at sea, resulting in mega-hauls of euros too. Figures of 350,000 to 500,000 euros ($525,000 to $750,000) floated about—for a single trip's catch! We knew that the harbor at Castletownbere is one of the largest in the southwest, and it's also Ireland's largest whitefish port, with tens of thousands of tons of fish landed annually. But we had no idea of the cash splashing about! There are regular flotillas of Spanish, Portuguese, and French trawlers here too—enormous creatures—crammed cheek by jowl beside smaller (but much larger than a decade ago) local craft. With so much technology and state-of-the-art know-how on full display every day, surely it wouldn't be that hard, we thought, to see how the whole trawling system worked and decide whether all the cries of repressive quotas, premature bankruptcies, depleted stocks, and anti-Irish prejudices could be substantiated. Our determination, however, was somewhat diminished when we realized that the world of mega-hauling is a rather secretive and cautious one where information is exchanged with reluctance and even the occasional drop or two of wile and guile.

Winks, nods, and knowing—but mainly silent—communication

seemed to be the rules of the game. And while we met some of the most delightful people involved in the trade, we still came away sensing that basic truths and solid data continued to elude us.

PEOPLE LIKE MARGARET DOWNEY were the epitome of graciousness. This warm, cuddly grandmother (with a spine of steel, as we later learned) invited Anne and me over for tea and cakes at her large home set on a prominent seashore site overlooking Bere Island. There she regaled us with tales of her family's long association with fishing. Following the recent death of her second husband, Frank, she and her son Kevin were now the primary controllers of a huge new 120-foot-long craft, the *Sea Spray*, which towers over the smaller Beara boats at the nearby harbor. She took us on a tour of this meticulously maintained masterwork of modern navigation. I don't think I've ever seen an engine room quite so clean and gleaming. Ditto the wheelhouse and the crew's quarters. Eerily spit-and-polished. And yet Margaret insisted that the boat was in regular use "during the quota period" but that no matter how arduous and wave-bashed the latest voyage might have been, shipshape appearances in port were obligatory.

As we stood high on the prow of the boat overlooking the square, it was curious—quaint, even—to see in the midst of all this huge high-tech clustering of trawlers, there were still fishermen scattered along the quay mending their nets by hand, as they have done here for centuries. We found this a rather reassuring time-warp glimpse of a far simpler era.

Through a long family association with the sea, Margaret was familiar with all the sagas—the destruction of the Calf Rock Lighthouse in a terrible storm in 1881; the loss of a large Spanish trawler and all nine of its crew in 1984 just at the entrance to the Bere Channel less than four miles from her house; the enormous financial penalties for "overfishing"; the crazy dodgem car antics of trawlers when they're all competing to fish the same shoal, and the illegal "beat-the-quota" selling of catches at sea to other international boats.

"Oh—I'm getting too old for all this," she said. (We didn't believe her.) "Especially when I go to the cemetery and realize I know just about everybody in it! Only problem is—when I walk into town, with all our scores of new Polish and Lithuanian immigrants, I hardly know anyone!" (We didn't believe that either, but we understood her point. Sometimes MacCarthy's sounded like a Warsaw café and the nearby supermarket boasted a whole section of Polish foods.)

We asked her about all the dire warnings of shoal elimination. "Lot of nonsense!" she replied emphatically. "There's still plenty of fish out there, 'specially mackerel. That's a real moneymaker. But the quotas keep us back. March to September is our dead time. And I've got a crew of eight, and some of them have been with us more than thirty years and then their sons are coming in too, and that's something you just can't cast aside lightly."

We nodded and I thought I'd test the waters of "truth in information" with Margaret.

"Well, it must still be worth it. There seems to be good money in it most of the time. One owner told us his boat goes out on three- to five-day-long trips, and he has a capacity of 450 tons, and depending on market conditions, he claims he can bring in around 1,500 euros a ton. So we did the math, and that seemed to top out 'round about 650,000 euros if he's got a full load. Which doesn't sound too bad to us!"

"Well, lucky him!" said Margaret with a twinkle that only half disguised the steely determination and strength of this remarkable woman. "But don't forget, full catches like that are very rare, plus the fact that the mackerel quota for the whole season for our boat is only 900 tons. On longer fifteen-day trips up toward Iceland you can go for tuna and whatnot if you can get a license. But you've always got the government inspectors snooping around. Most don't know the front end of a boat from the back end. But they're always trying to fine us—and drive us all out of business. Meanwhile, the Spanish boats seem to do whatever they want. They just use Castletownbere as a place to unload onto trucks bound for Spain."

It was obvious that discussing the details of catch prices and the like was not considered polite in these parts. And Margaret was too busy anyway listing all their challenges, such as needing 60,000 gallons of gasoline to fill their 600-ton *Sea Spray* and decrying the farm salmon industry for "their endless problems with pesticides, sea lice, red dye number 2, chemicals in the blood, spreading diseases and poisoned water which kills wild sea trout and other fish." She finally returned to the inequities of the quota system—"Oh, Lord," she grumbled. "I'm so all-at-sea with the quotas!"

"So are we!" was about the only reply we could give.

Even Grant Fulton, the inspector who supervises the quotas and enforcements for the government at the harbor, seemed to have problems clarifying the system for our neophyte understanding. Plus the fact you could tell he was uneasy being seen in public discussing such matters with blow-ins like us. He was a tall, lean young man with humor-filled eyes. And, by absolute coincidence (yes, I know—there are no coincidences), he was also the son of one of our favorite artists on the island of Harris, Willie Fulton, whose work we celebrated in our *Seasons on Harris* book. They both had that refreshing Pythonesque take on life and all its odd nuances, although in Grant's case, we sensed his frustration with his job and for the local fishermen.

"Oh, of course, there's always some that try to sneak around the rules, but we're really having a rough time compared to the Spanish and the French—we're being left the scraps, really. And you never know when a crunch point is reached with any particular species of fish. Like the shrimp on the Grand Banks off Newfoundland. They just vanished. One year you came back with brimming boats, next year—nothing."

Grant told us quite a lot more when he and his wife, Gillian, invited us over for dinner at his beautiful home near Adrigole, which he'd built mainly by himself. But it was all essentially "off the record." So we respect his position and responsibilities and leave it at that. Maybe we understood a little more than we did previously about the fishing industry, but I'm not really convinced. And it still seems to us that the Irish fishermen have been well and truly screwed by the EU—and even by their own government!

But we were utterly convinced by Gillian's superb soufflélike Yorkshire pudding that accompanied Grant's magnificent, perfectly cooked medium-rare standing rib roast. It simply was by far the best pudding we'd had in months—anywhere.

Gillian, with her research-based Ph.D., described her work with our old friend Jim O'Sullivan to ensure the continuity of his Beara Breifne Greenway, a trail of over six hundred miles commemorating that epic march of Donal Cam O'Sullivan, chief of the O'Sullivan clan, north to Leitrim following his defeat at his Castletownbere

Mending Nets by Hand

home of Dunboy Castle in 1602. More than a thousand followers set out on the march, but after skirmishes and decimating starvation along the way, only thirty-five finally arrived. An amazingly heart-rending—but ultimately inspiring—story.

And we also found Susan inspiring too. Susan Steele, a doctor of marine biology, is the beautiful, blond-haired, energetic, lean, elo-quent, and dynamic daughter of Norman and Veronica, the cheese makers at Eyeries. Her multitasking list of responsibilities for the Irish Sea Fisheries Board and other organizations was utterly mind-boggling.

The first time we met her down at the harbor, she'd just been given an additional responsibility as agriculture and business train-ing coordinator and was having "a bit of an off day." Apparently her husband, Andy, had just had a couple of ribs crushed by an ungrate-ful cow on their small farm off the Allihies Road as he tried to re-lease it from a tangle of fence wire. "If it'd been a bull, he'd be dead!" she said with a beguiling "make the best of it" grin. And apparently she had also just realized that she'd left her purse, wallet, and "Lord knows what else" at a doctor's office in Cork where she'd had to take one of her children the previous day in an emergency for a "terrible ear infection."

Then she remembered that her notes for a lecture she was about to give that afternoon on seaweed farming were also in her purse. Then she'd been told the motor was kaput on an inflatable boat she used to give classes in seamanship and safety at sea. (These were in addition to other classes she gave on kayaking.) Then someone had just told her that a party of twenty Japanese marine biologists had decided to visit her and her offices the following morning and would expect a guided tour, et cetera. And then she'd just been asked if she'd teach a "short fun course on the sea" for elementary school kids—starting next week. And then . . .

Enough! Point made. This young woman was a miracle of per-petual motion. A true new female Celtic Tiger restless and roaring to garner even more challenges. And laughing too—always laughing—as, with one of her gorgeous and equally energetic children, she led us around her "sample rooms" filled with scores of different seaweed species, a remarkable array of dead and living sea creatures, and her lecture room teeming with wall charts, more specimens, and copies of her books. (Yes, of course, Susan is an author too.) We were exhausted after an hour with her, but she looked as fresh and frisky as when we'd first met her.

She invited us up to her farmhouse for "a bit of tea" in the evening, so that's where we were around 6 P.M., drinking strong Irish-blend tea and selecting from a deluge of her home-baked goodies. Little kidlets flitted about like golden-haired angels. ("Soon as you've gone," Sue said, "they'll turn back into devils!" Andy, despite his bandaged ribs, insisted on showing us his extensively hand-built home and various pastures and paddocks on the sloping hillside overlooking Castletownbere.

In terms of learning more about the fishing industry itself, Sue seemed to agree with much of Margaret's synopsis. But she did offer one beguiling comment before we left: "Bearans are a bit like bulls. Normally pretty docile—but get us riled up and the bad guys had better start running for the hills—fast!"

AND RILING TIME MAY indeed be approaching. Like a friendly young fisherman from Cornwall told me at MacCarthy's one evening, some are ready to let fly: "I can't tell y' the real truth about our fishin'. It's all far too political. It ain't worth m'life t'tell y' those stories. They're unbelievable. But troubles are comin'. So I keep t'm'self. I've only got a small boat. Thirty miles out is my maximum—hooking pollock around the reefs and wrecks out there. Many of the boats were sunk by German submarines in World War II, just like the *Lusitania* was nearby. And I'm doing this all quiet like. Not treadin' on anybody's toes. That's not so good for your health in these parts. But we are losin' the big fishin' 'round here. We've been really messed up by the EU and our own government. But in the meantime if I keep m'head down I can still make a nice quiet living . . ."

"A NICE QUIET LIVING" is definitely not what Richard Murphy is making out at his enormous 20,000-square-foot fish and seafood processing and packing plant on Dinish Island near the Castletown- bere golf course. Founded in 1987 by Richard and his partner, Shell- fish De La Mer—winner of an Irish Seafood Exporter of the Year award and creator of over 130 different products primarily from local boat catches—appears to be one of Beara's true economic success stories.

"I've always been optimistic about Beara," Richard told me as we sipped coffee in his award-draped, file-strewn office. He was a handsome, strapping prototype of an ambitious, driven CEO, and I could tell he had a low quota of patience. That was particularly ob- vious when an urgent call came in from Spain while we were talk- ing from some unfortunate salesperson who'd obviously botched a huge shellfish deal. And, well, all I can say is that I was glad to be me and not the fellow a thousand miles to the south whose day, or maybe rest of the year, would be utterly wrecked by what transpired in that crushing conversation.

We toured the vast plant, watching whitecoat-clad and hairnetted employees do amazing things with crabs and prawns and a host of other aquatic creatures (making chowders, seafood pies, hors d'oeuvre platters, cute little crab claw bites, et al). Richard empha- sized that "what we need 'round here is a bit more initiative and risk taking. Another 'value-added' processing factory for local catches of mackerel and whatnot, for example. Then we wouldn't have to worry so much about the deadening effect of quotas. I'm sick of seeing the waste of boats and human expertise here. I started off myself as a crab and lobster fisherman who couldn't sell brown crabs except to local restaurants. So I decided we should make the meat—beautiful meat—more appealing and saleable. And now—well—we're supplying over a thousand restaurants with customized products. The key is not to wait for government handouts and all that nonsense. Just get in there with some reliable friends—and make something happen!"

You don't hear that kind of rhetoric on Beara too often. Richard is obviously one of the true Celtic Tiger types, and so far his vision is helping keep Castletownbere alive and thriving.

Which brings us right back to the fisherman at O'Donoghue's who complained: "It's getting worse and worse."

To which, I imagine, Richard would roar a Tiger-inspired reply of: "Not from where I'm standing!"

BUT THEN THERE WERE the all-too-human horror stories of the fragility of fishermen's lives among the pernicious coastal shoals and during sudden dramatic swings in local microclimates. One of the saddest events of our stay on Beara was in the late summer when two fishermen out in a small underpowered dinghy were capsized by a fierce squall under the black cliffs below Dzogchen Beara. One lost his life jacket and was drowned; the other managed to reach the jagged rocks at the base of the cliffs and scramble to safety.

The funeral was held in the massive church on the hill above main street and was packed to overflowing; fishermen and families from miles around stood outside in the dour, drizzling morning. "At times like this," one of the drowned man's friends told us, "we're all one family."

When the coffin emerged, it was taken for a ritual circular procession around the harbor past all the fishing boats, some partially cloaked with black cloth awnings. The streets and squares were so filled with mourners that the traffic was completely blocked for well over half an hour, but not a single horn was heard. Funerals here are major community events, and everything else ceases. Even lights were turned off in the stores and banks and all the offices along the main street. This was one of the saddest—yet most impressive—demonstrations of the solidarity and mutual support of Bearans we ever saw. In hindsight, the words of Oscar Wilde ring true for the people who live here and whose lives are tied to the ocean and the oh-so-fickle climate of southwest Ireland: "When people talk to me here about the weather, I always feel they mean something else."

Yes, indeed. The idiosyncrasies of the local climate may be intriguing—even amusing—to us blow-ins, but talk with the local fishermen whose fortunes and existences are linked inextricably to the moods and mayhem of the weather and you'll get a far different interpretation.

Margaret knows all about this, as do Grant, Susan, Richard, and the scores of fishermen who float in and out of the harborside taverns, trading tales and sharing somber wisdom. They all recognize the precariousness of their lives—and yet they continue to struggle, in larger and larger boats, hoping the shoals will keep running . . .

23

This Farming Life

:::

"THERE'S REALLY NOT A LOT GOIN'" on over the seasons beyond what you'd expect from normal farmin'," said Noel O'Sullivan. Anne and I sat chatting with him at his farmhouse near the cable car contraption that carries the few remaining residents and occasional hikers across to Dursey Island a mile or so down the road.

We'd been introduced to Noel by Jim O'Sullivan, our mentor and guide in things Beara. "If you want to get a sense of farm life the way it once was—he's a good man to talk to. And there aren't too many of his type around anymore. Farming's not what it used to be . . . but Noel's a true holdout!"

We were in his front parlor, which was painted a vibrant semi-gloss turquoise. "It was a cheap paint remnant—seemed a shame to let such a cheerful color go to waste," Noel said, his sixty-odd-year-old red-purple face glowing in the intense heat of his turf fire. A tray of tea, cookies, Jacob's Cream Crackers, Irish butter, Irish blue cheese, and thin slices of tenderloin lamb with fresh mint sauce lay before us on the low table. Every other surface in the room seemed to be crammed with framed family photographs. The mood was jocular and convivial. Previous chats with Noel, often in the company of Michael O'Sullivan, official chief of the O'Sullivan clan, had always been friendly and open, and we were beginning to feel almost like family.

"Help y'selves to whatever y'want. Y' don't need me to wait on you now."

We gazed out the small four-panel window set in the stone wall almost three feet thick at a million-dollar vista across the so-called Kenmare River (actually an enormous elongated ria estuary separating the Ring of Beara from the Ring of Kerry) to the soaring monoliths of the Macgillycuddy's Reeks range.

Way in the west on the horizon we could just make out the two dragon-backed profiles of the Skellig islands—Little and Michael. Immediately below us, gentle lines of surf lapped an almost-white sand beach. Then, abruptly out of the ragged, rock-bound bay, rose a tumble of velvety green meadows with not a scintilla of gorse on them to mar their verdant perfection. Ancient drystone walls, sage green and mossy with age, wriggled snakelike up the steep hillsides. These were Noel's fields, along with others he rented elsewhere on the peninsula, and they were littered with the woolly balls of his sheep and their now-large lambs.

"Bin a good year, all in all. One point five lambs per ewe on average, and a good shearing too, though t'be honest, it's hardly worth it. The cost of cutting the fleeces is more than the wool brings in nowadays. No one seems to want it, even though they make such a fuss of pure wool fashions and whatnot. And this is good wool—not like the upland Blackface Cheviots. Their wool is coarse and hard to work. Only good for house insulation and the like. But I just don't understand about our fleeces. I mean—look at them. Look at how soft and fluffy they are. Not stringy at all . . . just gorgeous!"

We watched the sheep. There was something hypnotic in their slow, waddling movements as they munched their mellow way around the pastures, pausing occasionally to look around and check out the flock before easing themselves on, nibbling the vibrant green shoots of grass and frilly white daisies and golden dandelions and iron-rich clover. And they would do this for hour after hour, day after day, week after week. Cute, cuddly munching machines. Visibly plumping themselves and with nothing to do with their time except . . . eat. That and lambing was all that was expected of them. And apparently nothing much was expected of Noel either beyond the occasional bit of wall repair, supervising the biannual dipping of his flocks, organizing their ultimate marketing, and casting a proprietary eye over his little fiefdom of immaculate velvet pastures. And pretty well ditto for his cows too.

Beara Shepherd (a Rare Sight)

"So much then for the image of the poor, diligent, worn-to-the-bone farmer with hardly a minute of peace or comfort for himself," I said after Noel's "not a lot going on" remark.

"Who the hell told you all that nonsense?!"

"Well—it seems to be the typical picture in most other parts of the world."

"Ah well y'see, here we've learned our lessons from our own sheep. Sit back, watch, and learn to be wise, is what I say."

"So that's what you do, is it? Just sit back and watch them and become wise?"

"And sleep. There's a lot to be said for a good sleep now and then in the day."

"Sounds like a darn good life to me."

"Well—and who says it isn't? Certainly not me!" Noel laughed a cigarette smoker's laugh and proceeded to light up his sixth Benson & Hedges since our arrival. "Terrible habit, this." He chuckled. "Still—I stopped with the drink over twenty years ago. Not a drop has passed these nicotine-stained lips and teeth of mine in all that time. Which is perhaps a God-given blessing because what with two bottles of the Powers whiskey a day and a fine temper to go along with it and a tendency to treat the boreens like my own personal car racing track—I don't think I had much time in this world left for me, if you know what I mean."

"Not much time? As a farmer or a man?" asked Anne with a smile.

"Aha—mainly the man, though there was a time when farming was goin' bad in places like Beara. Obviously you know all about the potato famines of the mid-1800s—Skibbereen and down by the Mizen Head Peninsula well southwest of Bantry—that was one of the worst places. But farming's always been the backbone. Even now there's almost three-quarters of the land of Ireland used for agriculture. Which is pretty amazing when y'think of all the bog country in the middle of the country and the rock deserts of the Burren and whatnot in the northwest. But we were old hands at the job. Some of the earliest small farms in Europe were discovered at the Céide Fields in County Mayo—said to date from before 3000 BC. Then there were the Celts, who rolled in around 300 BC with the *brehon* system of tribal land tenure. Then the Normans in the twelfth century—they didn't mess around too much. It was those damned

Anglo-Irish 'Ascendancy' plantations in the seventeenth century that locked us into a feudal system, with almost all the land being owned by those bloody blueblood British outsiders. Took us three hundred years to start to get our farms back. Finally we had to boot most of 'em out, and good riddance!" Noel smiled, seemingly proud at his erudite recitation of Irish history. He was an odd but intriguing mix of blunt, back-to-the-earth farmer with a quieter, well-read, and sensitive persona.

"And you lucked out too when Ireland joined the EU—right?" I suggested, having heard of the extremely generous subsidies that had been made available to small farmers.

"Ay well—y'could say that. The fishermen round here definitely think so. We got the subsidies, and they got stuck with tiny quotas and buyouts of their boats. Y'wouldn't think so, but we're still a country of farmers—over 130,000 still left. And bigger acreages too. Mostly animals—sheep and cattle. The land never was much good for crops. Great for grass, though—the Emerald Isle and all that stuff."

"What about the famous potatoes—once your staple diet?" asked Anne.

"Well, after the famines, we kind of lost some of our appetite for them, although set a tureen of colcannon or *boxty* on the table, and you'll still see it gone in a flash! And listen, talkin' about food, I've laid out all this stuff here—some of my best cold lamb, fresh soda bread, some of Norman Steele's beautiful cheeses—so let's just get on with it."

So we got on with it, and a fine afternoon it turned out to be, chatting between the cheeses and watching those little woolly balls of sheep munch their myopic way across his salt-spray sea meadows far below by the churning surf.

"Magic," said Anne. "Again! That word just keeps popping up!"

Norman laughed. "Magic—y'want to know about magic? There's still plenty of it about, y'know. A lot of new people comin' in too.

Some have the powers. Definitely. When I was young, all raw and splintery, you always knew who had the powers—specially second sight and the like. A lot of people would go to them long before they'd go to the local priest. They could help solve problems. Not just pray about them—but really solve them, if y'know what I mean."

We both nodded. The conversation had taken an unexpected turn, and we were intrigued.

"Y'wanna hear a story? A true one, not a *piseog*—not a superstition. Happened to my friend's grandmother, who had special powers. Some said she was a 'changeling'—a mysterious being left by fairies when they steal a real mortal child. I think she was just very wise—and gifted in the healing powers. She helped many people round here through the fevers and suchlike. She was a fine 'keener' too at funerals—could let out real good banshee wails for the wakers. 'Course—don't get me wrong—wakes weren't all wailin' and moanin' by any means. They were big social events too, sort of honoring the spirit of the deceased with *céilí* songs, whiskey, flirtations, and all that. There was one pretty raunchy game—like a mock wedding that the clergy thought disgusting. Of course in those days it was all pretty innocent. Not like today, with young women as fresh and free as horny rabbits! Oh, and some claimed when she was younger she could turn into a *lianhan shee* fairy—sort of like a sexy seductress who lures fellas into Tír na nÓg—the underground fairy world, or as some call it, "The Land of Eternal Youth"—for a bit of you know what. And then she'd leave them to get lost or sit them on the back of a *pooka*—a huge horse spirit that whirls 'em off on a terrible wild ride before—if they're lucky—dumping them back at home to be battered senseless by a furious wife with a rolling pin!"

"Quite a life!" said Anne.

"Well, listen. This is how it ended when she got old and finally died. Y'know that when you're in your coffin and being carried into the church you're always supposed to go in feetfirst. Only priests get to go in headfirst. So what happened at her funeral was that they were carrying her in same as they would any other normal person, but the bloody coffin—soon as it got close to the door—turned itself and all the bearers around until she was headfirst. And they'd back off and try again and—wham! The coffin'd swing like a compass needle, and she'd be headfirst again . . ."

"So what happened?" asked Anne.

"How the heck do I know. I was just a little kid, but I imagine she got her way. People don't like to mess with fairy stuff, even if the church is involved. Once you start playing around with that, it goes beyond religion."

There was a sudden knock on the door and in walked a friend of Noel's from a farm just down the road. "C'mon in, Tom—I was just tellin' m'guests here the story of Michael's grandmother . . ."

"Oh yes, indeed—fine lady. Very gifted for the healing and suchlike. Tapping into special powers and all that. And talking about higher powers, did you tell them that story about the movin' Madonna statue?"

"No," said Noel. "We hadn't got that far yet. Why don't you tell it?"

Tom laughed. "I only came round to pinch a few cigarettes but—well, it just goes to show how you've got to be careful with

Old Tractor near Dursey Island

296 + At the Edge of Ireland

things y'don't understand 'specially at a time before the Celtic Tiger came roarin' in and things were pretty hard all around. Anyway, there was in this lovely little village of Ballyspittle a statue of our Holy Mother by the church that started to move. I mean move so you could actually see it shiftin'. And the papers picked it up and people started comin' from all over to see this statue, and the little village was getting' fat and flush from all this attention. And this, of course, was very nice for Ballyspittle, which got a premature taste of the Tiger, so to speak. But other nearby villages in a rough state economically were getting a little envious, and more reports of moving Holy Lady statues started to flood in. But the movements were always very small—more like little wobbles. So one imaginative young man in a village way up in Kerry decided he could create a real rocker of a statue. He was a trainee engineer and knew about pulleys and guy lines and the like, so he set up this elaborate system of nylon filaments like near invisible but very strong fishing lines—and started rocking the Virgin high up on her pedestal way above the main door. And people saw it and the word spread and the papers and TV came and all agreed that this was the best rocking virgin of them all and the village started to get rich from all the visitors . . . until . . ."

"Ah—the inevitable 'until,' " Anne said.

"D'y want me to finish this? We're just getting to the best bit . . . One night the young trainee engineer came down from his hidden nook where he'd been pulling the lines. There were a few people about but most had gone home. And as he came out of the front door of the church he didn't notice that one of those almost invisible fishing lines had somehow come loose and he caught his foot on it and it jerked the statue completely off its plinth and it started to fall . . ."

"A messy end!" said Anne.

"Ah—not so fast," said Tom. "It was coming straight for his head and would have smashed it like a fat juicy watermelon but—six inches from impact—the statue suddenly stopped apparently in

midair, and everyone round about gasped and shouted and photo-
graphed and videoed and the young man still didn't know what all
the fuss was about.

When the crowd pointed to the statue slowly revolving about his
head he lost his nerve and ran and was not seen around the village
for quite a long while after that. But the photos were, and everyone
agreed that, despite all the fakery with the lines, the fact the statue
had stopped in midflight and spared the engineer's life was a miracle easily equal in notoriety to all the other moving statues around
the country. And so the little village continued to prosper!"

"Fascinating," I said. "And the moral is?"

"Moral? I'm not too sure about that. Maybe—make the most of
whatever you've got—I suppose."

"Just like Noel with his beautiful little farm all those velvety
meadows, all those cute sheep, and a stack of money in the bank
from all those bottles of whiskey he never drank."

"I'll drink to all that!" Noel said, laughing, his warm eyes glowing in the brilliant sunset that was bathing the room in a golden-
scarlet light.

"Oh no, you can't do that!" Anne said, chuckling. And the evening rolled on . . .

24

A Scrap Odyssey

∷

ANOTHER CONVERSATION A FEW DAYS LATER reinforced a lot of what we'd learned from the "protean life" seemingly lived by many of the more creative individuals on Beara. I was chatting with Pete O'Neill, a burly red-haired fisherman in his early fifties who lived down in Kinsale but seemed to enjoy occasional sojourns up to Castletownbere. We'd met originally by chance at Breen's in the square and agreed to keep in touch. On this particular occasion we were sitting down by the ferry slip on a warm afternoon, and he was describing the appeal of our little town and his memories of one notable event back in the late 1990s.

"Y'see, this place always seems to lure in the mavericks and the magic individuals—with the occasional madman thrown in to keep the pot bubbling. In fact there was this one guy—back in '98, I think, maybe '99. He seemed to be a bit of all of that—maverick, magic, and definitely a touch mad too. I think his real name was Pearlman—David, Dennis—I forget. But he'd decided to call himself Neutrino—Poppa, Poppa Neutrino, that was it—after the name of a small particle so elusive and mysterious that he assumed it was unreal—a theoretical entity."

"And how did you meet this Neutrino fellow?" I asked.

"Oh, I didn't. I've been told about him. I wish I had met him, though. He became a bit of instant Beara folklore when he arrived here out of the blue—actually, out of the black, just after a tremendous storm had hit the town here. Floated in on a clapped-out piece of junk he'd somehow hobbled together with a few of his mates out of scrap lumber and Styrofoam and suchlike and sailed with this crazy crew—three guys and three dogs, I think—across the Atlantic from Canada to Ireland."

"Did the locals take him seriously?"

"Not at first. I mean, you wouldn't believe what a piece of crap that boat of his was—if you'd even call it a boat. More like a mini-masterpiece of discarded dreck! Some didn't believe he'd made the crossing at all, but after a while, as people talked with him, he became a bit of a zany saint-guru. He seemed to be all kinds of different people bundled up in one little individual. They said he was a singer, songwriter, violinist, poet, builder, craftsman, a lettering artist—I heard he painted quite a few signs for people around here.

"The guy was in his seventies, but he acted like he was in his early forties. Energy just radiated out of him, so they said. He seemed to be one of those people who refused to outgrow their vicarious vicissitudes. People'd come just to listen to tales of his adventures around the earth, especially his zany sailing odysseys on other crafts he'd patched together from scraps of this and that. I think he even tried to replicate Thor Heyerdahl's journey on his amazing trans-Pacific *Kon-Tiki* raft built out of balsa logs. They couldn't get enough of this chap around here. They even started quoting him— things like: 'The forbidden and the impossible are always the greatest aphrodisiacs.' And another—'Life is fire—you're meant to get burned. You can't escape it. The faster you learn to enjoy the smell of burning, the faster you learn what life is all about—an endless adventure!' I always remember that last bit—'an endless adventure.' Kinda makes you wonder about your own life—the way you've chosen to use your time.

"And that's another thing he kept saying too—about the choice always being yours. No matter what the circumstances—no matter how many justifications you have for living a straight-line kind of life—stifling the options—it's still you doing the choosing. 'Course he said there were penalties to be paid: 'He who dares not grasp the thorn should ne'er crave the rose'—bit of Emily Brontë so he said. You can blame God, fate, bad luck, obligations, responsibilities—all the usual stuff—but the choices are always there and only you can choose them, release them, sailing on the whims of the winds—and release yourself, I suppose."

"Or your *selves*," I suggested.

"Yeah," Pete said and thought for a while. "Yeah—well, I think that's what this Neutrino chap was trying to get across. Some people got mad at him, usually behind his back, though, and called him irresponsible, a wandering bum, an escapist unwilling to live in the real world with real responsibilities. Others went the other way—they seemed absolutely fascinated by his ideas—and more important, the fact he'd lived out his ideas. Lived out his fantasies and dreams. Made them really real. He gave people a kind of release—at least that's what some of my friends who were around at the time tell me. He seemed to be living proof that zany things are possible—that life could be lived as a great adventure. He said something like, "The true adventurer goes out aimless and uncalculating to meet and greet unknown fates!"

"Well, sounds like this Neutrino chap gave Castletownbere quite a bit of a buzz."

"Yep. They said the quay was crammed with people as this piece of floating junk bobbed into harbor. It was all in the papers.

Poppa's Boots

Neutrino shouted out, so they say—'Sixty-two days from Newfoundland to wherever it is we've landed in Ireland—we've definitely broken the scrap barrier!'

"And scrap just about describes his floating creation. The major components were 'distressed' lumber nailed and then woven together with miles of frayed rope from local boatyards back in Canada, huge Styrofoam floats, an old parachute pulled over a web of ancient fishnets for a sail, broad outriggers of bamboo to stop the contraption from flipping over, and a huge piece of construction plywood as a daggerboard. And additional luxuries apparently included a full-size upright piano, an old radar that nobody knew how to work, an ancient oak bar for nightly 'sundowner' drinks, and—oh those three pet dogs . . . said it was all inspired by Buckminster Fuller's crazy concepts and constructions.

"He must have had God on his side—they were hit by two hurricanes, tipped over, blown three hundred miles off course, kept running out of food and having to beg from rare passing boats. They'd planned to piggyback on the Gulf Stream current all the way to Europe but never seemed able to find it! But they somehow finally arrived in Castletownbere, were celebrated mightily by the locals, and eventually had a video of their exploits shown on the National Geographic channel later on the same year. And when they interviewed him on the local TV and radio, he kept coming out with more pretty neat ideas—things that kinda stuck in your mind . . .'"

"Like?"

"Well, like . . . like what I was saying earlier on, really, and well, it's been a while . . . so I can't remember it all . . . but I know he kept saying you've got to 'break the alignment' . . . meaning, don't be too predictable. He said, 'When you die, the alignment's broken anyway, so have more fun and do it yourself from time to time. Step out of one life existence and slip into another. Let your possessions go—all those material distractions—give 'em away . . . Be a gypsy . . . Let go and trust and let the current carry you . . . Go a little crazy . . . You don't have as long as you think . . .'"

"So you do remember!"

"Well—maybe not his exact words, but that was the gist of it. He spoke what many of us secretly think or fantasize about—but most times we never do anything about it. Never get beyond the 'what if' stage."

"So what happened to him?"

"I'm not sure, really. I heard he'd gone back to the States to build another raft to cross the Pacific to Japan or . . . or maybe it was Thailand. He'd always have some wacky scheme going. For him, I reckon, it would just be following his life-code. Doing what he felt he should be doing. But I tell you, he left a lot of people around here wondering about their own lives and the way they were living them . . . He created ripples of restlessness, you might call it . . . which isn't necessarily a bad thing, is it?"

"Y'know," I said, "we've had quite a few friends visit us down here from England and the USA and they told us that Beara itself—this beautiful peninsula—has had a similar impact. Creating those 'ripples of restlessness' as you see other ways of living—other ways of celebrating life and being alive."

"Yeah. And it doesn't just happen to the blow-ins. I think many of us who've lived here for years—sometimes all of our lives and the lives of our forefathers—feel we can tap into these . . . ripples. Kinda keeps us on the right course . . . gives you a kind of whack on the side of your head once in a while. And that can be a very useful reminder of the important things . . . right?"

"Dead right," I said.

25
Walking the Beara Way
(or Not . . .)

∷

WARNING: THIS IS NOT A PROJECT to be undertaken lightly. Oh sure, it looks easy enough on a small map—a simple dotted line wriggling up and around the Beara's mountainous spine and encompassing its two islands, Dursey and Bere, and ending up among a very pleasant cluster of restaurants in elegant Kenmare.

Even the official guidebook is disarmingly encouraging in its summary description: "Using tracks, old roads and mountain paths, it takes in some of the most breathtaking scenery in Ireland . . . One could walk sections by following the easily recognized marking posts or a map. It provides a delightful and easy way to discover and explore the peninsula."

The actual length is a little disheartening, though—125 miles is a lot longer than it looks on the map—but having once in my more ambitiously exploratory days conquered England's Coast to Coast Walk (75 miles) and the mighty Pennine Way (at 270 miles, the longest of all the nation's "long-distance" footpaths), I convinced myself that the Beara Way must be something of a dilettantish dawdle. Particularly as almost half of it is along narrow paved boreens and not across (so I was assured) thigh-deep bogs and snap-your-ankle rock deserts, as it was on the wild and soggy moors of England.

I thought I might do it in sections, and indeed my preparatory strolls on the two islands were both enticing experiences. At the tip western end of the peninsula is the enchanting, almost abandoned isle of Dursey. Barely four miles by one and a half miles, it is described by Penelope Durell in her richly informative book, *Discover Dursey*, as a "long leviathan at rest, gazing out at the boundless ocean—up-tilted nose, smooth domed head, back formed by the curvaceous contours of five hills."

The island may appear at first somewhat docile and even dull. But closer inspection reveals dramatic tide races in the narrow channel separating it from the mainland, rugged beachless cliffs rejecting easy access, and the stump of a lighthouse built in 1866 on Calf Rock and battered to pieces by a hurricane in 1881. This is indeed not a friendly place, as its history of hardship and horror would indicate, most notably in a massacre of all its three hundred inhabitants—supposedly members of the O'Sullivan clan—following the destruction of Dunboy Castle at Castletownbere in 1602.

The description of this event is spine-chilling in its ferocity:

> *Many of the people on Dursey Island at the time were refugees from the mainland, and they had fled in terror on the arrival of the forces. These were English forces under the command of Sir George Carew who was sent over to challenge local chiefs and even the forces of King Philip III of Spain who had sent supplies and men to aid the struggle for sovereignty against Queen Elizabeth I in 1601. Following a disastrous rout for the Irish, Dunboy Castle became an important but fragile garrison against the imminent attack. When disaster seemed apparent, many of the occupants fled to Dursey Island. Some had entered the small fort there, others ran away to hide or placed their hope in the sanctuary of the church. It was all to no avail, for after dismantling the fort, the soldiers set fire to all the houses as well as the church. They rounded up the people and shot down, hacked with swords or ran through with spears the now disarmed garrison and others—old men, women and children—whom they had*

driven into one heap. Some ran their swords up to the hilt
through the babes and the mothers, who were carrying them
on their breasts, others paraded before their comrades little
children writhing and convulsing on their spears, and finally
binding all the survivors, they threw them off the cliffs into
the sea over jagged and sharp rocks showering on them shots
and stones. In this way perished about 300 Catholics.

It's hard to juxtapose such hideously cruel events with the mellow moods presented to visitors today who take the time to explore Dursey. The Beara Way here on the island is a ten-mile loop on paths and boreens and is particularly pleasant in early fall when the gorse is in radiant golden flower across the bare treeless dome of the island. The climax experience, though, is not so much the walk itself, but access to the island by a creaking, rickety old cable car that crosses the tide-race abyss at the eastern extremity of the peninsula. The tiny metal cabin with a capacity of "six persons or a cow" seems alarmingly fragile and subject to a nauseating swinging and swaying as winds buffet it eighty feet or so above the roiling waves below. Occasionally dolphins doing flips and leaps in the turbulent channel can distract from the traumatic experience, but if windy heights are a worry, just stare straight ahead and promise yourself a tipple of the hard stuff when you finally arrive on the other side.

So why come? Well, certainly for the peace and silence, as only a handful of hardy residents call this place home. Also the evocative remnants of a monastery, fort, signal tower, and villages in addition to fine vistas of Bull Rock, Ireland's second largest gannetry, plus a breeding ground of storm petrels, fulmars, razorbills, guillemots, choughs, and even occasional peregrine falcons. But for those relishing the rich mysteries of Beara, Dursey's tales of strange boats, mystical lights, sea and animal apparitions, ghosts, and fairies are a far more tempting lure.

Anne and I visited Penny Durell to learn more about some of these oddities.

"So—how long have y'got?" was Penny's laughing response after we told her of our mission to learn from her more of Dursey's strange folkloric heritage.

"Well—we have your book, so we've got a bit of a head start," said Anne.

Penny smiled. Or rather, she glowed. She was one of those intriguing individuals who seemed to float about buoyed on their own auras of happiness and contentment. Despite a recent and obviously still painful injury to her right hand, her smile exuded radiance and humor.

"Oh, well—if you've already forked out for the book, you're very welcome indeed. Cup o'tea? Homemade biscuits?" (This had obviously now become one of our "Beara rituals." A substantial part of our diet seemed to consist of cups of tea and homemade confectionaries in other people's homes.)

"Yes to both," I said. "We need restoration. It took quite a while to find your place. You're way out in the middle of nowhere . . ."

Penny giggled. "Well, I don't know about nowhere. It's certainly a bit isolated but . . ."

"And almost lost in your own massive windbreak trees and bushes."

"Yes, and that. But, be honest now, isn't it worth it just for the view!"

She was right, of course. The all-embracing vista of the whole of Dursey Island, the foaming tidal rips of the narrow sound and the faint hazy outlines of the two now familiar Skelligs twelve or so miles out there in the Atlantic, was magnificent.

"I'd never get tired of that view," Anne said, sighing.

Penny laughed, "No, you're right. It's very beautiful . . . when you can see it! But you know how our weather is here. We can go days—even weeks in winter—when you can barely see the trees at the end of our garden."

"Yeah—we've had quite a few experiences with those local

mists—more like the old London pea-soupers. But I was looking at your garden. Lots of stuff you're growing out there . . .'

"Well, I guess David, my loyal mate, and I are still maintaining some of the old counterculture spirit—y'know, self-sufficiency and all that. We grow a mass of tomatoes and other veggies, gorgeous apples and soft fruits and herbs galore. But when we first moved here some people thought we were a bit suspicious with all our herby stuff. Thought it might be something a little more . . . y'know, radical—but we invited them in to help themselves, and they eventually accepted us as harmless old ex-hippies still living the simple 'good life.' "

Penny's "tea" was one of her own herbal brews and full of fruit flavors. Her homemade cookies were the kind that you find your fingers reaching out for despite edicts issued by the responsible part of your brain insisting that your quota has already been outrageously exceeded.

And Penny's stories were wonderful. We could fill chapters galore with her tales, but as her book *Discover Dursey* already does that, why be redundant. Suffice to say, we delighted in her historic vignettes and descriptions of pre-Christian superstitions or *piseogs*. Apparently the old feast of Bealtaine on the first day of May celebrating the coming of summer was the climactic event of the year here and spawned a wealth of customs, many revolving around cows, milk, and butter making. The animals were blessed by marking the sign of the cross over the byre doors, which would then also be tightly locked up in the morning to prevent mischievous fairies (as opposed to the "good little people") from stealing precious milk and butter. May Day itself was particularly rigid—no butter could be churned on that day no milk could be given away, as such a gift would drain "the luck of the farm." And woe betide any cow giving birth to a calf, as they were both certain to die and bring doom upon the household.

And then, as summer moved on, there came the lighting of great bonfires on St. John's Eve to ward off disease and entice blessings, and the furious flurries of semi-erotic singing and dancing for the Lughnasa pagan harvest festival. But then things became a little more onerous with the strange antics of Halloween and All Souls' Day, the Celtic festival of Samhain when, in Penny's words, "only a thin veil separates the physical world from the realm of the spirits."

She went on to tell us that, because of that terrible massacre on Dursey in 1602, residents would be "very wary of greeting any stranger encountered on the road at night because the ghosts of those tragic victims still wandered about, lost and hopeless, under cover of darkness."

The local fishermen also had their own rigorous codes of super-stitious conduct. Conversations on their boats out at sea were bound by strict taboos forbidding any discussion of pigs, foxes, or priests, which, they claimed, could jeopardize a decent catch. And if a fish-erman should encounter a red-haired girl on his way down to his boat, he would be well advised to return home promptly and aban-don fishing for that day.

"Oh," added Penny, "and if he'd forgotten to put some coal in his trouser pocket before he left home, he'd also better go back and get some. And then he'd need to drag his wife or one of his kids down to the jetty to throw an old shoe after the boat—supposedly a very aus-picious good luck gesture, although it must have cost them a small fortune in shoes. But if all these precautionary customs failed and there was a death at sea—a drowning—then there were more strict rules to be followed. For example, a close family member had to wear the victim's clothes at Mass for the three Sundays following the funeral service—and any woman pregnant with child could only attend the service, as she was barred from the actual burial. How-ever, if she heard a bell-like ringing in her ear, she should pray for the deceased immediately. Oh—and if she wasn't married, she should watch out for houses where sparks from the peat fire flew out of the chimney, because money would be coming in for the fortunate occupants. And if one of them happened to be an eligible bachelor who picks up a hairpin in the road and then immediately meets a woman, she should be ready for a serious proposal of marriage. Of course, if there's a ginger cat crossing her path 'round about the same time, she should refuse the offer, as she would be constantly plagued by bad luck for the rest of her life."

"So complex!" Anne laughed. "Surrounded by so many fears and fantasies . . ."

"Oh, that's just the start," said Penny. "In the old days, little old Dursey was a hotbed of hauntings, fairy ships, fairies themselves, ghosts, huge fantasy galleons, strange lights, sea apparitions, hidden treasures, disembodied voices, and many other manifestations of overactive imaginations."

"So, you're a believer in all these things?" I asked. 'Have you experienced any apparitions yourself yet or found any hidden treasure?"

"Well—we certainly found treasure. This house for starters! But no, I can't really claim firsthand experiences, although when you talk to some of the old folk around here, they can make you almost believe . . . almost anything! But how about you, David—you've walked around the island. What were your feelings?"

"Well," I said, "I've a hunch that, if I'd read your book and talked to you earlier, I'd have come away with a rather different take on Dursey. I mean—I certainly sensed a loneliness there . . . I think I only saw one other person . . . Who knows, maybe even that was an apparition . . . It was definitely an odd figure by the southern cliffs there, near where they threw the bodies over in tied-up bundles during that ghastly massacre. He or she was all hunched over and very dark in silhouette—even though the sun was way over by the Skelligs, behind me . . . I waved and the person turned but seemed to completely ignore me. So I carried on a short way toward the old village of Ballynacallagh and then I turned around and looked back . . . but he or she or it was gone. Whatever it was. And for the rest of the walk it was just me and the birds—hundreds of 'em, and . . . utter peace."

"Ah, yes, the dulcet spirit of Dursey," said Penny. "And for a tiny place, it has so much history—Viking invasions, the Normans, pirates, famines and evictions, emigrations, shipwrecks, collapsing lighthouses and storms like you can't imagine, and of course, all those—what did Anne call them—superstitious fears and fantasies. Well, it's amazing it can still offer the kind of peace and calm that can stay inside you and with you for days . . . weeks."

"Yes, it can . . . it did. It still does!" I said.

Penny giggled again. "Ah, c'mon. You've got a bad case of the Dursey Dreamtime!"

"Is it very infectious?"

"Oh—totally!" Penny laughed.

"You're right," said Anne. "I haven't even been there and I'm utterly enticed . . . I'm just not sure I want to go across in that cable car contraption."

"Never a single accident," insisted Penny.

"Oh, good," said Anne.

"Yet," said Penny.

A SECOND LITTLE SIX-MILE loop appendage of the Beara Way is on Bere Island itself, an appealing fifteen-minute ferry ride from Castletownbere. Renowned for its fine harbor, the island was the site of a major British naval base until 1938.

With a small population of around two hundred, a couple of pubs, and some basic accommodations, the place seems far removed from the quayside hullabaloo of Castletownbere, packed with huge trawlers and all its now-familiar bars and restaurants increasingly redolent with Polish and East European accents.

The island doesn't look very different from the mainland with its neatly walled fields, scattered farms, and beautiful patchwork quilt of greens and ochres featured in so many photographs of this part of Ireland. But it certainly reveals its own strong character in the remnants of fortifications, gun batteries, a Martello tower, and fine views of Dunboy Castle, where the O'Sullivan clan was massacred by the English general Carew after a siege of eleven days in 1602.

There are other island delights that make a hike here worthwhile—the late summer explosions of golden gorse flowers, the scarlet profusion of fuchsia hedgerows, a Bronze (2000–500 BC) Age standing stone on a high point marking the exact center of the island, and the wonderful, wind-buffeted wildness of the moor itself with panoramic vistas in all directions.

MEMORIES OF THESE TWO walks are true keepers: mists writhing like semitransparent serpents around the wrinkled strata of the hills; the swirl and scurry of hungry seagulls hoping for tail-end scraps from my sandwich lunches; burpy recollections of large breakfasts to bank up the energy supplies prior to my explorations. Anne's fine repasts would honor royal palates—thick pinhead porridge with cream and treacle, gorgeous slices of pan-roasted gammon ham liberally scorched with caramelized brown sugar, a couple of oh-so-golden eggs fresh from the farm down the road and tasting like eggs did pre–World War II (or so I'm told!), and finally, whiskey-flavored orange marmalade thick with pungent zest slathered on hot buttered soda-bread toast. And of course—tea. Good old stand-a-spoon-in-it Yorkshire tea.

Such abundances make you feel ready—indeed, obligated—to sally forth like a squire inspecting his estates. And in doing so you forget your sedentary tendencies and launch into that delicious stupor of "earned exhaustion" and frisson flashes that occur in those high barren places where the wind whips away all the crud of civilized torpor and reveals your true "creature of nature" beneath. This is the one that hunted with stone ax and rough-hewn spear, the one that sensed the power of the Creator in every daily moment and act and understood the sheer glorious surge of nature in all her moods and terrible cruelties. That's the fellow you don't get to meet too often in the comfortable confines of domesticity. That's a transcendency that transcends all mundanity and moroseness and lingers in the spirit for days—even weeks. Until the next time and the next revelation on these high wild places.

AND SO IT WAS that I was finally ready to begin my own odyssey of self-rediscovery on the Beara Way itself. And where better to put myself in an appropriate mood than by making my start at the four white stones at Allihies, otherwise known to the cognoscenti of Irish folklore as the Children of Lir.

An alternative starting point, and a place to which Anne and I return regularly like dogs exploring the scents on their favorite tree, could have been the remarkable remnant of a neolithic stone circle on the back road just to the west of Castletownbere. Among the tumultuous tumble here on Beara of standing stones, circles, cairns, souterrains, megalithic tombs, dolmen, and ring forts, this strong and ancient entity of Derreenataggart is one of our favorite and most dramatic places on the peninsula. We came here with good old Carey Conrad, our early mentor and guide, during our initial explorations, and it has remained one of our key touchstones of ancient authenticity here.

However, I chose the Children of Lir as my starting point. Anne drove me down on a windy morning from our Allihies cottage, patted my rucksack to ensure I had my sandwiches and water, and gave me an unusually clinging hug, as if she sensed some uncertainty about the likelihood of an imminent return.

We stood together, looking at the four famous stones. As stones go, these hardly seemed icons of mega-significance. In fact, they were barely more than large rounded beach rocks a couple of feet or so across and set closely together in rough-cut grass just above our beautiful Ballydonegan Beach.

"They hardly seem to reflect the importance of that great Lir legend," said Anne. "I mean, isn't it celebrated all over Ireland as one of the keystones of all their vast Celtic culture˚ Four little white stones doesn't really seem to do it . . ."

And yet it was rather moving in its own modest and sad way. The tale has many versions, with subtle variations and nuances that only true folklorists could relish. We prefer the short, relatively untangled one that goes something like this:

The wise and revered ocean god-king Lir of Sidh Fionnachaidh, intent on bringing peace to the tribal feudings of ancient history, married Eve (Aobh), daughter of King Bodhbh Dearg the Red, a powerful member of Tuatha Dé Danann. They were the people descended from the mother-goddess Anu, who, according to Irish legend, arrived here from Greece around 350 BC. Much later on, following a series of lost battles with the Celtic Milesians from Galicia in northwestern Spain, these people became the "fairy people"—sole possessors of the underworld.

But prior to all that, Lir was blissfully married to Eve, who conceived two sets of twins. Unfortunately Eve died in the second childbirth, so to maintain the peace, Lir married her sister Eva (Aoife). However, Eva was not so nice a character as Eve and became extremely jealous of Lir's love for his four children. So one night she secretly carried them off to Lough Darravagh and transformed them into swans.

Unfortunately, while immediately recognizing her impetuous sin, she regrettably lost the spell to release them (or so she claimed). But it was too late anyway, because King Bodhbh Dearg discovered her terrible deed and turned her into a demon condemned to float alone in the air forever. So according to the legend, the four children of Lir remained swans for nine hundred years until the coming of

Christianity in the fifth century. After the first three hundred years or so, they moved from Lough Darravagh, and many other lakes across Ireland are claimed as their second home. But eventually they settled on the Atlantic Ocean for the last three hundred years. Then finally, attracted by church bells rung by a monk, St. Mochaomhog, at the Christian church in our little community here of Allihies, they finally came ashore. Immediately the spell was broken and they regained their human form, but alas, in doing so, they also became ancient, shriveled-up nine-hundred-year-old beings and died almost instantaneously—but not before the saint had rushed down to the shore from the church and baptized them.

And thus it was that they came to be buried beneath these four white stones, which are still revered by the locals and whence I began my Beara Way odyssey.

AND SO FINALLY I was alone and striding eastward, thinking what a glorious day's adventure on the high fells lay ahead. I was looking forward to disappearing into the deep solitude of the moors—that shimmering, humming stillness that I sensed on shorter walks around Allihies and Ballydonegan beach. Then, next thing I knew, I was stopping and wondering where the hell the fells had gone. I'm sure they'd been there when I set off a short while ago. In fact, I know they were. But now they weren't. A cloud out of nowhere had snuck in when I was studying the map or daydreaming about Anne's fabulous breakfast or wondering where to camp the night after a long hike. Except I wondered if my hike might be interrupted. There was a strong suggestion of imminent rain not yet fallen.

And then, of course, the rains fell. Also out of nowhere. In fact, I could still see sunlight like jagged golden rips in the ever-accumulating black cloud mass. And of course it was your typical southwestern Ireland deluge—unforecast, unforgiving, and unforgettable. I don't believe—except maybe in the height of the Indian

Beara Way Scene

monsoon season—that I've ever known a rain that can so quickly turn a mood of bucolic bonhomie into a pure bloody mayhem of mud-slimed, buckled knees, clobber-soaked, heart-pounding, ankle-cracking chaos. And of course I'd left all possibilities of shelter behind me. Around me was nothing now but moor dotted with flesh-ripping huddles of ogreous, spike-laden gorse Not to mention an unusually odiferous collection of cow pies rapidly dissolving into the mud of the path, which in turn was rapidly dissolving into the adjoining tangles of tussocks and marsh grass and—of course—also disappearing into my now-sodden boots.

There was no choice but to slosh and plodge on, hoping that somewhere in the murk ahead I'd find respite from the helter-skelter furor. Childishly optimistic, of course, but that's the way you feel at the beginning of a hike. And my mind, searching for softer consolations, conjured up an image of an early morning a few days back as I'd sat by the sliding glass door of our cottage overlooking Ballydonegan Beach and watched a robin pecking crumbs from around our wooden picnic table. Such a tranquil scene—the little creature proudly thrusting its ochre-colored breast outward as it surveyed the scene to locate its next morsel and occasionally cocking its head in my direction as if to say: "C'mon, mate, time for a bit more bread, if y' please—this crumb-peckin' is f' the feekin' birds. Other birds, that is—not this one." And I'm sitting, smiling, and nodding and doing nothing because I know as soon as I get up to fetch more crusts and scraps, he'll lose faith in my benign tranquility and fly off. And what was so enticing was—

"Ah! Halloo. A nize day, I zink! Ha-ha!"

I must have been so very deeply reveried, almost fetally curled, in that captivating bubble of memory that I had completely failed to notice two figures looming out of the teeming murk. They were obviously fellow hikers but serious ones with far larger rucksacks than mine.

"Ah . . . oh . . . sorry. Didn't see y' there . . ."

The taller one with a dark dripping beard smiled patronizingly: "Ziss iss not zerprizink, I zink. Ze rain, she iss very wetz."

The other man, smaller and with a rather more feminine face despite a thick brown mustache, nodded seriously. "Ya. I zink zo too," he said.

I couldn't help an hospitable chuckle. The rain was so bloody obviously wet that to even mention it seemed ridiculous as we all stood together, drenched from tip to toe and with our boots squishing and our noses and other appendages dripping like chronically leaky faucets.

Making idle and convivial conversation in such conditions seemed a bit odd, but there again, we had nowhere to go for shelter and were so soaked already as to be beyond restoration anyway. So we removed our rucksacks, sat on them by the side of the path—which actually was now a thick mud stream—and chatted together like old buddies. I passed around a bar of chocolate. They—far more sensibly—passed around an unlabeled liter bottle of what I thought (hoped?) might be Irish poteen moonshine, but they insisted it was

German schnapps—"from ver ve are comings . . . Stuttgart . . . You know Stuttgart?"

I apologized profusely for a very significant lack of familiarity with Germany while insisting that Anne and I intended to make amends in the spring with a planned visit to Eastern Europe via Berlin.

"Ah yez—Berlin. Very fine place. Ve like ver much. Goods foods. Goods beers. And ver goods ladies . . ."

"Ah," I said, "in that case, maybe I should come alone."

They both stared at me curiously. Humor, I then remembered from prior conversations with fellow German travelers, is not always such an easy form of comradely communication.

"You know—what you said about the good ladies . . ."

Still no recognizable response.

Last try. "What I mean is—maybe I should not come with my wife if the Berlin ladies are—"

At last. "Ah! Aye . . . yez, yez—yez. I zee vat you zay. Ya! Ver funny. Ver good idea! Ha-ha!"

"Ya. I zink zo too," added the one with the mustache.

God, this is going to be hard work, my inner voice whispered. Yes, I whispered back, but the schnapps is just too good to up and leave. So somehow we chatted on inanely and the schnapps eased the edges of our conversational confusions. And when we finally parted, I encouragingly confirmed that they were almost at the end of the Beara Way and they, not so encouragingly, told me that I was indeed just at the beginning and it would very quickly get worse as I headed up into the high hills to the east.

I tried to think of some lighthearted aphorism to end our chat, but for some inane reason, all I could come up with was: "Well— may I just say that as you slide down the banister of life, I hope the splinters never point the wrong way!"

Not surprisingly I received only blank, uncomprehending stares until the smaller one with the thick mustache reiterated his "Ah, ya, I zink zo too."

I'd like to boast that I then pulled on my rucksack, straightened my back, set my mental and physical sights at the high ground, and marched onward and upward like a true "bog-trotter," determined to conquer all the climatic chaos, all those little incisors of insecurity, and other demons of the Beara Way.

I'd like to, but in all honesty, I can't. Because that's not what I did. I was deluged not only by the rain but by memories of my own early ineptitudes. On previous hikes, particularly as a young Boy Scout, I gained the inauspicious reputation of "the lost one," as a result of my uncanny ability to confuse marked trails with meandering cow tracks that invariably ended in pernicious, cow-pie-filled bogs. So—determined not to repeat such a fiasco—I continued on up the path until it finally merged a few miles later on with a narrow boreen. Here I checked my map for the location of our cottage and hitchhiked home from the Beara Way with visions of a hot bath, a large Irish whiskey, a loving welcoming wife, and a huge dinner of roasted chicken and cabbage and colcannon. The visions dangled like gorgeous fat carrots on the end of an extremely wet stick.

And it all came to pass just as I had envisioned! In fact, come to think of it, Anne's splendid chicken dinner was just a little too extravagant and well prepared—almost as if she was expecting me back home as soon as the storm hit. And as usual, she was correct in her somewhat demeaning expectations.

Anyway—blaming the notorious fickleness of the southwest Ireland climate—I decided to walk the Beara Way thereafter in shorter segments within relatively easy reach of boreens and pubs. It's a fine experience if you can put up with constant fogginess, snatching clumsy fistfuls of knife-edged marsh grass, and occasional break-a-leg confrontations with rocky outcrops. And of course, if you're a true marathon-masochist and the 125 miles of the Beara Way seems far too modest a challenge, there's always Jim O'Sullivan's 600-mile O'Sullivan Beara Breifne Greenway. Commemorating the notoriously decimating march of the O'Sullivans following the devastation of their Dunboy Castle in 1602 by the English Elizabethans, the route roams northward deep into County Mayo and ultimately to the city of Leitrim. And if you attempt to complete the whole course, then my hat's off to you and I'll toast your progress while watching our almost-tame robin seeking his bread crumbs around our table and sipping my Jameson by our warm fireside at the cottage, or out in the cow-cropped pasture in gorgeously drenching sunshine.

Onward!

26

Weather Signs
(and Visions Too)

IT ALL BEGAN WITH ONE OF those throwaway remarks over lunchtime at Murphy's. I was chatting with a sprightly-eyed young woman and happened to mention the zaniness of our peninsula's weather pattern—"utterly unpredictable and fickle" was the euphemistic way I described it following my Beara Way fiasco.

She chuckled and thought for a moment. "Listen. I'm a teacher over in Bantry, and I've been working on a class project about weather lore and whatnot. It's time the students had a chance to show off what they've learned. Would you like to be a spectator? You might enjoy it . . . even learn something!"

I wasn't too sure I felt like spending an afternoon in that particular fashion, especially as it was quite a long drive to Bantry.

But there I was anyway a week or so later, in Bantry, perched on a very small chair in a classroom with twenty or so kids in the ten- to twelve-year-old range. The teacher was ready to go—the students looked a lot less enthusiastic.

"Sean—you won our last class competition. Tell the gentleman a few of the most important signs we look out for in the weather here."

No one said anything. No young Sean arose to face the teacher.

"Sean . . . Come along now . . . You did very well in the test last week. Stand up now . . ."

Still no movement. Somewhere a very sensitive Sean lurked, wishing he was the size of a dust mite.

"Sean!"

Actually, he was huge. Relatively speaking, of course, in this class of preteens. And unusually adipose. And unusually red in the face. He towered above his peers—a picture of pure terror caught in a cross fire of smirky sidelong glances.

"I forgot . . . miss."

"Sean!"

Sean took a deep breath. "Well . . . ," he began, "if the stars look dim, very bad weather will follow on the morrow . . . but when the swallows fly very low, it is a sign of good weather . . . uh . . . uh . . ."

"Tell the gentleman about the winds."

"Winds, miss?"

"Sean—you know all about the winds. That's how you won the prize, isn't it now? Why don't you start with the east wind . . ."

After a long pause, "Er . . . the east wind . . . brings hard cold weather and very often frost . . . The west wind brings the fine weather . . . The southwest wind brings the rain . . . and er . . ."

"The north wind, Sean?"

"Er . . . the north wind . . . um . . ."

The teacher was obviously becoming most disappointed by this particular student. His performance was not reflecting well on her prowess as an educator, at least in the area of weather signs.

"Anyone else?" she asked lamely.

Sean immediately sat down and hid behind a sea of heads. His aura of relief was tangible, despite the fact I couldn't even see him now.

"Me, miss! Me!"

An obviously excitable young girl with bright auburn hair and a flurry of freckles across her cheeks jumped up and down in her chair, waving her hands.

"All right—Maria . . ."

Maria leapt up, delighted to be the focus of attention and obviously used to it. "Miss, a north wind over the ancient stones brings cold showers, Miss."

"Very good, Maria . . ."

"And the wind that blows down the chimney and makes the soot fall into the grate is a sign of rain coming soon or late."

"Excell—"

"And when the wind raises up the fine dust on the road—that's rain coming, and if there's light blue smoke on the hills in May, that means the fine weather will come and stay . . . and—"

"Thank you, Mar—"

"And if there's a ring around the moon, it means rain is on the way very soon . . ."

"Maria—thank you."

"Yes, miss." An abrupt break in her eloquent, well-rehearsed flow.

Ancient Stones—A Fallen Dolmen

"That's very good now. Thank you."

"But there's more, miss," said a frustrated, on-a-roll, precocious Maria.

"Yes, I know, but let's ask . . . Finbar. Finbar, stand up please . . ."

At the far side of the classroom a tiny Finbar rose slowly from his desk, his face pale and sallow. Obviously the sudden spotlight of attention had been unexpected, which caused what one might call a sudden embarrassing and noisy explosion in his preteen gut. He gave an odd gurgle, clutched his stomach, and rushed out of the classroom, leaving the poor teacher uncertain as to her next move.

"So—well now, let's continue to show this nice gentleman what we all know about our weather. Brendan, it's your turn now."

Brendan was obviously destined for stardom. He was a charmingly urchin-faced boy with apple cheeks, a welcome-all smile, and a disarmingly confident "I'd-be-delighted-to-help-out" manner. "Yes, miss—thank you . . . there are some I really like—the ones that rhyme like, when the stars run bright and low along the darking sky, the frost and the freeze are both close by . . ."

"Very good, Brendan. Now go on and tell the gentleman about insects and the like."

"Ah." Brendan smiled confidently. "Sure indeed I will." (Oh, yes. I could see this lad on TV in no time at all with his broad grin and twinkling green eyes. A real Irish charmer.) "First, there's the ants—the ones with the wings—and if they should fall to the earth, it's a sign of good weather coming. But then, with the bees, if they are noisy and buzzy around the hive, then rain will be coming before the day's out—as with the midges; if they're all over in moving clouds over your head, that means rain too."

"Excellent, Brendan!"

"Miss—I have one, miss . . . better than Brendan's!" Brendan laughed as a complete clone of himself rose up at the back of the classroom. Obviously his twin brother.

"All right, Ryan, let's have it. You won't be happy until you give it to us anyway." The teacher grinned, obviously used to their sibling rivalry.

"Well, my grandfather used to say: 'Mackerel sky and mare's tales make lofty ships carry low sails.'"

"And what do you think that means, Ryan?"

"It'll soon be pissing it down," came a whispered response, but not from Ryan. The class burst out with pent-up laughter.

"Now—who said that?!" demanded the teacher.

The laughter continued. No one rose to admit responsibility.

"We do not use that kind of language in front of guests!"

"No—only at home!" came another subvocal wisecrack from the opposite side of the class.

"Now—look. Who said that?"

A whirling of questioning heads, but still no admittance of guilt from anyone.

"Miss—I haven't finished yet," said Ryan as the laughter faded into sniggers. This was obviously a fun class to be in. Although maybe not for the teacher.

"Yes, I know, Ryan. And I know who's being rude too. I will deal with you both later." (I don't think she did know, but she had to maintain face somehow. I nodded with a stern grimace, trying to show my support for her, but giggling like a loon inside.)

"Continue, Ryan, please . . ."

Ryan smiled as brightly as his TV-destined brother and began again: "Well—when the sun is on the rocks and makes them shine like glass, it's a sign that rain will very soon come to pass."

"Good . . ."

"And another . . . 'When the new moon is on its back, it is a sign that of bad weather there'll be no lack . . .'"

"All right, good . . ."

"And another, miss—'When the sea goes a-whistling on a summer's day, it is a sign there'll be rain without delay.'"

"Excellent, Ryan. You can sit down now."

"Just one more, miss—it's really, really good . . ."

"Miss!" said sibling Brendan. "Tell him to sit down. It's my turn again now."

"Brendan—sit! And Ryan, you, too, sit!"

But Ryan, while slowly lowering himself onto his seat, had to have his way. "If the sun comes out too bright on a winter's morning, it will certainly rain in the evening without warning—"

"Ryan! Be quiet!"

In the midst of all the frenzy a tall, thin girl arose waiflike from her chair, and as she did, the class immediately quietened. Was she a class leader, I wondered? She seemed to exert a sudden powerful influence over her peers, and even the teacher.

"Ah, Bernadette . . . you have something to say?" asked the teacher in what seemed to be an almost fawning manner. Bernadette made no reply, merely stood, princesslike, looking over the scattered heads, staring intently at the blackboard. There was total silence. And then she began in a chantlike monotone: "When the smoke rises straight from the stack into the sky, it'll be long-fair and warmly dry . . . When a star falls into the sea, it is a sign of a full rain to be . . . When the swallows are flying high in the sky, it's a sign of fine weather in the bye and bye . . . When seagulls rest on land a fair distance from the sea, a storm will be coming, just you wait and see . . . When the house cat's back is turned to the turf fire, it means bad weather is coming, likely dire . . ."

Bernadette nodded to indicate she'd completed her litany and demurely sat down. There was silence again. No wisecracks, no sniggering remarks, nothing even from the two twins, who were obviously the appointed class clowns.

Finally the teacher gave a brilliant if slightly servile smile. "Excellent, Bernadette . . . and beautifully expressed. Don't you all agree, class?"

And—wonder of wonders—the class responded with a unanimous murmur of approval. Who was this girl? What was the hold she appeared to have on this class? And the teacher?

Later, when I was leaving, I asked the teacher about Bernadette. "She seemed kind of special. She was certainly treated with great respect by the class."

The teacher leaned close to me and half whispered, "Well, she . . . she's had a hard life, let's just say that . . . oh—and then, of course, there was the sighting thing."

"Sighting? You mean like second sight . . . seeing into the future?"

"Well no . . . not exactly," said the teacher softly. She was obviously uncertain about continuing this discussion. "Y'see, there was talk of a vision . . . kind of thing . . ."

"Of . . . ?"

I could tell the teacher was becoming even more uncomfortable, but she'd aroused my all-too-rampant curiosity.

"Well—they say . . . who knows if it's true. Bernadette won't say anything more about it . . . and the priests are not too happy . . . even the bishop . . . It's something you have to treat very carefully nowadays, y'know."

"What is?"

"A vision . . . thing . . . of the Blessed Virgin. But listen—I'm sorry, I've got to go back in. They're terrible when they're left alone. I'm sure somebody will tell you the whole story . . . far better than me."

But the odd thing was that no one ever wanted to talk about Bernadette's "vision thing." It was hinted on a couple of occasions that it would be "best for everyone" if I forgot the whole story.

Which, for the moment at least, I did.

27

Danny's "Song of Beara"

▪
▪
▪

A FAINT VOICE EBBS AND FLOWS on the other end of the telephone line. A line that ends somewhere in the wilds of New Jersey far from the toxic wastelands of Interstate 95 and "Chemical Alley" and the strange, ever-diminishing swathes of reedy marshlands around Newark and its ever-expanding airport. A line that stretches way over three thousand miles to this little battered phone box outside Eileen Kelly's post office in Allihies from a quaint colonial cottage on the eastern fringe of the USA set among huge shade trees by a skittering stream.

"So, I'm flying into Shannon next Friday—with Rob and Celia. That's still okay—right?"

"That's just wonderful," I gushed. "You'll have a great time. I've told a few of the pubs around here about your splendid reputation in the States as an Irish folksinger and recording artist supremo and they say come on in and give them a *seisuin* anytime. Tourist season is pretty well gone—although there weren't too many of them this year anyway—and they say they're ready now for a bit of true Irish *craic*."

There was a chuckle at the other end. I knew that chuckle well. It always preceded Danny Quinn's latest jokes, which he scattered randomly throughout all his conversations. In fact, most of our chats seemed to be mere interludes between his jokes, which he invariably laughs at long before he gets to the punch lines. "Did y'hear the one about . . ."

"What?"

"The one about . . . What the heck's wrong with your line . . . ?"

"Oh, nothing much, except it's pouring outside and I can hardly hear a word from your end . . ."

"Okay—I'll save it . . . It's too good to lose in the middle of a Beara cloudburst . . ."

"What?"

A frustrated pause at the other end and then, "When are you gonna get a decent world cell phone or something so we can kvetch like normal people . . ."

"What?" The last was lost in the thundery roar directly over the phone box.

"Forget it. See you Friday. And tell Anne . . ."

The rain was now deafening as it crashed in columns on the leaky cast-iron shell of the phone box.

"Yes, okay, I will. Have a great flight . . ." I had no idea what I was supposed to tell Anne, but I knew that one more "What?" would eradicate the limits of our mutual patience.

"What?" That was him, not me. Followed by more of his gurgling chuckles.

"Get lost, Danny . . ."

So THERE I WAS, rudely dismissing my friend, the mighty Danny Quinn, one of America's finest Irish folksingers, creator of a dozen or more popular albums, composer of countless fine songs, compatriot of Tommy Makem and the Clancy Brothers and, when he was into one of his joke-laden, giggle-laced monologues, one of the funniest of all our friends. And—finally—after much pestering, we had lured him from his rigorous schedule of concert, club, and pub dates in the USA to spend a few days with us at our Beara cottage along with

Robby and Celia, longtime buddies from our lakeside neighborhood in the Hudson Valley.

"Anything you need me to do . . . or bring?" Danny had asked in a previous phone chat on a bright sunny day when conversation from the phone box had been a little more coherent.

Back in the USA Danny would occasionally stay with us at our home when on one of his laboriously long East Coast folksinging tours. And it had now become a most enticing ritual for him to bring a bagful of British goodies—Stilton and (real) cheddar cheese, chocolate biscuits, treacle, British bangers and bacon, and his latest finds in fine red wines.

"Well—you might as well bring a few of your CDs, because as soon as they hear your voice, you'll be a local star . . . Oh—and one more request—actually it's a condition of our hosting you at the cottage and catering to your every gastronomic and other whims . . ."

"This is sounding good . . . especially that thing you said about 'other whims.' I've always got a few of those floating about, y'know."

"Yeah—and it's just a simple request . . ."

"Okay—I'm waiting . . . But I'm getting just a wee bit nervous."

"Well, I've told you what a fabulous place this Beara is—the scenery, the people, the history, the traditions, and a sense of touching something authentically Gaelic-Celtic . . . very Irish."

"Yeah, yeah—I know all that. Why do you think I'm coming?"

"Well—to spend time with us primarily, I assume."

"All right—that too . . . I suppose, if you say so. And what is it you want from me?"

"A song."

"A song?"

"Actually not 'a' song, but 'The Song' . . . the 'Song of Beara'. No one's written one as far as I know. There are plenty of Celtic long poems and all that, but not a really good folk song that captures the unique character of this place."

A long pause at the other end.

"Danny . . . ?"

"Yeah. I'm thinking . . . You kinda hit a bit of a soft spot there, matey. I hate to remind you, but I haven't written a decent song . . . come to think of it, I haven't even written a lousy song . . . in over two years. Plus . . ."

"Listen—you remember that Baudelaire quote, something about poets and artists being riders on the storm, exiles here on earth, trying to fly, dragging their giant's wings?"

"Oh how very literary of you. Is that meant to make me feel better?"

"No—but this place will. Believe me. Beara will set all your muses in motion."

"Are they the female kind—all sort of wrapped up in slinky, diaphanous, silky things?"

"Absolutely!"

"And young, and nubile, and pretty and . . . very . . . inspiring?"

"Oh, boy—you'll be inspired like you've never been inspired before."

"In that case, like good old Oscar Wilde, I'd admit that 'I can resist everything except temptation' and . . . I'd like one to be named . . . Daphne."

"No problem. I'll have a Daphne ready and waiting."

". . . and maybe another . . . called Felicity."

"Okay—Felicity and Daphne it will be, Oh Honored Guest and Great Composer."

"Ah! Now I know you're lyin' . . ."

"No, no, not really. Merely a wee fleck of 'expedient exaggeration'!"

"Well in that case, I may have a few other conditions of my own, David . . . like seeing you pick up your own guitar again for once."

"Not a chance on that one, Danny. Sorry. My fingers are as twisted as a turf carrier's back.'"

"Oh, how very . . . colorfully ethnic . . ."

"So, we're set then? You get your seductive mélange of muses and we get 'The Song of Beara.' "

"I'm only coming for a week or so, y'know . . . and I haven't even seen the place yet."

"How do you think I felt when I arrived to write this book?"

"Yeah—but you've been there months now!"

"So I'll distill all my impressions for you, give you a fabulous drive around, pour pints of the strong black stuff down your throat at all the locals, introduce you to some of the nicest people you'll ever meet this side of heaven . . . and then give you a pen and a note- pad and wait for the splendid result that I know will flow quickly and mellifluously!"

"I've always loved that word—*mellifluous.*"

"So—deal?"

"Okay. Deal. But I should tell you. I've got my fingers crossed at this end, so it doesn't really count."

"No problem. If we don't get our song, you'll have no fingers left anyway—and no nubile muses either!"

"Oh, very nice. Thank you so much for that."

"Looking forward to seeing you, Danny."

"Likewise."

AND LO!—IT CAME to pass as it was written, or at least verbally agreed. "The Song of Beara" emerged from our friend's previously composition-blocked brain and spirit. And it came in a remarkable tsunami of inspired creativity on his fourth day on Beara, no less, after we'd all returned from a roiling ride around the peninsula that had impressed our guests with its raw power and bold immensity.

"Fantastic!" gushed Rob, who for the whole of our six-hour odys- sey had never once mentioned his Corvettes and antique Cadillacs and Chevys back home and had sat apparently mesmerized by the power and beauty of the cliffs, coves, and soaring Caha peaks serenely bathed in sunlight from a sky dimpled with soft lilac clouds.

"It's even better than I expected—far, far better." Celia, Rob's wife of thirty-five years and always a trustworthy enthusiast of any place we lure her to, grinned. (She had joined us on both of our prior book projects for *Seasons in Basilicata* and *Seasons on Harris* in Scotland.)

Danny Quinn by Celia Teichman

Danny, now curled up like a little cuddly leprechaun on the backseat, had not tried to tell us a single one of his endless repertoire of jokes but rather had sat silent, smiling and stroking his beard for much of the journey, seemingly moved to muteness by the majesty of this place.

And then when we returned to our cottage overlooking the ocean and the distant Skellig islands, Danny vanished. Which was particularly odd, as cocktails were being served on the patio and cocktail time was one of his favorite interludes of the day.

"Where's he gone?" asked Anne as she poured the drinks.

"No idea," Celia half whispered. "But let's leave him. You never know . . ."

"Never know what?" asked Rob, impatient with mysteries and the like.

"Well—you know . . . the song," said Celia softly.

"Ah, yes," was the unanimous response. "The Song."

So, wherever he was, we didn't disturb him and were well into the cheeses and crackers and wines and even beginning to salivate at the aromas of dinner drifting out from the kitchen window when who should suddenly appear strolling across the gorse-flecked field in front of us but the man himself, grinning and waving a large note-pad above his tousle-haired head.

"Could this be the great Moses bringing us his life-transforming commandments?" shouted Rob.

"No—this is the mighty Quinn bearing the very modest first draft of his Beara song . . ."

A hearty round of applause and cracker and cheese sprays as we shouted out our congratulations.

"You've done it . . . already?" asked Anne, eyes bright.

"Ah well—when the muses move one . . ."

"So that's where you've been—dallying with the little darlings deep down in the dell." That was me, bemused by the delightful image of Danny being seduced by the sirens of song into writing his first composition in over two years.

"Oh yes—those delicious damsels dangled words before me like fairy charms, they did." Danny laughed. "Just let me get the guitar and we'll see how this thing really sounds."

It sounded great! Simple four-chord verse lines with a couple of seductive grace notes in the chorus to give it a uniquely evocative—almost plaintive—melody. We were all silent and entranced. After the first rendition, Danny made a few alterations, changed a couple of chord sequences, and then sang it once again—clearer and far more resolutely this time. And we just sat, with collective tingles scampering up and down our spines and, at one point, even traces of tears on a couple of faces as we realized just how effectively this master musician had encapsulated all the amazing characteristics of this magical corner of southwest Ireland. There were smiles galore in the humming stillness. The final shards of amber sunlight spot-lighted Danny's face as he smiled back—a very happy songwriter and singer.

Over the ensuing days, the stanzas were expanded and adjusted as Danny met more of our friends and gained even greater insights into Beara itself. But the basic energy and vision of the original composition, with all its "work in progress" flavor, remained intact. The final version, which has now been sung and celebrated in countless venues across Ireland and the USA, goes as follows:

"Song of Beara"

The fishing boats of Beara glide back to Castletown
The folks down at MacCarthy's have just bought another round
Some old ways that are changing, some things remain the same
In this place of ancient wonder, touched by sun and wind and rain

Chorus
You can hear the cattle lowing, you can feel the breezes blow
And the wild ocean crashes on the rocky beach below
Where the green and lovely Beara reaches out into the foam
It's a place you may have never been, but it always feels like home

The mystic Hag of long ago kept watch o'er land and sea
She knew all ancient languages, of wind, of bird, of tree
When strangers came with different thoughts they tried to
   change her own
And then her Celtic heart and soul found refuge in a stone

Chorus

In the desperate days of famine, when hunger ruled the land
Life hung in the balance, starvation was at hand
Some were cleared or emigrated, some died along the way
If you stand upon that Hungry Hill you can feel their pain today

Chorus

Slieve Miskish and the Caha Mountains, so craggy and so high
The magpie and the seagull share that ever-changing sky

Ring forts and stone circles can still be plainly seen
It's a terrible beauty—so wild, so lush, so green

Chorus

The word must have spread about Danny's song. How that happened, I have no idea, except that numerous times during our stay here, we sensed a kind of Beara bush telegraph in operation, whereby information mystically spreads around the peninsula. Actual fresh news seemed to be rare. Whatever snippets and crumbs were picked up on the grapevine and shared with friends already seemed to have been assimilated into the collective psyche of the populace. Of course, we knew there was magic here. The whole place seemed to float on a cushion of curious coincidences, telepathic exchanges, clairvoyant perceptions, and healing-restorative processes that no one fully understood but most accepted as part of the benign bonus of being a Beara resident.

Despite his brief stay, Danny's "Song of Beara" gained an enthusiastic following. Word had spread, even as far as Glengarriff. Despite the town's panoply of unique delights—including those world-renowned Italian-styled Garinish Gardens, created in the early twentieth century on an island in Bantry Bay barely a hundred yards out from the main street; the exotic Bamboo Park featuring an Edenic profusion of subtropical species; and a wonderworld of lush little enclaves in the old Glengarriff Valley (now a gorgeous National Park) reaching back into the mountains—we rarely spent much time here. In hindsight it was possibly our loss, but the little town seemed just a touch too complacent and touristically situated on the main Cork-to-Killarney highway. Maybe if our intended interviews with such renowned but elusive residents as Maureen O'Hara, Julia Roberts, and (a little farther south near Skibbereen) Jeremy Irons in his "pink castle" had materialized, we might have become more enamored of the place.

Certainly we were enamoured, though, when one evening Danny was invited to give an impromptu miniconcert here in the Hawthorn Bar to rousing applause (and free librations too). Then we all strolled across the road, entered the Blue Loo Bar, and found a traditional reel-and-jig *seisuin* in progress. And with a full retinue of participants too, featuring four fine fiddlers, three tin whistle exponents, two melodeon squeeze-box maestros, a *uilleann* pipes player (contributing intermittently from what appeared to be his permanent perch at the bar), and a bodhrán goatskin drum maestro thwacking away so rapidly with his little stick that his fingers were a wild blur.

It took a while to distinguish all the subtle variations in rhythm and notes between the tunes, but eventually we just kind of settled into the melodic mood of the place and stomped along with the rest of the enthusiastic hand-clapping audience.

"Oh yes—I know," said Deirdre Donnchadhi, a celebrated whistle player in the group who chatted with me during a well-earned break in the *craic*. "The tunes can seem awful similar if you're not used to the music. But once you've played them a while, they're as different as chips and colcannon. And yes, I know, most are in the same key, which doesn't help. I usually only need a D whistle, although once in a while they'll switch keys and I'll have to fake it a bit by half-covering the holes and sort of bending the notes. Sliding. Some of the real traditionalists don't like that, but, as they say around here so often: 'There's no right way. Only a wrong way!' Your ear will tell you if it's just not working—especially with a hard-core group like this one of ours tonight."

"Yeah," I said. "You all seem to take it awfully seriously. There's not much laughing or smiling while you're playing."

"Well, you've got to really focus when you've got three, sometimes four, people all playing the same tune on the same instruments. There's got to be exact precision, otherwise it sounds like a circus of cats. My mother's people were all great fiddle players from the Cork-Kerry border. My aunt Julia became quite famous and knew a lot of the older players, so we try and meet up like this—friends and family—every once in a while for a real good *seisuin*. We're still celebrating a tradition that goes back so far, no one really knows when it all began."

Danny eased himself onto the bench beside me. He nodded and smiled at Deirdre: "Yeah," he said. "That's part of the spirit here. Being part of an ancient Celtic and pre-Celtic culture that still resonates in modern-day Ireland. There's real power in this music—in your music tonight, especially."

Deirdre smiled and whispered a quiet "thank you" just as the lead fiddler laughingly reminded the audience crammed into the small taproom of the bar that "the more you drink, the better we sound—and guaranteed—the better you look!" She returned to the group, and off they went on another half hour of full-blast, foot-tapping, full-speed-ahead Irish folk music.

A few nights later, quiet thank-yous were replaced by tears and cheers as Danny became the star attraction at the end of one of Michael Murphy's week-long Love, Loss and Forgiveness workshops held at Dzogchen Beara.

It began as a very spontaneous suggestion on the phone by Michael, who was looking for something to "end the session on a real upbeat note."

"Michael—you're in luck! Synchronicity raises its beguiling head once again," I said. "It just so happens that we have one of America's finest Irish folksingers staying at the cottage right now, and I'm pretty sure he'd be delighted to help out. Oh, and he'll possibly feature a brand-new composition—his beautiful 'Song of Beara.' That do you?"

"Fantastic! Perfect! Listen—come early before the food. We have about an hour when all the individual participants are asked to summarize what this week has meant to them—sort of sharing their perceptions and breakthroughs."

Céilí *Faces*

"Michael—thanks, but I honestly don't think we'd feel comfortable . . . I mean, this is highly personal stuff for you all and I don't think they'd be too happy with us outsiders being present . . ."

Michael invariably gets his way. Through wile, guile, bloodymindedness, and gritty determination—oh, and charm too I guess—he has a knack of persuading all concerned that his way is indeed the best for everyone. So there we were on the final workshop evening, Anne and I, Rob and Celia, and maestro Danny, all sitting in a circle of workshop participants in a room with huge windows overlooking a magnificent sunset. In the far distance dark and ominously broken cliffs were bathed in gold. Their grassy tops had sheens of platinum playing across the undulations, and the ocean was ribbed in gossamer filaments of lemons, scarlets, and purples. The slow, deep rhythms of the foaming surf were hypnotic, soothing, and smoothing, conjuring up primal images and urges—maybe even "altered state" recollections of our aquatic origins in the womb, when water flowed through us and we existed in another fishlike form.

Michael suggested that we all spend a few minutes in silence watching the slow-changing light and celebrating that beguiling curl of time from sunset to dusk to dark.

It is in moments like these that hearts can expand and welcome the new.

Then began the whole ritual of summations from each of the twenty or so participants. It was a remarkable portrait of varied human dimensions as a "talking stick" was passed around, enabling each person to speak without interruption. A kaleidoscopic array of emotions filled the room. There were tears, muted cheers for particularly courageous participants who had obviously waged wars with themselves and apparently won, followed by laughter, applause, hugs, kisses—the whole gamut. We learned later that two couples had met and fallen in love, one married couple had agreed (amicably) to separate, another couple decided not to get married "just yet," and almost everyone celebrated a great cleansing of spirits, a release from "anorexia of the soul" and reaffirmations of self.

I watched Danny as the time drew near for him to provide Michael's "real upbeat note." For all his many years of experience as a folksinger par excellence in pubs, clubs, schools, and concert halls throughout the USA, Danny has always maintained a deep-seated modesty—almost a constant sense of surprise that audiences actually turn up in droves to hear and cheer him. So every event for him seems to be a new beginning coupled with a new determination both to please and move his listeners. And that evening he was entranced by the warmth and mutual love that rippled around the room. He knew this would be one of those special times when an empathetic, sensitive audience would listen to—and totally hear—every word of his songs.

And so it was. From that first E major thwack of a chord on his beloved Martin acoustic guitar he carried that small captivated audience through every nuance of Irish folk music—from bawdy ballads to tear-jerky melodies to songs of great battles (lost of course—the Irish always seem to prefer it that way), to one of the best a cappella versions of "Danny Boy" I've ever heard him sing. And finally to his brand-new "Song of Beara." He'd only refined the verses a couple of days previously, but it already sounded like a permanent part of his repertoire.

The room exploded with applause. He had to play three encores before he could finally enjoy the buffet, and as we reluctantly left a couple of hours later, Danny laughed and spoke for all of us: "I'm so covered in love and good stuff, I'm not going to wash for a week!"

And as if to celebrate that "love-bath," he decided a few months later to lead a magical mystery tour–type bus journey with sixty or so of his American fans, visiting key historical places through southwest Ireland, participating in nightly seisuins in pubs, and generally enjoying ten days of Irish-American craic, which led to the creation of two more Ireland-inspired songs.

In a recent chat, he hugged Anne and me, and said, "You know I want to thank you both again. Beara was my breakthrough. The echo of the whole experience is still here with me. And you two made that happen."

It was either smile or weep, so I chose the former: "Oh no, no—it wasn't us at all, Danny—it was those gorgeous nubile muses. We saw the smile on your face as you kept going off across the meadows to finesse your verses!"

Danny's usually the one to make others blush with his raunchy jokes and whatnot, but we swear we both saw a rising pink flush on his face. And to think I never really believed much in the existence of those muses at all . . .

POSTSCRIPT

We certainly learned to believe in muses following a visit to our Allihies cottage by Theo Westenberger, a dear friend and celebrated award-winning New York photographer, who seemed to be able to conjure up her muses at will despite her ongoing battle with cancer. Whatever aspect of her photographic repertoire she focused on—travel, animals, ethnic peoples, celebrities of stage and screen, presidents, and top-league politicians—she always tackled her projects with unique vision, humor, love, and sincere empathetic interest. Her subjects came alive, brimming with life and energy. She was never patronizing or sycophantic. We loved to watch her work. She glowed with true human intensity and luminosity. She made people relax and give of themselves without artifice or angst. Tightly scheduled shoots with "sorry-gotta-go-now" celebrities turned into spontaneous fun fests. One of my favorite zany shots is of dainty, slim-limbed Theo sharing a foam-filled Jacuzzi tub with a grinning, muscle-bound Arnold Schwarzenegger. (No, they were not naked—their swimsuits were hidden by the foam!) And we remember her last photo shots being made on Beara as she struggled with her illness to capture close-ups of dry stone walls, lichen patterns, cloudscapes, and abstracts of marsh plants reflected in still black peat water ponds.

Theo loved her projects for such magazines as *Life*, *People*, *Time*, *Sports Illustrated*, *Newsweek*, and *National Geographic Traveler*, where we'd both been contributing editors, but alas, we'd never worked together on a joint project. We kept promising ourselves we'd find something to lure our poor overworked editor in chief into giving us a lucrative round-the-world odyssey feature! We also started work together on a little book linking Theo's animal shots with humorous quotes from celebrated quippers. We had other ideas too . . . but they were not to be. A few brief months after her time with us on Beara, Theo passed away at her apartment in Manhattan's TriBeCa. We were there with her, along with many of her friends. We miss her deeply. This book's dedication to her is but a tiny token of our love and respect for this beautiful, multitalented human being. Thank you for your very special friendship, Theo—thanks for investing so much energy to join us on Beara—and thanks for all those great enduring memories . . .

WINTER

The Season of Samhain

AND THEN, OF COURSE, COMES OUR winter—brief, benevolently mild but with a few long dark and raw days, and a special majesty all of its own. The cream and amber rushes and dying reed grasses rustle in the winds across the barren wetlands below the Caha range. Carpets of green, spongelike mosses in the boglands turn bronze; lichens hang ghostlike in the chill mists. The light is thin and "shy," and time creeps by slowly through to the "short dour days" of February, relieved only by the "fearsome craic" revelries of singing, dancing, and other amusements.

Despite the lack of travelers and blow-ins during this season, there's certainly no lack of music. Everywhere you hear the flute and fiddle, the goatskin bodhrán drum and the melancholy drones of the uilleann pipes. Unlike the visitors, whose appreciation of genuine Irish music and folk songs often lacks what one might call "informed selection" (overheard from one jaded and whiskery singer: "If I get one more request for that bleedin' 'Danny Boy,' there'll be a dead body in here, and it definitely won't be mine!"), the locals applaud ancient time-honored ballads rarely sung during the summer céilí seisuins. Bonds are tightened during these colder months, old prides restored, and a more mellow pace of life adopted once again.

Although there's rarely snow here on Beara, those dark days and "weary wets," relieved by the occasional low-domed sun and a sear of golden light across the black-teethed ridges, tend to keep us inside and insular. Sometimes there are passing dolphins and whales—fins, sperm, pilot, humpbacks—some almost seventy feet long—that bring us out with binoculars. A lot of the time is spent reading books we've been promising ourselves to read for eons (Dostoyevsky seems most appropriate during this seasons); listening to good music; inviting friends to join us for "improv" dinners (we both enjoy the unexpected flavors that can emerge through a spontaneous blending of national cuisines and flavors), and generally allowing the mood and rhythm of each day to shape our activities.

And so the days move on, slowly lightening and warming until St. Patrick's Day races in again (although never quite so riotously self-conscious as the U.S. versions), and the whole splendid seasonal romp begins once more . . . on this wild and beautiful Beara.

28

Set Dancing at Twomey's

:

"SEEMS VERY QUIET TONIGHT," I SAID politely to the lady behind the bar at Twomey's. "Is the dancing canceled?"

"Is the what?" she replied with a pleasant smile as she waited patiently for someone's pint of Guinness to settle before completing the traditional three-stage pour.

"The set dancing. Your Friday-night special. It's advertised on your window . . . there's a poster . . ."

"Oh, yes. Very nice poster too, isn't it? Will you be joining us?"

"Yes. That's why I'm here. It says it starts at nine-thirty . . . and it's just about nine-thirty now."

"Is it now? Well . . . would you believe. How the time flies by s'fast doesn't it?"

"So, is it still on?"

"What?"

"The dancing . . ."

"Oh yes, yes—indeed it is."

"So, what time d'y think?"

"Oh, I imagine about an hour or so." She was still smiling so pleasantly that I couldn't allow myself to express the growing exasperation I was feeling.

"Y'mean it'll start at ten-thirty?"

"Ten-thirty—yes, that'd be about right . . . maybe eleven."

"So—a little late then. The start . . ."

"Oh, no—it's always around ten-thirty or eleven . . . when it gets full."

"OK—fine. But . . . well, your sign seems very definite—nine-thirty on the dot!"

"Well now—and does it really? Would y'believe . . ."

"So the . . . the sign's wrong then." (The hum of desperation in my head: I was beginning to wonder why I persevered with this line of questioning.)

"Well, to tell you the truth, I don't really know. I've never actually seen it . . . the sign."

Stalemate and silence before she continued in her happy, carefree manner—"So, you've got nice time now. You can relax 'til ten-thirty at least . . . so, what can I get you . . . a nice pint o' Guinness?"

I DIDN'T WAIT THAT night, but I did come back the following week. At ten-thirty. And this time there were more people in the bar. A total of twelve. The same bar lady was there, but I decided to ask one of the patrons if there was ever going to be any dancing here.

"Oh, not just yet," he told me with a fuzzy sort of grin and an even fuzzier pronunciation. "M'be another half hour or so, or an hour. Y'know. When it fills up a bit . . ."

Oh Lord!

SO—THIRD TIME LUCKY, I returned the following week. At eleven-thirty. And at least there was music this time. A young girl with a guitar and her male partner at one of those synthesizer boxes the size of a dog coffin that seemed capable of playing any instrument on the planet and a few interstellar oddities too. He went from the saxophone to bagpipes to pennywhistle to something like a didgeridoo all in the course of a couple of Irish folk tunes. But unfortunately there was considerably far less here than first met my eyes and ears, and his fancy machine didn't seem to improve the actual presentation of these once-fine ballads. The girl just couldn't seem to hold a tune, and the guy seemed to be playing in a different key from her guitar. And worst of all, there was no applause from the patrons. The death knell of any pub show. All the "entertainers" were offered was what I later called (having seen it on many subsequent occasions when "the entertainment" failed to impress) the "wall of backs."

Not a single person in that now increasingly crowded bar paid any attention whatsoever to the unfortunate duo. Silence towered up like a forest of giant redwoods. I was embarrassed for both of them, and despite the fact they'd have been far better off staying at home, I gave them my best hand-cracking clapping at the end of one of the worst renditions of "Fields of Athenry" I can ever remember hearing. And despite the fact that my clapping stimulated an unenthusiastic ripple of applause from other patrons, I felt a real phony. "Fields of Athenry," along with "Danny Boy" and Tommy Makem's "Four Green Fields," is one of the quintessential Irish ballads, recorded by just about every folksinger from our favorite—Danny Quinn—to the Clancy Brothers, the Chieftains, the Dubliners, DeDannan, Clannad, Christy Moore, and Planxty to Mary Bergin, Shane MacGowan, Ron Karenn, Paul Brady, Tommy and Sidbhan Peoples, Sinéad O'Connor, and even Enya, whose Irish-tinged mystery-Muzak is probably the most recognized sound in the world today.

Collin Irwin in his amusing travelogue *In Search of the Craic: One Man's Pub Crawl through Irish Music* describes the importance of this song throughout the island:

> *When the band went to "Fields of Athenry" that's when the*
> *bar crowd really erupted. There's something about the chorus*
> *that really just won't go away and it's hard not to be touched*

*in some way by the forlorn dignity of the lyrics about a
woman trying to be brave as she attempts to talk to her
husband on the other side of a prison wall and then watching
from the harbor as a ship takes him off with the other
convicts to Botany Bay in Australia and she knows she'll
never see him again. And his crime? Stealing a handful of
corn so his kids could eat during the famine . . . Heart-
wrenching stuff. And once you hit the big "Low lie the fields
of Athenry where once we watched the small free birds fly"
chorus, the eyes well up, the heart swells, we link arms and,
by God!—we have an anthem . . . it gets sung spontaneously
by crowds at Ireland's international football games . . . it's
sung by every street busker you meet and covered by
everyone . . . you can barely enter a pub in Ireland without
hearing it in some shape or form . . . in fact music pubs are
defined by whether or not you're likely to hear "Fields of
Athenry" inside and you can usually tell the minute you
cross the threshold . . . it seems to fulfill every musical
sentiment the Irish hold dear. It encompasses the national
tragedy of the famine, the heart-break of enforced emigration,
the outrage of legal injustice, the preciousness of the family,
and a deep enduring, harrowing, emotional love story to
boot. Ultimately, the spirit of rebellion, defiance, independence, and hope plays chords that run soul-deep in the very
bowels of the Irish psyche.*

Fine, fist-clenching rhetoric then from Mr. Irwin, who, had he
opened the door to Twomey's just a mere crack and heard the stuff
coming from our poor little duo, would have doubtless scampered
off the Beara Peninsula pursued by demons of discord, never to
return.

Anyway—I digress. I'd come to see the dancing. Set dancing, so
the flyer on the window said—and finally on this, my third visit, it
came. But not at all in the form I'd expected—the Riverdance whirl
of short flared skirts of young gazelle-legged girls moving in perfect
unison and the complex counterrhythms of their hard clicking shoes

A Seisuin *Group*

and the straight motionless arms held tightly down their sides, rigid
as flagpoles, and the flare of long hair in ringlets or ponytails and
eyes gleaming bright and staring straight ahead, as if inspired by a
mystical master of the dance just beyond our vision . . .

No, alas—none of this at all. Because I'd got my terminology
mixed up—it was *set* dancing here, as opposed to the world-celebrated
step dancing.

Actually, it turned out to be a bunch of locals, a dozen or so
stocky males and females, many well over retirement age, who
launched themselves into a series of jigs and reels with all the energetic enthusiasm of teenagers. Apparently the "sets" are based on
old "quadrille" dances brought over from Europe in the early 1800s.
There had been furious outcries at such outrageous importations,
particularly by the clergy of the time, but somehow they remained

here, glossed with Irish tunes—most of them pretty fast and furious. One elderly man, who exhibited the complex footwork of Popeye dancing the seaman's hornpipe, seemed to grow more and more purple-faced by the minute. I thought the evening was about to come to an abrupt end with a fatal heart attack, but he whirled on, sweat flying off his brow like a flailing prizefighter, laughing, encouraging the others, correcting swirling colleagues if they misstepped in the complex rhythms and counterrhythms, and giving out the occasional "Wahoo!" when sufficiently inspired by the cohesion of that stomping, whirligigging group.

And it was good. Obviously though, it wasn't what I'd expected. At all. It certainly wasn't Riverdance, and there wasn't a single flying ponytail or nubile teenager anywhere in sight. But it was great honest fun and flare—a bunch of Bearans putting on an impromptu show for another bunch of Bearans all bellied around the bar—but this time with no "wall of backs." Everyone turned to enjoy the show and applaud deafeningly at the end of each reel.

It was utterly exhausting to watch. But exhilarating too as I observed the little community—our little borrowed community now—at play, pleasing themselves and one another. Celebrating their traditions easily and naturally without striving for elusive perfection. Letting the *craic* just emerge and flow on through the night in the little pub on the waterfront at the edge of our tiny Beara town . . .

29
Tales of the Seanachaí

:

"OH LORD—WAY BACK THEN, SIX, seven hundred years ago, y'wouldna believe the things they did, d'y'know, to poor Celtic bards who got the sequence of the kings and other royals wrong! Jus' one name missed out of a genealogy of hundreds could do it! It beggars the imagination—important bits of them cut off, tongues and other things pulled out, blindings with red-hot pokers, snapping off their—"

"Okay. Got the point. Nasty. Risky business, then—this bardic storytelling life?"

I was chatting with Tom O'Ryan during a well-earned interlude in an evening of his tall-tale-telling at a pub in Kenmare. Tom was the featured *seanachaí*, although there were two other names on the bill that no one seemed to have heard of.

"Who's this Sean MacGowran, then?" I asked at the crowded bar.

"No idea" was the general consensus.

"And Jack O'Malley? Y'know him?"

"Not a jot."

TOM'S TALES HAD BEEN honed down with half a lifetime of crafting his talent in pubs and halls across the southwest. "O'course—there were perks too, in those old days, y'know." Tom continued his description of what he called "the best of bardic times." "If you could wangle y'self into a royal household and get the sequence of regal names right—often going back a couple of centuries or more—then you were in pig heaven. Y'see, it wasn't just for royal ego satisfaction. It was also about legitimacy—constantly reinforcing the memorized oral liturgy, because there was no written Celtic language—and also about the long and revered heritage of the royals. A royal bard might also have to be able to describe more specific things like the precise boundaries of the kingdom and particularly colorful—or bloody or heroic—deeds of past and present royals. In great detail too. And there were plenty of those to go around in that Celtic era."

"But the bards were more than just useful record keepers—they were poets and entertainers too, right?"

"Jus' a minute. Hold y'horses. Who's tellin' who this stuff . . . I'm comin' straight t'that point."

"Sorry." (I was still learning that one does not interrupt an Irishman, particularly a noted *seanachai*, as he's telling one of his tales.)

"Okay. Jus' don't mess up my train of thought. I'm not s'young as I was an' the old mem'ry's flaggin'! Next thing I know, they'll be loppin' bits off me, too! Anyway. Yes indeed—bards were poets and great entertainers, reciting—even singing sometimes—the great long songs like *The Cattle Raid of Cooley* or, t'give it it's correct title, *Taín Bó Cualnge*, or the tales of Finn MacCool from the *Duanaire Finn* . . . things of that nature. Fine powerful stuff. Some of them meant the bard had to act out dozens of different characters in gestures, voice tones, and body postures. And for a little light relief, they'd also become sort of stand-up comics and gossipmongers, spreading snippets of news and rumors and tabloid titillations to the assembled throngs. And that was particularly true of the wandering bards—the great *seanachai*—who carried hundreds of tales in their heads and made their living moving from village to village and—"

"Just like you do?"

"Ah well, they had to be a lot more talented than us modern-day *seanachai*. People expected a hell of a lot from them then. They were often the prime entertainment at fairs and in remote villages. When a *seanachai* arrived, everything stopped and everyone came to listen to his stories. Mesmerizing they must have been—theater, radio, TV, movies, all rolled into one man and his magic ways of making people forget their troubles and just listen. Letting his words and their own imaginations take over . . . and—well, allow them to fly . . . fly to places like Hy Brasil—that mythical enchanted isle floating somewhere in the haze off the west coast here . . . or anywhere at all. Anywhere he wanted to take them. And to some extent—that's still going on. There's quite a Celtic revival at the moment . . . all over the country, in fact y'might say all over the world."

While Anne and I were in Dublin at the start of our Beara odyssey, we were amazed by the number of young bard-singers—some call them balladeers (others were less complimentary)—on the street corners, guitars rampant and guitar cases littered with the confetti

Tom O'Ryan

of coins. We talked to a few of them between their spontaneous gigs. One young girl told us how she'd never forgotten her grandfather's old "street songs," the musical cries of hawkers and barrow boys, the children's skipping chants her mother used to sing, and all those beautifully sad and lilting Irish love ballads. And of course—always—the songs of the great battles expressing courage and fortitude invariably in the midst of disaster and doom. She laughed—"so typically bloody Irish—always celebrating defeat!"

And so typically Irish too was the fact that many of the ancient songs were almost lost. Throughout the eighteenth and nineteenth centuries the ruling Protestant "Ascendancy" of Britishers issued edicts banning the use of the "barbaric" Celtic language and the singing of "superstitious and silly songs" about fairies, leprechauns, and a host of other folklore "little people." But, spurred on by the remarkable success of such books as *Grimm's Fairy Tales*, a Celtic cultural renaissance began in the early nineteenth century. Thomas Croker of Cork published one of the very first books of Irish folktales—*Fairy Legends and Traditions of the South of Ireland* in 1826.

Later in the century Oscar Wilde's parents—Sir William and Speranza Wilde—became enthusiastically involved in recording authentic Celtic music and stories. They in turn encouraged William Butler Yeats and his creative philanthropist-partner, Lady Augusta Gregory, cofounders of the Abbey Theatre in 1903, to publish *The Celtic Twilight* (Yeats) and *Visions and Belief of the West of Ireland* (Lady Gregory).

Yeats also went on to celebrate Ireland's mystical Celtic heritage in his beloved and world-renowned poems—in particular "The Wanderings of Oisin" and "The Lake Isle of Innisfree." The two of them also embarked on numerous "collecting expeditions" in Connemarra and Sligo and realized that the preservation of Celtic songs and poems required a renewed nationalistic retention of the Irish language. So eventually the Gaelic League was formed, and by 1906 it boasted almost a thousand branches and more than 100,000 members. The Irish government then reinforced it by creating the Irish Folklore Commission in 1935.

"So it was things like that, y'see, and a new pride in our land and in our ancient Celtic culture that allowed people like me to do what we do today," said Tom, "retaining and respecting the role of the *seanachai* and keeping the Gaelic revival alive and well—thank you very much!"

"KEEPING THINGS ALIVE AND well is not always an easy thing," said Teddy Black, one of Beara's most notable "mod'rn-day" *seanachai*. His name had been mentioned to Anne and me on various occasions when the old Gaelic tales were floating about during evenings of *craic*—tales of fairies, tinkers, lovely naked ladies on horseback, the perils of drink, vows of eternal abstinence, and the like.

"The man's a living miracle," a young Teddy Black fan had gushed after a particularly raucous evening of Irish folk songs at Twomey's. "He reminds me of m'dad—he's got stories galore. People come alive when 'e tells 'em. Y'can see his characters an' what's going on in the tale. M'dad had Beara instincts buried deep inside him. He could forecast the weather for a week just by going down on the shore here an' listenin' t' the sounds an' lookin' at the sand—the slap o' the surf an' the crack o' the wind-chop, the tone o' the pebbles growlin' an' grindin' in the shallows, patt'ns on the wet sands, the way the dry grains moved higher up the beach. He was hardly ever wrong. An' Teddy's like that—Beara's folk historian and much more besides."

So obviously I went off in search of Teddy Black and finally traced him to his home on the eastern edge of Castletownbere set on a high bluff overlooking Bere Island and the narrow channel and the town's small, enchanting (but difficult, so they say) golf course.

His bright-eyed wife, Ann, greeted me and invited me in. I needed no further inducement, as the hallway was full of the most delicious baking aromas. Almost every time we went to visit someone at their home, there was always some baking going on. Very odd . . . there was definitely some kind of grapevine messaging system here that had signaled our fondness for just-baked cakes and the like?

"I'm hungry already—and I've just had lunch!" I said.

"Good—because somebody's got to eat these new-baked biscuits an' it might as well be you," said Ann with a chirpy laugh.

"I'll only protest through politeness. Then I'll finish the plate."

"That sounds like my kind o' fellow . . ." A voice boomed from the adjoining living room. And out stepped this stocky, blue-eyed, white-haired gentleman, radiating auras of energy and good humor, and I liked him before we even got to the hand-shaking ritual.

The next couple of hours raced by in a welter of stories, punctuated by Ann's plates of still oven-warm cookies. Apparently Teddy had sort of "slipped sideways" into the *seanachai*'s role after spending much of his life as an insurance salesman. "I could always tell a pretty good tale—but so could a lot of people on Beara. It was part of the local tradition, really—before the days of radio and TV and videos and a dozen other demonic distractions! Y' had t' find something t' keep y' going through those long dark winter nights, an' I guess I learnt it through m'grandfather. He came from Oban on the west coast of Scotland and worked on some of our southwestern lighthouses. Ann's grandfather was one of those who survived that terrible disaster at the Calf Rock Lighthouse just off Dursey Island."

"What disaster—I don't really know that story. Penny Durrell mentioned it briefly to me, but I never heard the actual details."

Teddy's eyes gleamed with delight and a broad grin almost made an ear-to-ear leap across his happy round face. "Oh!—so y'don't know about Calf Rock. Ah well . . . I suppose I should put on my *seanachai* hat an' give you the official version. Or at least, *my* official version!"

And so he proceeded to do precisely that—relishing the rich details of the saga from the very first day the project was conceived in

1846 ("very stupid . . . you couldn't have chosen a worse, more storm-battered place than that pathetic little piece of broken rock off Dursey") to its arduous construction from 1862 to its first lighting in 1866. "An' o' course—like everythin' else connected with this crazy project an' all its disasters—the light rotator didn' work and the lens had t'be turred by hand by one o' th' two keepers. An' then a couple o' years later durin' a terrible gale someone misread the signalin' flags from th' lighthouse an' thought they needed urgent rescue. So seven men set out in a small boat an' the storm got worse an' worse an' finally they capsized jus' a hundred yards or less from the rock an' all seven men vanished in a flash, never t' be seen again. Not a single body was ever found."

When the traumatic events reached a gripping climax early on Sunday morning, November 26, 1881, Teddy's eyes were ablaze and his speech increased in speed and timbre. He was a true storyteller, telling the tale as if for the first time with none of the stagy antics I might have expected from a professional *seanachai*. He raced me through the deadly phases of the event—a terrifying hurricane with winds from the northwest over a hundred miles per hour; the enormous crashing waves leaping over the top of the little lighthouse; the sudden disappearance of the lantern and the whole upper level; the dash by the keepers for the tiny lighthouse cottage across the rock, and their imprisonment in a ten-by-fourteen-foot kitchen awash with stormwater for . . . and at this point, Teddy became almost purple with excitement . . . "for twelve days . . . can y' imagine, twelve whole days until Thursday, December eighth . . . they were in that horrible dark, wet, foodless, waterless—at least in terms of freshwater—hole. For the first six days their families thought they'd all been killed. The storm was so bad the men couldn't even open the door of the kitchen to signal rescuers. In fact, they didn't know if there were any rescuers! But all the time they were trapped, their story was being transmitted around Ireland—and the world. And when they were finally rescued during a lull in this storm to end all storms, their names and the names of their rescuers had become almost legendary. In fact, Michael O' Shea, a fifty-three-year-old fishing boat captain from Ballynacallagh, was so revered for his bravery in leading the rescue, that he was awarded a special medal for gallant conduct and became known locally—and proudly—as 'Michael O'Shea of the Medals.' And," continued Teddy, "like I said, Ann's grandfather—God rest his soul—was one of the men rescued by Michael and was never short of a pint at the pubs for the rest of his long life!"

I congratulated Teddy on a fine tale superbly told. He laughed. "Oh, I always love t' tell a tale—and listen to the stories of others. It started, I suppose, when I was very young. We had a boardinghouse, and over dinner in the evenings there'd be all this wonderful storytelling by the residents. I guess I learned a lot from them. I learned—most important—to adjust the telling—the pace, the tone, the punch line, the humor—to the audience. I'm not one of these rigid storytellers, but it's still very important for me to be called a storyteller—as opposed to a yarn spinner or a raconteur. I bring in modern tales too—not just the grand old tales. Some do that and they go on the American circuit, and big names they are too. But I love Beara as much as any man and I love to tell its tales and legends here. Once a month I go to a place in Cork called the Yarn-Spinners Club and they have storytelling gatherings that bring people in from all over the country. Last time we had three from New Zealand—wonderful storytellers. I've done radio an' the like an' so I've been invited to join many of these kinds of groups.

"I think if I'd taken the whole storytelling thing more seriously, I would've done quite well. 'On the circuit,' so to speak."

There was something about Teddy that reminded me of our folk-singer friend Danny Quinn. Maybe his genuine modesty coupled with a rich bedrock soul tingling with humor and Irish benevolence.

"I admit I like a little bit of adulation now and then, but there are others who deserve it much more than me. The real traditional *sea-nachai*—like just down the road—is Mary Madison. She reflects the heart 'n' soul of this place—the days when storytelling was an important part of communicating at *céilís* and between different parts of the country. An' it kept the old deep earthy pagan Celtic soul alive. Kept us proud. Helped us celebrate this amazing treasure trove of archeological sites we have here and all our amazing legends. A sense of entitlement to the richness of our history and all the tales and legends behind it

"It was hard because, when I was younger, we had a town here that had closed up completely. The mining was dead, the navy and army had pulled out of Bere Island, Dunboy Castle and the Puxley mansion had been destroyed by the rebels. We were living in what you might call the 'tumbleweed era.' Every second house on the street was empty. Everything was dying out, all the old traditions. But—thank the Lord—things are a lot better in that area now, and I've got so many stories in my head that have been passed on to me. I see myself as like a bit of a folk historian—being responsible for trying to keep them—keep the old oral traditions and the people whose lives they reflect—keeping them all alive. For us—and even for the blow-ins too. They're desperate to identify with something and somewhere because they've lost their own roots—forgotten where they came from, if they ever knew. And they reach out to us and our stories, trying to find an anchor. Americans particularly. They're very 'rootisk'—always looking for their own histories over here. Well, it's hardly surprisin' is it, in a country that—let's face it—is less than two hundred years old in terms of real emergence as a power—*the world power*! And I don't have any problem with that at all. We need all the stories we can get nowadays. And when I watch the faces of my audiences—when I see the stories grab 'em and carry 'em and excite 'em or even make 'em cry a little—why, then I'm a very happy fellow—a very satisfied *seanachai*!"

"So you even make 'em cry?!"

"Oh, yes—indeed! And especially lately, since my latest poem-song. It's one of those things that came to me out of nowhere . . . well, no, that's not really true. It came out of years of concern for this beautiful country of ours and all its Celtic Tiger antics. So-called progress has changed people. Tremendously. We're in risk of losing so many of our best qualities, I think . . . as I say at the end of the second verse . . .

> *"It seems that our nature and kindness have gone*
> *And even the Lord is finding it hard*
> *When it seems that He's needed no more."*

The conversation had taken an unexpected turn. "Teddy, could you play me that song?"

"Here. Better still—take a CD copy with you and play it back at your cottage. Then let me know what y'think."

So, I did, and this is what I heard:

> *We say that it's progress*
> *When we've sold off the land*
> *the fish the sea the sand*
> *and even the gray rocks as well*
> *then from mountain to shore*
> *we have ripped up and torn*
> *the heart and the soul*
> *from Ireland*
> *with no time to wait or to stand at the gate,*
> *and chat till the cows come on home,*
> *our stories the* craic
> *our songs and folklore all drifting away from our shore*

Chorus
> *We say that is progress and just what we need*
> *could it be that we're drunk on new money and greed*

and as our old country she gets up to speed
will our people be heard anymore?

For too many years we have cried bitter tears
as our young were being forced from this land
for the thousands that never came home
and now that we're able to have a fine table
it seems that our nature and kindness have gone
and even the Lord is finding it hard
when it seems that He's needed no more.

30

A Trip to Tuosist
(and Way Beyond)

"I WOULDN'T BE PARKING THERE IF I W' YOU," said the white-haired lady at the post office door. She reminded me of my Irish grandmother. Tightly bunned hair, frowny, strict expression hiding a reluctant smile, and a determined manner that forbade contradiction or even the slightest hint of a question.

But I did have a question. After our dramatic nail-biting drive over the switchback challenge of the Healy Pass, I'd parked across the road from her tiny post office/grocery store at Tuosist, which despite its nebulous size, is the key parish of the County Kerry section of the Beara, stretching twenty-three miles from Kenmare to Ardgroom. I'd parked on a grass verge off the winding narrow back road and well away from the frantic antics of Cork drivers. Not that there were any around here. We hadn't seen a car for miles.

"You don't think it's okay here?"

"That's what I jus' said," she replied sternly.

"Well—we're just coming into your store for a minute. I'm sure it'll be fine."

"Is that so, y'think?" was all she replied before she vanished inside.

We followed her, bought a couple of oranges and some oversugary Brit candies (our guilty favorites—Fry's Cream Bar, Rowntree's Rolos, and that Aero chocolate stuff patterned with thousands of tiny air bubbles). We explained to the lady (still unsmiling) that we were looking for Tuosist parish hall. We'd heard from Jim O'Sullivan that there was some kind of annual festival of local folklore and other regional peculiarities going on over there.

"Well now, y'jus' passed it. It's barely fifty yards away," she said, regarding us skeptically as hapless foreign tourists. "There it is." She came to the door and pointed from the corner of the post office down a lane to a small school building with a substantial whitewashed depiction of the Crucifixion towering twelve feet over the road. "Don't know how you could have missed that."

"Looks like we're not going to miss this, though," gasped Anne as round the corner from our parked car came a herd of thirty or so cattle swaying, lumbering, and mooing through the mud and constantly trying to break free from the two ankle-nipping dogs controlling them. The post office lady was smiling now. Her face creased and wrinkled with mirth and a defiant look of "Now didn't I tell y'so?"

From the cows' point of view, our car was obviously an obstacle to be enjoyed—a way to escape the dogs. So they rubbed and scrunched against it, tried to hide behind it, or ran circles around it, all the while churning up ribbons of mud and murky grime from the soggy grass verge and relieving themselves copiously along their erratic ways. When they'd finally been corralled and moved on down the lane it was rather difficult to distinguish our previously bright and shiny silver rented Opal from all the mire and muck surrounding it.

We had to laugh. "Well—I guess your advice was good," I said as we tried to remove the goo from the door handles. At this point, God bless her, the post office lady finally let her warm Irish heart show through her stern carapace. "No—wait a minute now. Let me be getting you a bucket and a cloth. You'll never get all that stuff off with your fingers—the idea of it!"

So giggling, she brought the water and cloths for us to wash it back to something recognizable as a car.

The Healy Pass

"Well—I hope you enjoy the Eigse—our little local folklore gathering," she said as we left to drive down to the hall. "We have one most years in memory of Dr. Sean O'Suilleabhain . . . Lovely man he was . . . Collected all our folklore and poems and stories and whatnot around here . . . We all helped him . . . His favorite saying was 'Neighbors—don't let your fine talk go under the clay.' If he'd lived, he'd be well over a hundred by now."

Then the postmistress smiled sweetly and sadly—quite a transformation from the battleax demeanor we'd first sensed. "But, well, of course he never really died, did he? All those tales and legends and proverbs and folk prayers and charms and songs and airs told by the *seanachai*. Thousands of them he collected. We called him 'the master'—some of us were children when we first helped him collect all these things . . . It's good you're going to the Eigse. You'll be learning a lot, I'm thinking . . . *slán leat* and *Bail ó Dhia ort.*"

I didn't feel I deserved such a pleasant good-bye and the blessing of God after I'd ignored all her advice at the outset. But I smiled and wished her a long life—*saol fada chugat*. Slowly—very slowly—I was learning these little bits of Irish, and my efforts always seemed to bring a chuckle or two.

We'd really come to hear a talk by Connie Murphy or Conchur O Murchu, as he preferred to be called, another one of our key mentors in the arena of Beara traditions and folklore. His subject, "Is There a Future in Our Past?" sounded intriguing, and we entered the meeting hall—one of those all-too-familiar bare spaces with creaky chairs, a small stage, and a stale aroma of disinfectant, as if the room had been used for far more nefarious purposes the night before. Unfortunately Connie was not there. Somehow we'd mixed up dates and times and found ourselves listening (and yawning) to a young archeologist whose lecture ended up being, when his PowerPoint machine functioned properly, a rather nebulous set of slides and lists of ancient stone piles on nearby mountains whose functions, age, and significance seemed to elude him and certainly everyone else.

Brochures in the hall on previous Eigses, however, reflected a fascinating glimpse into the folklore collected by Dr. O'Suilleabhain— tales of witches and kings and giants and moorland creatures and "hags" and death omens and resonant memories of ancient gods.

One of his most popular books, *Irish Wake Amusements*, had an oxymoronic appeal to it, but apparently wakes were not quite the grim occasions one might assume and were often an excuse for a wealth of rough and rowdy games and rituals that seemed to relate little to the individual being mourned. They were also occasions for violence, particularly if bodies were transported over the mountains from County Cork into County Kerry. Before the construction of the dramatically serpentine Healy Pass road, an impressive project to link the two counties funded at the time of the Great Famine to provide much-needed employment for the starving and poverty-stricken inhabitants, it was not unusual for "stopping the funeral" skirmishes to occur (over something about burial rites, we were told) on the high ridge near the huge flat stone where coffins were usually rested after the arduous climb.

"We were not the most civilized of people in those days," explained one of the elderly men huddled at the back of the hall after the lecture.

"Well—are you different today, then?" I couldn't help but ask, grinningly of course.

"Oh well, what with all the TV we've got now and the stupid high price of Guinness in the pubs, we don't get as much of a chance as we did to do the mischief. Isn't that right, Dermont?"

And so Dermont joined in and then Patrick and then Sean and then "Old John," and the tales began to roll. Some we found utterly incomprehensible, others were such a mishmash of English and Irish that we couldn't understand the punch lines, but a couple stood out—little flickers of ancient folklore, fears, and superstitions.

"Old John" Kelly claimed to recall an old woman always dressed "bog black" who lived near his family house and "used to go about with the fairies." "A couple of farms from us was a child of four years who couldna' walk at all. So the old woman came—I think they asked 'er, y' know—to see the child, and she told the family that the cure was in the kitchen. Now in those days you often kept the hens in a coop in the kitchen. Nothing unusual 'bout that then. Quite normal. So they asked—whereabouts in the kitchen?—so the old woman points to the large cock and says 'It's in that old gentleman over there, so take him out of the house and wash his feet three nights in a row and then wash the child's feet each night in the same water.' And would you believe what happened—the little girl was walking within the week. Within the week, I tell y'!"

"Old John" acknowledged the murmurs of appreciation at his tale. "Sean would have liked that one," said Patrick. "Did y' ever hear his story of the mermaid horse, then . . . ?" A shaking of heads. "Well, it appears that a farmer lived down by the sea not far from here, near

Lauragh, and one day he sees this beautiful strange horse coming in with the tide—big chestnut brown creature with a long black tail—and wearing a fine-looking leather and brass collar. So the farmer went down to the strand and stroked him and removed his collar and led him back to the farm. And he kept him as a workhorse for seven long years—plowing and pulling loads. But then one day they were clearing out the barn and they left the horse's collar outside. And the horse sees his collar, runs over, and puts his head into it, and races off toward the beach. Then they say he stopped, turned, and gave this great roar that echoed all around the Caha mountains—then disappeared back into the sea, never to be seen again . . ."

More murmurs and smiles of appreciation.

"Good story, Patrick," I said. "Actually it reminds me very much of those Scottish island tales of silkies that emerge like seal men or women from the sea with a sealskin belt, and so long as you keep the belt hidden, he or she will stay with you, but once the belt is rediscovered, the silkie is off back to the ocean. And like your mermaid horse, for some reason it's usually after seven years on land."

"Aye." Patrick nodded. "I've heard tales like that from Scotland—but that's hardly surprising, is it? It was all the Gaeltacht—all part of the Celtic-Gaelic heritage."

"Maybe it still is," I suggested.

Another murmur of assent and appreciation—a bonding in the mysteries of tales told down through the centuries, collected and preserved by such individuals as Dr. Sheain Ui Shuilleabhain or Sean O'Suilleabhain or Sean O'Sullivan, the English version of his revered name. No wonder this part of the Beara—the Kerry part—is so proud of his long and contributive life of research and as a storytelling *seanachai.*

AND LIAM DOWNEY WAS very proud of his research too into "bog butter."

Traditions and tales of traditions come in all peculiar shapes, sizes, and guises, but this most certainly must be one of the more esoteric and elusive fields of academic study.

I'd been told that one of the regular meetings of the Beara Historical Society was being held at Twomey's (where else?) one Thursday evening, so I wandered down for a peep into the back room to see if anything of interest was going on. And there was Liam Downey, an eloquent, smiling-faced gentleman of very mature years, boggling the audience of fifty or so in the cramped, stuffy room with tales of his years of research into the obscurities of *"booley* huts." These were temporary summer shelters way up on the peaty hilltops where younger farming family offspring would take the cattle from May Day to early October for upland grazing to give the lower pastures a chance to recover from overuse.

"And what did all those lovely young people do up there all day while the cows were chewing away?" asked a middle-aged gentleman with a sly wink and nod at the audience.

There was snickering laughter, but Liam, who was not in the mood for licentious innuendos, insisted that "oh, don't you be thinking things like that—there was an awful lot to do that kept them busy. They had to watch the cows all the time, then milk them twice a day, make and salt the butter in the old wooden churns, which takes a lot of time and effort, maybe make cheeses with the spare milk . . . And of course they had to make votive offerings to the gods of the earth in the form of 'bog butter.'"

There was a ripple of giggles through the audience. This was obviously a new term for most of them.

"No, I'm very serious," said Liam. He was obviously not one to tolerate undue levity on the part of his listeners, especially if it reflected adversely upon his years of arduous study and compilation of learned papers. "We have scores of examples of where they buried butter in the bogs—often in communal drinking vessels known as *methers*, or in less sophisticated hollowed-out tree trunks, or tight-woven wicker baskets, kegs, churns, or even in animal intestines and bladders. And radiocarbon dating on the bog butter finds in Ireland cover a very wide range of time spans, from 400 BC up to at least the thirteenth century. And it wasn't just in Ireland. Many similar offerings have been found in Scotland and Scandinavia. It's thought they were left as important offerings to the forces of nature and fertility."

"How do you know if the butter wasn't put in the bog to keep it cool or something, and then th' eejits just forgot where they'd put it. Or maybe it went off, so they just left it . . . Or maybe they hid it in the bog to keep it from their greedy neighbors . . ." This was from a younger member of the audience. Someone with a distinctly British accent, which caused a distinct swiveling of heads to see who was making such facetious suggestions.

Liam realized it was time to ignore such digressions and impress his audience with a welter of his scientific data. "So, using high temperature gas chromatography in combination with GC-mass spectrometry enables researchers to develop the capacity to distinguish between fatty acids from different sources by using GC-combustion—and isotope ratio MS to determine core values for the dominant fatty acids present to confirm the chemical composition of milk-based butter.'

That did the trick. No more comments and questions from the audience now. The man next to me whispered conspiratorially with a lopsided grin, "Liam's almost always right, y'know. Not because he's a know-all y'understand, although he's a very bright man, but because he hardly talks about anything he doesn't know backward and inside out." And to substantiate his well-justified claims of intensive research, Liam handed around copies of his published papers full of graphs, charts, dating profiles, bog butter chronologies, radiocarbon records, fatty acid profiles, and sample "discovery" locations throughout Ireland.

What else could his admiring listeners do but burst into genuine applause. *"Booley* huts" and "bog butter" would now enter the vocabularies of attendees and be used to boggle their compatriots out in the bar.

An evening well spent indeed.

Then, after all the Eigse and bog-butter folklore, I was abruptly and unexpectedly introduced to the secrets of the *sheela-na-gigs* by way of a booklet I bought after the meeting (on the enthusiastic recommendation of Liam).

And talking of being "boggled." That was definitely my reaction when I first studied the book's grainy black-and-white photographs of Ireland's most bizarre totemic creatures.

Considering the blatant sexual flagrancy of the objects themselves, the introductory paragraph of the outrageously illustrated booklet on the origins and functions of these bizarre entities was a splendid little euphemistic masterpiece of modest and decorous prose. It begins:

> *Sheela-na-gigs are carvings usually of naked females posed in a manner which displays and emphasizes their genitalia . . . They were first brought to scientific attention in the 1840s by antiquarians, some of whom regarded their aggressive sexuality in negative terms. More recently the images have come to be regarded in a positive light. By some they are seen as a symbol of Irishness and by others, particularly Irish feminists, they are a symbol of active female power.*

The term *sheela-na-gig* derives from the Irish language and is interpreted as "the old hag of the breasts," although on most of these arm-size, powerfully primitive carvings, the breasts are far less emphatic. As my booklet explains politely, they invariably depict: "widely and acrobatically splayed legs and sagging genitalia . . . and the commonest position of the arms is with the hands placed in

Sheela-na-gigs

front, gesturing toward the abdomen or, more explicitly, toward the pudenda."

While the primitive nature of the hundred or so *sheela-na-gigs* so far discovered throughout Ireland might suggest prehistoric origins, they were in fact created primarily following the Norman invasion of Ireland from England in 1169. At that time the papal power of the Catholic church, headquartered in Rome, fully supported the invasion. Apparently as the Irish had come to be regarded as a "sinful and licentious people" particularly in regard to their "ambiguous" attitudes toward marriage and divorce and the freewheeling marital status of the priests, who, according to one prominent Norman lord, "celebrate fornication rather than celibacy and themselves do outrageous deeds of concubinage."

As the Irish church was brought into fuller accord with Roman practices under their new conquerors and with such reforming churchmen as St. Malachy, it became obvious that women were seen as the prime instigators of lust and licentiousness (males seemed to be criticized more for their avaricious and pecuniary natures) and closely allied with the great and powerful earth goddesses—Tellus Mater, Terra, Gaia, Cybele, Anu, Demeter, and her daughter Persephone.

Some suggested the figures depicted the primary forces of fertility and procreation, but others claim that, as sinners were said to be punished in hell through the bodily organs by which they had offended, the vastly enlarged genitalia depicted the dangers and ultimate denigration of the body resulting from the sins of carnal lust. Certainly that could explain how, despite the fury of sanctimonious priests, these carvings still exist in all their graphic explicitness.

It seems, from the *sheelas* that did survive the destructive "reformations of paganistic church sculptures" in the seventeenth century, that their creators had considerable freedom and license in the realization of their creations. In some instances the pudenda is over half the size of the whole figure. In others, the poses range from distinctly masturbatory to multi-orificed and ghoulish depictions of both male and female sexual contortions of almost Hindu-like dexterity and in some instances, purely male in all-too-obvious phallic enormity.

In almost every instance, the eyes and often the fanged mouths are hugely out of proportion to the rest of the torso. Ears are often enlarged too and protruding, and striations on cheeks on foreheads may be indicative of ritual scars or tattoos.

These are indeed powerful and even fearful entities, but some scholars decry the negativity of the female spirit that others claim they depict. On the contrary, they suggest that in Ireland, particularly as a result of the devastating events of the fourteenth century, including the Bruce invasions from Scotland in 1315–1317 and the decimating Black Death of the mid-1300s, the *sheela-na-gigs* were seen as urgently needed societal reinforcers or protective icons, warning sinners of both sexes of the hellfire-and-damnation repercussions of unrestrained lust.

Another interpretation and possible explanation as to the survival of so many of these vulnerable stone carvings is the Gaelicization of the Anglo-Norman conquerors, who, according to some historians, became "more Irish than the Irish." They adopted the

Gaelic language and traditions and even such epic tales as *Taín Bó Cualnge—The Cattle Raid of Cooley*—which encompass numerous heroic female figures. Other tales celebrated the powers of Brigid, Macha, Aine, and Cliona—all "earth mothers" to one extent or another.

Today the *sheelas* are celebrated by more militant feminists as powerful touchstones of female sexuality and procreation, which ironically may have been the original Euro-Asian origins of such carvings prior to the male-dominated feudal society.

Thus their symbolism may have come full circle, reflecting the very cycle of birth and regeneration that their female attributes emphasize so blatantly and boldly.

One has to admire their centuries of tenacity and endurance—an easy match for those unearthed containers of ancient bog butter.

31

Celtic Conversations

.
.
.

"TODAY IT'S DEFINITELY VERY HIP TO be Celtic," said Ralph White with an ironic chuckle that shook his stocky frame and made his thick beard and long mane of dark hair jiggle. He had joined Anne and me up at our house in New York State during one of our return trips from Beara, and he was quoting a line from his remarkable work in progress, *At the Edge of Cultural Change*, a memoir he's been slowly compiling over the last five or so years.

Ralph and I have known each other for well over a decade, although our actual face-to-face meetings have been far too few. As a community member and organizer at Findhorn, that world-renowned mystical "garden-commune" in northern Scotland, a former program director of the Omega Institute in Rhinebeck, New York, and cofounder and creative director of the world-famous New York Open Center in Manhattan and a myriad clones, Ralph has been deeply involved in the evolution and devolution of holistic, ecological, and spiritual thinking throughout the USA and Europe. His current editorship of the online magazine *Lapis* is now sending out even wider ripples of knowledge and insight across the planet.

I told him that I thought the *At the Edge* part of his book's title was far too modest and diminished his amazing role as creator-catalyst of new ways of thinking, understanding, and living. *In Deep*, I suggested, might be a more appropriate title, but Ralph, a

Britisher with Welsh-Irish blood, resists any insinuation of self-congratulation and hyped-up promotion.

I tried to persuade him to join us on Beara, but the demands on his time and energy from emerging holistic centers around the globe never allowed us to settle on a date. His spirit, however, was well and truly present, particularly his deep fascination with the Celtic world and its labyrinthine web of legends, mythology, and ancient wisdom. "The Celtic soul is far more prominent now in the world today than ever," he told me, his eyes alive with enthusiasm.

Ralph has met and often befriended just about every major and celebrated proponent of holistic spiritual thinking and life-ways on earth. I found it fascinating that a man who has organized seminars, workshops, and conferences involving scores of these individuals—Christian scholars, yoga masters, Tibetan Buddhists, Kabbalists, Zen Roshis, Taoists, Native American medicine men, Amazonian shamans, and Sufi philosophers—would ultimately return to the roots of his own ancient Celtic culture to find the depth, resonance, and perception he has been seeking for decades. He has managed to condense a vast diner-sized menu of philosophical and spiritual options in to a far more modest and balanced repast. He has journeyed long, hard, often dangerously—and invariably penuriously! In fact his odysseys of discovery—his inner discoveries particularly—began as a child: "I lived within a few hundred yards of the Irish Sea and went to school in tram cars that traveled through wide open fields to the shores. The mountains of Snowdonia to the south were visible through our kitchen window, and the patchwork of pastures, hedges, and hills stretching inland expressed a magic mixture of harmony and wildness that brought great joy and excitement to my child's soul . . . I was always moved by the cry of gulls. What was it that touched my little soul so deeply in this most common, but also most evocative, of bird calls? Years later in Ireland it came to me that what I heard dimly, echoing as if from some ancient past, was the lost holy wisdom of the Celtic island saints. As a child I knew nothing of them, but as an adult I became an aficionado of Celtic sacred islands off the coast of Scotland, Wales, and Ireland."

But all that was only after Ralph's "wonder years" of wandering from Central and South America and Machu Picchu, Eastern Europe and Russia, to some of the remotest and dangerous regions of Tibet, the Celtic centers of Europe, and the "ancient alchemical world" of Renaissance Bohemia.

In between his journeys, described with great vigor and verve in his still incomplete memoir, Ralph was involved in founding and/or organizing three major catalysts of holistic thought and action, which attracted a vast spectrum of thinkers, practitioners, and participants. Ralph was deeply enmeshed in not only the mundanities and minutiae of creating organizations but also the miracles of megachange and transformation that he sensed emerging from these amazingly energetic and effervescent centers.

But somewhere deep in his own soul and in the mind-boggling mélange of philosophies and "isms" he'd studied, he constantly sensed around him the great archetypal figures of Welsh mythology, Merlin and Taliesin—both beloved shamans with knowledge and understanding of the deepest mysteries of nature. "They were always present," said Ralph with his soft voice and irrepressible grin, "reminding me—and all of us—of the earth wisdom we need as we so belatedly attempt to restore a sustainable earth."

"But surely they're figures of myth—not reality?" I said.

Ralph's gentle grin became a chesty guffaw. "Well then—they're in good company with all the mythical Greek gods from whom we draw so much insight and wisdom—and even the Creator Himself/Herself/Itself and dozens of other legendary figures who function as metaphors for our own growth and enlightenment. The Celts had a natural affinity for altered states of consciousness—an intuitive acceptance of shape-shifters, magicians, and fairies. Merlin and Taliesin were all part of that wonderful tableau. I mean, the

Celtic world possesses a panoply of mythical figures, but it also has an intrinsic soul very much linked to reality and the earth itself. I discovered that truth in the 1970s when I spent time on the island of Iona in the Scottish Hebrides, long famed for its sanctity as the birthplace of Celtic Christianity. It was here on this wonderfully wild and windswept place that St. Columba came from Ireland in the late sixth century and carried with him a pure, nature-infused spirituality to the wild Scots and Picts who had remained beyond the control of the Roman Empire, north of Hadrian's Wall."

Ralph sat quietly for a while, smiling at his memories. "Iona's a truly magnificent place—a primeval haven with spirituality permeating the rocks, cliffs, caves, fields, waters . . . It's everywhere. Alive and throbbing. I enjoyed some of the most perfect, soul-nourishing experiences of my entire life on this little holy island. I don't have much interest in organized formal religions, but here I sensed an ancient spirit of true sanctity that felt eternal and essential . . . I sensed the island offering itself as a sublime location for the deepening of spiritual life. Certainly my spiritual life and, from what I know, the lives of tens of thousands of other seekers."

Another pause and then: "I mean . . . the feeling of peace and strength and delight I used to get just standing on top of Dun I, the island's highest hill. Late summer afternoons on cloudless days gazing west across that turquoise ocean—I can still remember those sensations of utter calm years and years later. And if I ever sense tensions or anxieties, I return to Dun I in my mind and let those beautiful memories restore that sense of inner peace."

"So the Celtic heritage still has real power even today?" I asked.

"Oh my gosh yes! And not in a theme park nonsense way, and not among esoteric—or more likely fake—crystal channelers and the like. I honestly feel that the Celtic mysteries still possess a power that can rival anything that's emerged out of Tibet or India or Native America, or anywhere else, for that matter. And—as you know from

A Collage of Celtic-Christian Symbols

living on Beara—the west coast of Ireland is a Celtic wonderworld brimming over with gods like the Celtic sun god, Lug, a whole array of Celtic-Christian saints, hermits, poetic bards, storytellers, folk healers, seers, shape-shifters, healing shamans, magicians, heroic kings, wizards, Druids, mighty warriors, banshees, and *shee* fairies—the Tuatha Dé Danaan—the spirit of Wicca, and neopaganism—all living on the fringes of Tír na nÓg—the 'Land of Eternal Youth'—that otherworldly paradise. And even during the early centuries of Christianity when hermit-monks lived on those remote western Irish isles like the Skelligs and Caher—Celtic traditions and mythology often linked with Arthurian and Holy Grail legends survived intact."

"Even today?"

"Yeah, well, it's like I said—it's hip to be Celtic today. Look at all the neo-Celtic music—all that Riverdance craze—movies like *Braveheart*, lots of Celtic-revival bands, new interest in the Celtic languages themselves, and all the great legends and song-poems. Sometimes, though, it can get very distorted. Until the recent peace in Northern Ireland, paramilitary groups on both sides would use the figure of Cuchulain as their own icon, the warrior-hero of that great song-poem *The Cattle Raid of Cooley*—in their initiation rites. One of the problems is that in their legends the gap between the Celtic bloodthirsty warrior culture and their deep, nature-loving spirituality was very narrow—almost invisible. And yet its essence is very human—recognizable in its strengths and frailties. It's easy to identify with. I think that's one of the reasons for the survival of Celtic traditions—that and maybe a deeper attunement to the wisdom and beauty beneath the surface of the Christian tradition. It's tremendously life enhancing—it binds you very strongly. Whenever I'm in Europe and need stillness and inspiration away from all the crush and stress of cities, I'm off to the Celtic lands and islands. Places of natural silence. Places to rediscover deep and enduring threads of connectivity with all the essential elements of life and living."

There was silence for quite a while. "Well, I guess that pretty well sums it all up," I said.

"Yep. I guess it does . . . for now."

"So all that's left is for me to get hip and get Celtic . . ."

"Right"—Ralph laughed—"and also recognize just how subtle Celtic ideas were about the unity and balance of man and nature. St. Brigid, one of the most revered Celtic deities, is still a symbol for appropriate ways of interacting with the natural world. You could argue she was in contemporary terms a real 'Greenie'—an avid supporter of conservation, recycling, reduced consumption, and increased sustainability by stopping our mad pursuit of mutual self-destruction."

"So I guess you could claim that, in the midst of our overwhelming consumer capitalist culture, the Celtic spirit seems to stand for something way beyond obsessive materialism?"

"Absolutely," said Ralph in a voice that sounded distinctly adamant and absolute. "It evokes a sense of music, soul, and poetry, of 'the other world' beyond the mundane chores of existence. I think we yearn for this desperately in the midst of all the money, gadgets, and obsession with work that characterize contemporary America. James Macpherson's poem *Ossian*, which evoked the heroic world of the ancient Celtic warriors in the highlands of Scotland, had a huge impact on the emerging Romantic movement at the end of the nineteenth century. As Europe was evolving from the rationality and classicism of the Enlightenment, it was this Celtic world that offered inspiration to figures as diverse as Goethe and Napoleon, both of whom were great admirers of *Ossian*. In the late nineteenth and early twentieth centuries, during the time of the Celtic revival and the work of W. B. Yeats, Irish myths and fairy tales summoned magic into an increasingly commercialized and industrialized world."

"So today the Celtic archetype returns once again to summon up the deeper mysteries of the Self?"

"Oh yes—to remind us of the need for a society in tune with the natural world, which stands for imagination, intuition, and mystery at a time when our psyches are barraged with an ever greater volume of data, trivia, and noise. As we see so many becoming gormless slaves—slaves of fleeting fads, slaves to the meaningless opinions or judgment of others, even slaves to the search for self-gratification and godless 'self-fulfillment.' As our longing for silence and beauty inevitably grows stronger in the face of this relentless stream of shallow stimulii that characterizes the early twenty-first century, the Celtic world reminds us of different and far more enduring values and a different form of consciousness. It certainly seems to me that the lure of those sacred islands, the pull of those holy places, the fascination with an ancient but living culture imbued with soul and spirit—all these will only grow stronger as the human psyche demands a new wholeness with the power to create a far more sustainable and increasingly just world."

Another long pause.

It seemed all that needed to be said had been said—elegantly and emotionally—by Ralph.

But then I think I surprised my friend: "Okay, I guess I get the last word because I've been doing some reading too. So I'll offer you a blessing based on the wisdom of the Celtic ogham—that ancient alphabet that possessed special spiritual qualities: 'May the trees of the forest take root in your heart that you may grow in wisdom, joy, and love for all who live in the earth's embrace.' "

Ralph looked a little surprised. Then he smiled, and then he gave one of his big laughs, which made me realize what a great experience we could have had together if I'd ever managed to lure him down to Beara.

"Maybe next time." He chuckled.

"Yeah . . . maybe."

32

Returning to the Stones

:

"Oh—just look at that!" Anne gasped and pointed ahead to our right. "It's fantastic . . ."

And so it was. We were on our way back to our Allihies cottage after a lively evening in Castletownbere, and a full moon was slowly slipping out from behind the distant Caha range, bathing the long swaths of peat moor in a phosphorescent light. I stopped the car and we got out. The air was chill but motionless. The silence was tangible, and we stood without talking, watching the moon ease slowly upward into the sky.

Then Anne pointed again toward the mountains. "What are those over there?"

I stared hard. Slowly an image appeared . . . large, silhouetted objects rising out of the dark immensity of the land . . . strange and yet familiar.

"I don't know . . . Ah! Wait a minute—it's Derreenataggart. Of course. The great stone circle. I'd forgotten we were so close . . . They look so eerie at night."

Anne nodded. She was not a great lover of eerie things. Especially at night.

"Let's go visit them again. In the moonlight," I suggested.

"You sure you want to do that? It's so late . . ."

"Aw, c'mon. It won't take a minute."

I took her silence for agreement (not at all the way Anne intended it), and then I spotted an odd vehicle over by a cluster of stumpy, wind-cowed trees. It was a bizarre, custom-made contraption. Part school bus, part caravan, part old hot-dog-and-burger wagon, if the faded sign over the side windows was any indication.

"Looks like an overnighter," I said. "Travelers. It's one of those Traveler vans."

"Our modern-day gypsies."

"Reminders of when we were writing our early travel books!" I said.

"Yes—but that was just the two of us in one tiny camper. Some of these Travelers move about in huge packs. They're quite a problem over in England. I remember they settled in a field one time—just opposite my parents' home . . ."

"Well—there's only one here. So let's leave them in peace and get to the stones. It's cold . . ."

And there they were, a circle of monoliths, sheened by luminescent moonlight and enclosing the great central stone itself. It resembled some mighty leader surrounded by his (or her) loyal acolytes.

Our previous visits here had always seemed a little underwhelming. In the daylight, the stones certainly appeared smaller than we'd expected, although in actual fact, this five-thousand-year-old creation predates the Pyramids of Egypt, and is one of the most impressive circles in the southwest. But on this particular night it felt very different—in more ways than one. First of all, the stones seemed far larger and more dramatic than before. And despite the benign moonlight and the shimmering festoon of stars—almost more stars than space—there was an air of menace about the enclosing circle. Anne, of course, sensed it immediately.

"Will we be long here?" she whispered plaintively.

"We've only just *got* here!"

"I'm not sure I like this place . . . at least not at night!"

It was then I saw the lights. Faint flickers at first, like fireflies, but as I focused, I realized they were tiny flames. Five of them. In a line.

"What is it?" Ann asked nervously. "What are you looking at?"

"Lights. Candles, I think. Down there—beyond the circle."

Anne saw them too. "Let's go now," she said with a slight tremor in her voice. "It's really late . . ."

"No—just give me a minute. I want to see what they are—"

"I'm not coming with you," she said. But she came anyway, and we walked together slowly and cautiously, not knowing what to expect. And then a voice, soft and definitely feminine, whispered, "Hello."

"Hi," I said, nervously looking around for the owner of the voice. And then I spotted her, half hidden by a huge round stone. She was dressed in very dark clothes. If the moon hadn't been out, she would have been virtually invisible. "I'm sorry—are we disturbing you . . . ?"

"No—please. Join me."

She seemed very small and waiflike, hardly more than a teenager by the look of her young face bathed in the soft moonlight. She wore a dark cloak, wrapped like a security blanket over her slight shoulders. Five tiny candles in windproof jars were placed in an arc around her.

"Is that your van back there?" I asked, not quite knowing how to address this odd little figure.

"Yeah—a real mess, isn't it? We're in the middle of doing it up."

"We?"

"Bob, my boyfriend—partner—and me. He's gone off walking over there somewhere . . ." She pointed vaguely down into the darkness beyond the stone circle.

"And are you . . . celebrating something? You know, the candles . . ."

"Right. The winter solstice . . . the longest night . . . usually around December twenty-first . . . it depends on the moon."

"Well, we won't disturb you . . ."

"No, no. Sit down if you want. Not many people come up here at this time."

Anne seemed hesitant, but we both eased ourselves down on the soft grass anyway.

"So—what happens at the winter solstice then?"

"Ah well—it's the time of Cailleach—the Winter Spirit. Some call her The Hag. She has different names in different parts of the Celtic world. Last year, we were way up in the north of Scotland. We were lucky, we got the aurora borealis too—you know, the northern lights—but the moon was often too bright. They're so beautiful—have you seen them?"

"No," said Anne, finally deciding to join in. "Even though we spent some time on Harris in the Outer Hebrides, we never got the full show."

Derreenataggart at Night

"Oh, it's great! It usually starts with a sort of hazy, ghostly rainbow—white—right across the sky, and then things come that look like huge searchlights but softer, misty . . . and then these sort of colored curtains rise up and dance really slowly—they look like they're throbbing . . . very gently . . . honestly, it's fabulous! And they're very important to tribal people—y'know, people living way up north around the Arctic Circle. The Inuit in Canada say they're lanterns carried by spirits of the dead lighting the way to heaven. The Lapps say they're gifts from God to relieve the disappearance of the sun in winter. Oh—and Galileo too—he called them 'the sunrise of the north.' "

"That's an enticing idea—a northern dawn," I said.

"It was best on the nights of the dark moon—not like tonight. Although tonight is special too."

"Is that what the candles are for—the Winter Spirit?" asked Anne.

"Yeah. Absolutely. Celebrating Cailleach. Knowing that from now on we're moving into shorter nights and longer days. Moving through Imbolc—that's the end of January—a time of one of the celebrations for Brighde—the earth goddess. And then comes the spring equinox in late March when the new light comes . . . that's the time of fertility and fresh life . . ."

"You know, I've heard some of these terms," said Anne. "I just never linked them to exact dates and names. All I remember is the summer solstice—around mid-June . . ."

"June twenty-first—the longest day."

". . . and all that crazy stuff that goes on in England at Stonehenge and Avebury, and Silsbury and Glastonbury . . ."

"Yeah, it's become a bit ridiculous nowadays—pseudo-Druids, New Agers, crystal planters, trance dancing, weird music, and TV cameras galore! It's all so fake, it's sickening . . ."

"And those Wicca exponents too, I suppose?" I asked.

"Well, Wicca's a little different, isn't it. I'm becoming more interested in that. Bob's not so sure, he thinks it's a bit too . . . 'witchy.' I try to explain that Wicca is like 'white' as opposed to 'black' magic—y'know, 'the black arts.'"

"Well," said Anne, "you've picked the right place to sense all these things. And on the winter solstice too!"

"Yes! And it's so beautiful, isn't it? This place is so . . . resonant. Part of a huge network of circles and standing stones and ley lines—you know—lines of earth energy . . ."

"Right," I mumbled. "Ley lines . . ." (a subject I've always regarded with some suspicion)

"You feel you're touching something timeless—a great mass of ancient knowledge and truth and wisdom—thousands of years old. A power that used to be understood, but it's been forgotten for so long. The power of the Earth Mother—all these great eternal forces of nature . . ."

Suddenly she stopped and giggled. "I'm sorry—really I am. I don't normally talk so much . . . honestly . . . I hope you don't mind . . ."

"No, no, not at all," said Anne. "Go on. It's very interesting."

Obviously complaints about the cold and the deep dark and the menacing stones had been forgotten for the moment. And that was just fine, even though the skeptical me was wondering about the veracity of this strange little person sitting all by herself in her black garments surrounded by these tiny candles. All very odd.

"What do you and your partner do . . . you know . . . living in your van. Do you do crafts . . . are you writers?"

"No—and yes," she said ambiguously. "We kind of do whatever we feel like doing. I'm trained in calligraphy, so I usually find someone wanting signs or wedding invitations . . . anything. I'm also an illustrator, so I make cards that sell pretty well down south, in Kent, where I come from. And Bob—my partner—oh, I'm sorry. I'm Mary, by the way—I forgot to introduce myself."

We all introduced ourselves and she continued. "Bob is a fantastic carpenter and builder. And a folksinger. He's well known in the south. Gets a lot of gigs and stuff . . . oh, and a lot of other things we do. It seems to work. We get by. Living on the road isn't that expensive—except for the petrol! That monster drinks the stuff like a thirsty camel. That's why we call it the Camel . . ."

"Great name," I said to Anne, and we smiled reminiscently. We'd begun our own traveling lives in a similar fashion eons ago, long before I started writing and illustrating travel books. In a way listening to Mary was like listening to our earlier selves—except for all the stuff about solstices and equinoxes and Earth Mothers. Somehow we'd never seriously explored those particular avenues. But I was certainly willing to hear more.

"So—why are you doing all this? What are you personally looking for?" I asked.

Mary giggled again. It was enticing. She didn't come across at all like one of those "I've found it, and you haven't" New Age converts. There seemed be no complacency. No preaching. She didn't seem to demand control of the channel changers. She seemed to be just someone reaching out to aspects and forces in our world that most of us either scoff at, reject, or blissfully ignore.

"I'm not always sure what I'm looking for. I'm not even sure if there's any specific 'it.' I think it's more of a process of letting go and opening up and seeing what comes . . . does that make any sense?"

"Yes," said Anne adamantly. "Yes, it does."

Mary continued. "I don't think there's any end-thing I want or need. I'm just excited to . . . 'go with the flow.'" She laughed out loud. "Clichéd—but it's what it feels like, you know. Flowing. Seeing where the flow takes us. There's so much inside us—all of us—that we rarely use. We don't even know it exists much of the time. I think the ancients knew. I'm sure they felt themselves intuitively to be part of these powerful forces—a huge network of forces—that linked them with . . . well . . . everything."

"That's the impression you certainly get when you read about ancient cultures—tribes in Amazonia, the Australian Aborigines, Native Americans . . . ," I said.

"Yeah—right. They were all tapping into energies that we don't seem to understand anymore at all nowadays. We've got too many distractions—we're all so . . . separate, I suppose. The people who placed these stones were fully in tune with the power of the seasons—Bealtaine, Lammas, Samhain—the Celtic New Year at the beginning of November when they light those huge bonfires. I mean, the whole layout of the stones here—and other places on the island and all over Britain—reflect the exact phases of the seasons. They show the great turning circle of Earth's energies—the circles of everything in creation. From the tiniest bits of matter—all those revolving bits and pieces of atoms, right out to our own solar system, the galaxies . . . all circles . . . life, death, and back to life again. Round and round. You can sense all that here . . . circles within circles within circles . . ."

As Mary spoke, her hunched little frame rose straighter, higher, but then she stopped, slumped back to her former dark crouch, and giggled. "Or something like that. It's hard to explain."

"I think you've explained it beautifully," said Anne softly.

"Yeah," I agreed. "Thank you."

Mary smiled. "I know we're living a bit of a crazy life—Bob and me. And who knows how long it'll be . . . before we're sucked back into the everyday things. But at the moment it feels right. We're touching things we don't quite understand . . . and it's beautiful . . ."

"And you're learning—and sharing," I suggested.

"Yeah . . . we're learning . . ." Mary smiled. "We're very lucky to be able to do that."

I wanted to give her something. A small thank-you gift. But all I could find in my pockets was a bar of chocolate. "I wish I'd got a bottle of brandy or something to keep you warm," I said. "But maybe some chocolate . . ."

"Oh, thanks," said Mary with what looked like genuine pleasure. "That's really nice of you. I'll save it until Bob gets back . . . well, some of it . . ."

We left her crouched down in the moonlight by the monoliths with her candles. We turned one last time as we passed out of the stone circle, and they were still flickering. Tiny warm glows in that dark, chill December night . . .

33

ROOTING AROUND
A Final Adventure
in Search of My Irish Heritage

∷

"WELL—I KNOW YOUR GRANDFATHER, WALTER Wade Yeadon, was a famous comedian and singer . . . right? And Yorkshire-born too, like you and Anne."

It seemed odd to be chatting with my cousin David, whom I'd met only on the rarest of occasions during our lives. We're not a particularly close extended family, but by the amicable tone of our conversation, you'd think we'd been buddies for years. And somehow our chat now began encompassing aspects of our mutual family history and one character in particular who had always intrigued me—the great black sheep of our Yeadon clan. My father's father. My grandfather. Walter Wade Yeadon.

I'd heard only tantalizing bits about him in the past. No one in the family seemed willing to discuss him or his life. It was, quite simply, a taboo subject. You just didn't mention his name. I explained all this to David.

"Yes, well, I suppose that's understandable." He chuckled. "He was quite a rake. A naughty old boy of the first order. Used to travel with those music hall shows—and, of course, lots of those music hall chorus girls—all over the place . . . Australia, New Zealand, South Africa, South America, the USA—you name it! I think he went up the Amazon once or twice to that weird city—the one that used to control the rubber trade. The one with that enormous opera house!"

"Manaus."

"Right—Manaus. I think he went there. And then, when he was home in England, he performed in all the big music hall theaters. He was billed as 'Walter Wade—The Great Yorkshire Scot' and also 'Yorkshire's Harry Lauder.' He pinched the real Harry Lauder's act—you remember the famous Scottish guy with the kilt and the crooked walking stick? Did a kind of Andy Capp Yorkshire take-off of Harry's spiel—flat cap, baggy trousers, wooden clogs, and all that. Apparently he was very popular. Kept on going for years with pretty much the same act . . ."

"Right—and he kept on going past my grandma's house too, hardly ever popping in. And according to Gran, God bless her, when he did, it was a quick 'So how are you and the kids doing and here's a bit o' cash for a few treats' and then he was gone again, leaving four children behind and my gran weeping and furiously sticking knitting needles in his old music hall posters . . . or so my dad told me. Normally he wouldn't talk about him at all. Well, actually, he wouldn't until the last few years of his life. Then he seemed to make peace with his memories and forgave old Walter, who was long gone by then, and he began to talk about him . . . just a little at first and then later on with what seemed to be something approaching real affection. And he even gave me Walter's battered, stringless violin—I still have it back at home. On display, even!"

"And," said David, "y' seem proud to know your grandmother was Irish."

"Yes—well, yes I am, but that was another one of those family taboo subjects. Especially as I think she came from the south somewhere. Too many problems up in the English north with Sinn Fein and the IRA . . ."

"She was from County Mayo originally," David told me, "but the family moved to Yorkshire in the late 1830s. Her maiden name was

Forkin. Annie Forkin. And where is it you're staying in Ireland—doing your book?"

"The Beara Peninsula."

"Ah—Kenmare. And Glengarriff, right? Lovely little towns, those."

"Indeed they are. And Beara itself is a wild and wonderful place. A bit of true 'old Ireland.' "

"Sounds great. I never went farther west than Glengarriff, unfortunately. But look—it'd only be a three- or four-hour drive to County Mayo. You should go and check out your roots and whatnot . . ."

There was a long pause at this point. David is one of the few celebrities in our extended family. He's a well-known TV actor, but I had no idea he had any interest in "rooting forays" and all that messy business of family trees and genealogical whatnot.

"Oh, I've been dabbling in charts and trees for years," said David. "I guess I'm the family historian now—by default! I can send you some stuff, if you like—you might find it interesting. You never know."

David was, indeed, a man of his word. A hefty package arrived the following week. In addition to a massive tome of photocopied birth, death, and marriage records going back in some instances to the late 1700s (he was right about our family when he described their Catholic breeding habits as 'like rampant rabbits'!—more like a biblical bonanza of begatting). He also enclosed some rather more intimate—and touching—items. My grandfather, the one none of the family wanted to discuss, suddenly came alive. All I had previously to confirm his existence was that old violin. But now came a cornucopia of other tangible evidence. Most fascinating were photos of his stocky figure and ruggedly handsome face and copies of old music hall bills featuring his name prominently along with other favorites of the era, including Norman and Leonard in their "Old Time Melodies Musical Extravaganza"; Eddie Wells, "King of the Jugglers"; hoop manipulators; gentlemen performing novel singing and dancing scenes; Tiny and Mite, two very vertically challenged contortionists; a couple of short varioscope films, and an amateur talent competition "open to every kind of entertainer."

Then, more sadly, were papers confirming his residency in a hospital at his death in 1923 at the relatively young age of forty-eight. Records from that last part of his life describe him as: "excited, aggressive, resents being questioned and makes threatening movements under examination. He says he has a huge hidden fortune but contradicts himself in all his statements and says he has the most beautiful ideas and could write the best book that has ever been seen."

That last bit naturally captured my interest (was book writing possibly a family genetic trait?), but further reports portrayed him as: "Face flat and flabby. Complexion yellowish. Expression staring and vacant. Teeth very defective. He says his false teeth are platinum, but they are only gold. Rambling, garrulous and confused. Full of delusions. Says he must get discharged quickly as he has to go on tour to America."

Gradually this multifaceted individual, also described in hospital records as "strongly built, well nourished, charmingly childish and exalted," was slowly becoming reincarnated in my mind. And then David sent us a copy of some memoir notes made by my father's younger brother in 1931, and we could sense Walter's almost tactile presence:

> On the theater posters I saw Walter Wade was always
> top-billing. I faintly remember that he, my father, was a close
> friend of Houdini. Mother took me to the Empire in Leeds to
> see his act . . . I can still remember some of his clever patter.
> He could be very funny. He was quite a dandy, too, and I saw
> him once with his paramour. Rosalind somebody. He even
> once played nearby at Yeadon Town Hall (how nice to have a
> town named after our family!) but he didn't make any
> contact with Mother or any of us. I remember how angry I

was at his attitude and having a strong desire to punch him
in the nose, young as I was!

Now I began to understand my poor grandmother's great sad-
ness, my father's anger, and why the family had decided to relegate
Walter to taboo status. But I was also now even more curious to dig
deeper.

"So, why don't we go to County Mayo?" suggested Anne. "See if
we can find some lost members of your family—go out on the limb
of your tree, to coin a phrase."

I gave her a curious look. She was not normally one for puns.
"You're joking . . . right?"

"Well, that lousy pun was a bit of a joke, but otherwise I'm being
serious. It could be a lovely drive up by Killarney and the Ring of
Kerry and the Dingle Peninsula and then over . . ."

Anne had obviously been looking at a map, and as previously
mentioned, that's another thing she doesn't do normally. Maps and
my good lady wife are utterly incompatible. The worst suggestion I
can make if we're out driving is to ask if she might just want to
take a peep at the map and provide the odd bit of navigational
guidance from time to time. Of course in Ireland the maze of
boreens is a navigational nightmare, so she always had a ready—and
convincing—excuse for our invariably getting lost. But, to give Anne
her due, she'll invariably pick up the map (with a heavy sigh), unfold
it with the reluctance of a kid taking a rigorous calculus exam, and
then spend a good five minutes trying to figure out which particular
part of said map is relevant for our journey (and trying hard not to
ask for my input). Then she'll sit like a frozen statue, eyes downcast,
staring at the confusion of colored lines and blobs and words, as if
they were the key to an incredibly complex cipher code.

"Darlin'—you don't have to look at the map all the time. Enjoy
the scenery. It's so beautiful . . ."

The most I can expect at this juncture is a growling "huh?" while her eyes stay focused on the map, as if waiting for a sign from above to determine the next set of directions.

Eventually I give in. I can't bear to see my mate suffering these pangs of outrageous misfortune and missing the exploratory joys of the drive itself, so I pull over and offer to have a glance at the map myself.

"It's okay," she'll normally insist. "I know exactly where we are . . ."

"Okay—but let me just have a look, uh . . . Darling . . . um . . . you've got it upside down."

"Yes, I know, I know. I'm just holding it the way we're going. South. Makes it easier. Otherwise everything's backward."

Bit of a difficult dilemma here. Especially as we're actually going north, which would explain her last two odd instructions. But I have no intention of spoiling what will now be a splendidly serendipitous journey as we try to get back on track. So very gradually, I turn the map right way up while pointing at some fascinating bits of scenery to distract her, and off we go and the day is saved . . . until . . .

"I saw you do that, y'know," said Anne in a somber voice.

"Do what, love? What did I do?"

"You know. You turned the map over."

Fortunately I'd just made a right-angle turn off the previous road: "Oh, no no no. I've just changed direction so it's better this way up now. Look, look—aren't those rabbits over there . . ."

But she knows. And she knows I know. And I know she knows I know. And isn't marriage wonderful.

Anyway. Back to the roots foray. Or actually not. I think it's perhaps best to leave it where it is for the moment. Partially because nothing conclusive has been unearthed yet, and partially because it's been such a strange and beguiling experience to date that I think the whole story is going to need far more pages and patience than I currently have left.

And so with apologies and a sincere by-your-leave, I'll let the tale dangle for a while and see how it grows and blossoms and possibly morphs into the early part of a sequel . . . if there ever is one. Who knows? Meanwhile, my grandparents, the rambunctious ghosts of Walter Wade and the angry, ill-treated Annie Forkin, continue to lead us on, roiling and rooting down the narrow boreens of County Mayo . . . and way beyond.

Wish us luck on our ongoing ancestoring quest . . . in fact, please wish us luck in all our quests, both inner and outer, generated by our experiences and adventures deep in Ireland's beautiful Beara. It was an amazing time here, and we continue to carry with us the *craic* of indelible memories—the long-genealogy locals and the blow-ins alike, the creators and healers, the fishermen and farmers, the *seanachais* and the *seisuin* musicians, the seekers and the finders—everyone who touched our lives and made our experiences so richly rewarding.

And we both leave you with a final enduring memory—of sitting together on the grass by our cottage, long after the sun has drifted

Castletownbere Boats

down behind the Skelligs, watching the moon-blanched mountains slip into the ocean beyond our beautiful white sand beach. And listening to the silence. And the silence listening to us. And little bubbles of new insights and perceptions rising. And laughing softly together at the simplicity and synchronicity of our wandering lives.

THANK YOU, BEARA! *Saol fada chugat* and *slán leat*—farewell and long life to you all.